Acknowledgments

Integral Ministry Training Design and Evaluation is the product of many hands, and no book would be possible without the combined efforts of the supporting team. In particular, I wish to acknowledge my co-editor Jonathan Lewis. This project moved forward with a confidence I would never have shared were it not for his mastery of the subject, and previous publishing and editing experience.

Together, we would like to express our sincere gratitude to the following people for their munificent volunteer assistance: First, to Robert Ferris who broke this ground with the previous edition published in *Establishing Ministry Training: A Manual for Programme Developers;* second, to William Taylor, not only for the initial and ongoing encouragement to pursue this project, but also for his continued input and contribution in the form of an inspiring foreword; third, to the contributing authors whose chapters and preface were offered generously without expectation of any remuneration; fourth, to those who contributed case studies and additional evaluative resources compiled in the third section of this manual; and fifth, to the editorial team whose input served to make this manual what it is.

For the design and layout we recognize the thorough efforts of Koe Pahlka. Peter Mitchell of Simple Graphics contributed an inspired cover design. Dawn Lewis, and Jackson and Laurel McAllister happily served to proofread the manuscript. To these we extend our heartfelt thanks.

Robert Brynjolfson and Jonathan Lewis

Editors

Integral Ministry Training

Design and Evaluation

Edited by:

Robert Brynjolfson &
Jonathan Lewis

William Carey Library
Pasadena, California
www.WCLBooks.com

Integral Ministry Training: Design and Evaluation

Copyright © 2006 by World Evangelical Alliance Mission Commission

All scripture quotations, unless otherwise indicated, are taken from the Holy Bible, New International Version. ©1973, 1978, 1984 by the International Bible Society. Used by permission of Zondervan Publishing House.

Book Design and Layout: Koe Pahlka
Cover Design: Peter Mitchell, Simple Graphics
Copyediting: Dawn Lewis, Jackson and Laurel McAllister

Published by William Carey Library
1605 E. Elizabeth Street, Pasadena, California 91104
www.WCLBooks.com
William Carey Library is a ministry of the U.S. Center for World Mission, Pasadena, California.

Printed in the United States of America

Library of Congress Cataloguing-in-Publication Data

Integral ministry training : design and evaluation / edited by Robert Brynjolfson & Jonathan Lewis.

    p. cm.

Includes bibliographical references and index.

ISBN 0-87808-457-6 (alk. paper)

    1. Missionaries--Training of. I. Brynjolfson, Robert. II. Lewis, Jonathan, Ph. D

BV2091.I56 2006

266.0071'1--dc22

            2006034437

Contents

Section 3: Additional Resources

Foreword

To Be Read...

William D. Taylor

As We Engage this Book and the Issues—Three Encounters

A few weeks ago, my wife, Yvonne, and I sat with a young, dedicated and creative group of African missionary candidates in training. They represented at least six African nations and more cultures, and were half way through the Focus Team Leadership Training program in Pretoria, South Africa. They peppered us with honest, strong and thoughtful questions about mission work, about challenges in life, about prayers not answered, about mistakes we had made in life, about how to stay in mission for life, about workable and unworkable African mission structures, about generational changes. It was a valuable exchange on all sides, and for us, a chance to listen to the younger voices so committed to long-term mission.

Last year I taught a doctoral seminar at Columbia International University, with a group of six veterans in cross-cultural ministry—spanning five continents. We became a missional/educational community of five days; eating together, listening to each other, praying together, learning and growing in our understanding of the kind of educational delivery system that best equips women and men for effective, longer-term ministry/mission service.

Next week I will attend a luncheon of local mission pastors, where a report will be given on how a local church alone can train missionaries. I know many of the players but I'm wondering what new ideas will come forth. Who will challenge some of the assumptions made? Which churches realize that they must create a strategic partnership with dedicated training/equipping/mission education centers to provide the more complete teaching/learning context for effective missionary training? I shall learn much.

Reflections on Ministry/Mission Training/Equipping Around the World

My three encounters of a close kind reflect in microcosm the macrocosm of ministry training programs in the world. I have personally visited at least sixty schools and programs on every continent that claim to "train missionaries". I have friends and colleagues that serve in at least another fifty centers around the world. This is part of my personal data base, and I also teach doctoral seminars on the training of women and men for ministry/mission.

First, we discover the obvious—the enormous diversity of training/equipping/shaping models in the mission world today. Some of them are church-based schools of spiritual transformation; some are small, dedicated missionary training centers that focus exclusively on the equipping of cross-cultural servants; the curriculum for some comes from high quality DVD recordings which are being translated into other languages, while others are privileged to have strong, full-time faculty on board; some are old but many are very recent in our mission history; they are found on every continent; some are church-based or agency-driven, and others desire to serve agencies; some proudly do not offer a diploma, certificate or a degree, and others with pride offer either a B.A., an M.A., a Th.M., a D.Min. or a Ph.D. in mission and or inter-cultural studies. At times I conclude that I have truly seen it all, and generally I am encouraged by what I have witnessed.

Second, the WEA Mission Commission forged a unique path to generate vital, contextualized and viable literature on missionary training. The first published book on the topic, *Internationalising Missionary Training: A Global Perspective* (The Paternoster Press, Exeter, UK and Baker Book House, Grand Rapids, USA, 1991), was a landmark on missionary training literature. No other book had dedicated itself to address issues of context, models and educational issues that impact missionary training. A product outcome of our 1989 Manila consultation on the topic, it set the standard for the Mission Commission publications: a global perspective to address global needs by global authors. It was translated/adapted into Spanish.

In 1993, Jonathan Lewis edited another unique book that went through two editions *Working Your Way to the Nations: A Guide to Effective Tentmaking* (InterVarsity Press, 1996). It rapidly was produced in Spanish, Portuguese, Korean, Chinese and Arabic. Here we thank Singaporean architect and mission leader, Loh Hoe Peng, for the original ideas that were then given shape by Jonathan.

That book was followed by a 1994, Pasadena, California, missionary training consultation that generated three more books in 1995: David Harley's practical handbook on the subject, *Preparing to Serve: Training for Cross-Cultural Mission* (William Carey Library, 1995), the *World Directory of Missionary Training Programmes*, a second catalogue now of over 500 training options around the world edited by Raymond Windsor (William Carey Library, 1995), and the seminal book edited by Robert W. Ferris, *Establishing Ministry Training: A Manual for Programme Developers* (William Carey Library, 1995). Harley's book was translated into Spanish and Portuguese.

Note: while some of these publications are no longer available for sale, they can all be read or downloaded from www.wearesources.org.

Time passed, and around the world new training models emerged, others truly changed and a few were proud that they had not changed at all. In our first book we presented a diverse family of models, and in the last fifteen years some of these schools have almost disappeared, only to come back in another form. Others schools have changed significantly; and some frankly never made it beyond a conceptual stage. We tracked these centers/programs over the years to see how they are doing today. In this new and also seminal work, *Integral Ministry Training: Design and Evaluation*, edited by Robert Brynjolfson and Jonathan Lewis, some of the 1991 models reappear. But significantly, the field has radically changed with new ones, which deeply gratifies those of us who are passionate about missionary/ministry training around the world.

Third, there is no doubt that some of the most fundamental challenges to the field of ministry/missionary training/equipping have come from local churches, whether in the Global North or South. We rejoice that the empowering Spirit of God has been at work in refreshing ways as churches have claimed their stake as major players in the global mission movement and its necessary structures—missional churches, training programs, sending and supporting systems. The fact is that in many regions of the world (Latin America as a continent exemplifies this truth) churches have been the initial and prime mission players. In other regions, the churches are attempting to reclaim their voice, and this is happening around the globe, not just in one region or nation.

While we rejoice in this vital church role, at the same time we have some questions. Can a church of small to modest size (and "size" depends on whether it's Korean or Japanese, Nigerian or English, Brazilian or German) expect to offer the complete menu of mission equipping? Is this luxury only for the mega churches with a wealth of resources? Frankly, we are encouraged when churches do all they can, but also delegate or sub-contract to dedicated mission training centers some of the components they cannot offer in the local context. This would include vital courses of ministry and church planting amongst Muslims, Hindus, Buddhists, animists and seculars; it would also include some of the foundational theology of mission and cross-cultural issues, as well as contextualization, among others.

Let us affirm the right role of the church to do what it can do best—to focus on character formation, on spirituality, on cross-cultural practicums within their near context, and practical church-based ministry in community and in accountable relationship with others. When we collapsed the major causes of attrition of missionaries in our 14-nation study, we realized the clusters of problems with inadequate spirituality and character formation, weaknesses in relationality and community, and the absence of instrumental knowledge and skills for the tasks before us in missions. Just peruse *Too Valuable to Lose: Exploring the Causes and Cures of Missionary Attrition*, William Taylor, Ed. (William Carey Library, 1997) and discover the many issues directly related to the lack of effective, pre-field training. And so many of these issues are best dealt with in the context of the local church.

But we cannot continue to do "missions on the fly", in a McDonaldized fashion, or assume that a brief home-grown program led by one or two people can do an effective job of preparing our longer-term cross-cultural servants. We will guarantee much higher painful attrition if we do not equip them well.

One of the most significant and recent studies on pre-field missionary training comes from the substantive work commissioned by Global Connections (GC), the UK mission network (http://globalconnections.co.uk/findresources/training/missiontraining.htm).

The research investigated four topics:

- The current demand for mission training.
- The current supply of mission training.

- Perceptions of trends and developments in mission training.
- Views of quality of mission training.

The study also makes some specific and realistic recommendations, with a full report that can be purchased. We are grateful to GC for permission to include their summary as part of our final section of Additional Resources. GC also offers in their website the diverse options for different mission training, whether the certificate, degree, diploma, online and distance learning, postgraduate studies, short courses and tasters. Would that similar research projects would rattle the Christian educational and training centers and systems of the Church around the world!

Fourth, regretfully many of us have concluded that most formal education institutions in both the Global North and South are the least willing to change, to examine their training assumptions, or to learn from others. Some of the greatest creativity in ministry/mission training takes place not in the Global North (though there are seminal exceptions), but in the Global South. But the pressures of supposed "excellence" and accreditation are just too much for some of them. To my knowledge, only one educational institution in the West, Columbia International University, worked through the "profiling process" presented again in this book. We are grateful for their courage and for the role Bob Ferris, CIU faculty leader, played there.

Fifth, this new book summarizes many years of practice and evaluation, incubation and reflection on the how to train/equip/shape women and men for ministry, whether within cultures or cross-culturally. The book applies equally to all kinds of training centers, programs and institutions, whether they focus on non-formal or totally formal education. All the writers of this book, and I join them (educators, program developers and reflective practitioners), agree on the imperative core issues that must characterize the best of integral ministry training—whether within culture or cross-culture, whether close or far, whether with mother tongue or as a result of learning a new language. The book builds on our previous publications, but it clearly moves the agenda forward with boldness, challenging again some of the treasured assumptions we have defended regarding training/equipping of called and gifted servants for ministry.

The seven prime writers have personally dedicated themselves to training, and they impart some of their magnificent deposit of training experience and reflection. This book also offers an educational template for all who claim to equip/train/shape for ministry. But it cannot be done as if we considered training of secondary value, or something to be purchased cheaply. The book demands serious reflection and self-examination of the key stakeholders in integral ministry training.

We share the deep commitment that the best equipping for ministry is done in community, and this has radical implications. What do we do with the rightful place of the exploding educational options through the Internet? Can they be combined with working teams in the same geography? What does this say to formal schools who offer day, night and weekend courses, in part driven by needs and in part by financial markets, in light of the demands of a high-pressure lifestyle and economic challenges? How can we presume to offer a master's in mission when our students have not been in any kind of accountable community that is integral to their training?

We are profoundly committed to an equipping that shapes men and women in their essential spirituality, their relationality, and the acquisition of knowledge and skills that will allow them not only to survive, but to thrive even in adverse circumstances. So this book on integral ministry training comes to us at a good time in mission history. As with our other publications, it reflects global issues and invites us to listen to voices from around our world.

The new Mission Commission periodical, *Connections: The Journal of the WEA Mission Commission*, dedicated its Summer 2005 issue to the topic of "Holistic Training for Cross-Cultural Ministry." This issue can be read and downloaded for free at the *Connections* archives at: http://www.worldevangelicalalliance.com/resources/connections.htm.

How might you read it? Slowly, carefully, pausing to reflect, to apply, and to consider what might be done differently, asking the Trinitarian Missionary Community to visit you in your journey towards more effective integral ministry equipping.

About the International Missionary Training Network (IMTN) and the Authors

The Mission Commission (MC) sponsored a consultation on international missionary training in Manila in 1989. Many issues surfaced and led to the production of several publications and an occasional bulletin. A cadre of "Associates" was also formed with key players like David and Rosemary Harley, Bob Ferris, Barbara Burns, Steve Hoke, Ray Windsor, and MC staff members, Bill Taylor and Jonathan Lewis. These associates traveled widely, visiting training centers and conducting national and regional consultations. Out of these efforts, the International Missionary Training Fellowship (IMTF) was born.

In subsequent years, the IMTF existed primarily as a loosely knit fellowship. Jonathan Lewis edited the occasional bulletin, *Training for Cross-Cultural Ministry*, soliciting practical articles from the IMTF's widespread constituency. Through an ongoing dialogue, it soon became evident that best practice in missionary training had to focus on the whole person—not just theological and missiological understanding. Additional books and articles published by the Mission Commission bore this out. All of the MC books and bulletins can be found at www.wearesources.org as free, downloadable pdf files.

In June 2003, during the Mission Commission's triennial consultation in Canada, members of the training community prayerfully met and elaborated a series of recommendations intended to invigorate and "re-engineer" the IMTF to become a more proactive organization. The ensuing "white paper" called for 21 initiatives. Perhaps its most salient request was that the Mission Commission find a full-time director for the network. The IMTF also changed its name to the International Missionary Training Network (IMTN). In January 2005, the MC leadership appointed Jonathan Lewis to focus on implementing the suggested initiatives. A year and a half later during the South Africa 2006 MC convocation, Rob Brynjolfson became the IMTN's first full-time director.

The IMTN is dedicated to encouraging best missionary training practices among its global evangelical Christian constituencies, and to assure that quality training is available to all those who are called to serve as missionaries. The IMTN carries out its purpose in diverse ways:

- Promoting whole person (integral) ministry training and best training methodologies.

- Providing training in how to design and implement integral training.

- Developing culturally appropriate curricula and training packages.

- Conducting research and consultations.

- Offering assessment to specific programs.

- Delivering internet resources for missionary training in widely used languages of instruction.

While the IMTN shares a common vision, projects and programs depend primarily on regional leadership. The IMTN staff exists to help coordinate and support these initiatives, but without these proposals and the participation of active expert volunteers in each region, the IMTN cannot accomplish its goals. More on the IMTN can be found at www.missionarytraining.com.

The authors of this work, *Integral Ministry Training Design and Evaluation*, each have a wealth of experience in missionary training and have participated actively as resource persons for the IMTN. Let us introduce them to you:

Rob Brynjolfson left his home in Vancouver, BC, Canada at the age of 18 to serve his first term as a missionary with International Teams in Bolivia, where he was involved in church planting. Upon his return, Rob studied at Northwest Baptist College in Vancouver, and then at Regent College where he earned an M.Div. At Regent he met and later married Silvia from Argentina. Together they served with WEC International in Spain and Equatorial Guinea, focusing on leadership training and development. Upon their return to Canada, Rob and Silvia were asked by WEC to start a "hands-on" missionary training program. This led to the founding of the Gateway Missionary Training Centre in Langley, BC, where he continues to serve as program director. In 2006, Rob completed studies and was awarded a D.Min. from Trinity Evangelical Divinity School in Deerfield, Illinois. In July 2006, he stepped down as the pastor of Esperanza Multicultural Church in Burnaby, BC, to provide direction to the International Missionary Training Network (IMTN). Rob and Silvia have three children, Karis, Walter, and David. They live in Langley, BC, Canada.

Robert W. Ferris' initial exposure to cross-cultural ministry came when his parents followed the Lord's leading into missionary service in Liberia when Bob was 12 years old. God used the years in Liberia to awaken Bob to the need for ministry training in churches of the Majority World. Following graduation from college and seminary, Bob and his wife, Sue, went to the Philippines with SEND International, where Bob taught theology at FEBIAS College of Bible. In 1977, his growing awareness of the educational challenges of cross-cultural teaching led Bob back to post-graduate studies in educational administration and curriculum. In 1988, following 21 years of service to the Church in the Philippines, Bob was appointed missionary scholar in residence at the Billy Graham Center in Wheaton and wrote a book, *Renewal in Theological Education*. Bob's service with the WEA Mission Commission dates from 1989. He was part of the team that developed the Mission Commission's workshops on developing curricula for missionary training, authored several articles for *Training for Cross-Cultural Ministry*, and edited the book *Establishing Ministry Training*. Bob currently serves as associate provost of Columbia International University, in Columbia, South Carolina, USA, and as teacher and consultant to ministry trainers in the global Church. In 2006, Bob and Sue celebrated 45 years of marriage. They have two married children and three grandchildren.

Lois K. Fuller served and taught in Nigeria from 1974 to 2004. Her preparation for ministry included studies at Emmanuel Bible College, the University of Guelph (linguistics), Trinity Evangelical Divinity School (New Testament) and London School of Theology (formerly LBC) in the UK. She is now working on her Ph.D. at McMaster

Divinity College in Hamilton, Ontario. Lois' ministry in Nigeria was heavily invested in ministry training. For 21 years she taught Greek, Bible and Missions at United Missionary Church of Africa Theological College (UMCATC), and she served for six years as the first Dean of the Nigeria Evangelical Missionary Institute (NEMI) in Jos, Nigeria. She has helped develop mission curriculum and materials for that school as well as for a number of other training programs and theological schools in Nigeria. She is the author of *Going to the Nations*, *The Missionary and His Work*, *A Missionary Handbook on African Traditional Religion*, *Adventures for God*, and *A Biblical Theology of Missions*. Following her doctoral studies she plans to teach in Canada.

Rodolfo Girón is an architect, a graduate of San Carlos University in his native Guatemala. Rudy has been active in ministry since 1978. An ordained bishop of the Church of God, Rudy completed his M.Div. in Cleveland, Tennessee. He then served as National Director of Theological Education for the Church of God in Guatemala, overseeing both residential and TEE programs. From 1990 till 1997 he served as president of COMIBAM, promoting and facilitating missions throughout Latin America. He also served COMHINA (Cooperation in Missions for the Hispanics of North America) as a founder and its first executive director. During that time he was also the coordinator for the Mission Commission's international attrition study (ReMAP). From 1997 to early 2006 Rudy left Guatemala to serve as founder and president of the Eurasian Theological Seminary, a Church of God educational institution in Moscow, Russia. In January, 2006, Rudy became the USA Director of Hispanic Educational Ministries for the Church of God. Rudy and his wife, Alma, have four children and four grandchildren. Rudy enjoys spending time with his family, reading good literature, making music, and visiting with friends.

Evelyn Hibbert was called to missions in her home nation of Australia at the age of eight and grew up in Papua New Guinea and Australia. After completing training in medicine, she served with her husband, Richard, in Turkey and Bulgaria for 12 years. Along with church planting, her ministry focused on developing leaders for the rapidly growing movement to Christ among Muslim-background Turkish-speaking Gypsies. Since 2002 she has served as the International Director for Equipping and Advance for WEC International. In this role she and her husband are developing a flexible, accessible, practical, and on-the-job training approach for missionaries. She has an M.Ed. in vocational education and is working on a doctorate in education focused on multicultural team leadership.

Steve Hoke is Vice President for People Development for Church Resource Ministries (CRM; Anaheim, CA), and serves on the Staff Development and Care Team. He was formerly professor of Missions at Seattle Pacific University (1977-1985), Director of Field Training with World Vision International, and President of LIFE Ministries (Japan). Steve is the author of over 50 articles on missions and is the co-author with Bill Taylor of *Send Me! Your Journey to the Nations* (1999). He lectures widely for the Perspectives course and does training with ACMC, teaches in the IFMA-EFMA Leader-LINK series around the world, and speaks widely in church missions conferences, helping churches refocus their mission vision to become more strategic. His passion is to equip and encourage front-line mission leaders to minister in the power of the Spirit and with spiritual authority in the difficult places of the world. He lives with his wife Eloise in Fort Collins, Colorado, USA.

Jonathan Lewis was born in Argentina as one of eight children, and is a third generation missionary. He and his wife Dawn served as missionaries from 1976-1997 in Honduras, Peru, Mexico and Argentina. The development of ministry training resources and programs has been the predominant thread in the Lewis' ministry. With a vision to support and train those involved in the emerging missions movement in Latin America, they developed the *World Mission* course in Spanish, first published in Argentina in 1986. Jon and Dawn spent much of the following years in Argentina with their four children, promoting missionary training, serving the COMIBAM missions movement, and helping establish the Center for Cross-Cultural Missionary Training (CCMT) in Cordoba. Jon also pursued studies in Human Resource Development and was awarded a Ph.D. from Colorado State University in 1992. From 1992-2006, Jon served as a staff member of the World Evangelical Alliance Missions Commission. For five of those years, the Lewises lived in Canada and helped develop the Gateway Missionary Training Centre, while Jon also initiated the ACTS Intercultural Ministry Centre at Trinity Western University and taught in their cross-cultural ministries program. He continues with his commitment to missionary training, working with International Missionary Training Network. Jon and Dawn live in Ferndale, Washington, USA, and enjoy the outdoors.

Drawing to a Close

As I gaze into the incredibly diverse world of the Church in mission, truly the most globalized facet of globalization today, I find many causes to encourage me related to training of the cross-cultural missionary. New models are emerging, local churches are trying to improve their programs, and creative training options are increasingly available on the Internet and in many languages. We have highly dedicated and gifted women and men who are deeply committed to revisit the established training models and to seek a new wind of the Spirit in their programs.

The way forward calls for valiant mission leaders and educators who passionately desire to collaborate even as they revisit the assumptions of ministry training, who incubate younger and creative leaders, who are not bound by the strictures of formal academics, who see the need to learn from others, whether it's the North learning learn from the South, even as the South learns from the North, and all listen to each other.

We are committed to emphasize with all of our resources the vital importance of integral pre-field and life-long equipping of servants who will minister in a cultural context different than their own—whether in close or distant geography, and probably crossing linguistic lines and ethnicities. In countless cities and nations, the "peoples" are on the move and resettling. Thus one can "reach" Muslims in Pakistan or Toronto; Buddhists in Sri Lanka or London; Hindus in Mumbai or Vancouver; Maya peoples in Guatemala or Los Angeles; animists in Haiti or Miami.

May God give us grace and creativity to push the boundaries, to create, to re-evaluate, to change, to redesign, and to serve with greater effectiveness and servanthood.

Preface

Fighting the Enemy with New Methods

Rodolfo Girón

1 Samuel 17 records the account of David and Goliath. It also tells the way Saul responded to David's brave offer to fight the giant. This historical text relates one of the most significant moments in the life of the people of Israel. It is a model passage, demonstrating the importance of using appropriate and contextualized methods to fight the enemies we face as the people of God.

This application is particularly true for the missionary movement from the Two-Thirds World, as it relates to traditional missions from the West. Methods, tools, and strategies that may have been of great value to the development of the historical movement may not fit the needs and potentials of emerging Two-Thirds World missions. In the area of training, this recognition is especially valuable. We may have a tendency to adopt the methods of others uncritically, because we feel they have worked well for some cultures. At the same time, some may attempt to impose their methods on us, just because they believe theirs is the right way to do missionary training.

In its own battlefields, the non-Western missionary movement is facing a lot of giants like David's Goliath. This man was physically greater than David. He was almost three meters (9 feet, 9 inches) tall, and David was but a "young man" by comparison. Goliath was there to fight the trembling flock of Israel. No one, not even big King Saul, was ready to fight him.

David came as someone simply willing and able to fight the great giant. David proved to be a man of vision, courage, and valor, but beyond this, a man filled with the Spirit of God. The way David faced the battle using his own methods, his own experience and tools, is an example to us as we try to approach the challenge of developing training methods and strategies to train our missionaries who are going to face the big giants on the mission field. We can simply repeat what others traditionally have done, because such an approach is believed to have worked well, or we can identify and use our own methods that fit our realities and needs.

Let's see how David faced the different challenges before him.

The Challenge of Confronting Opposition and Criticism

One of the major problems we can face when we offer to fight giants is the opposition and criticism that comes from our own people. It doesn't make sense, but we can be defeated even before entering the battlefield. This is exactly what David faced when he decided to ask, "What will be done for the man who kills this Philistine and takes away the reproach from Israel? For who is this uncircumcised Philistine, that he should taunt the armies of the living God?" (v 26)[1]

First, David encountered opposition from his brothers (vv 28-29). According to verse 28, when Eliab, his older brother, heard of David's interest in what was happening, he spoke to him saying, "Why have you come down?...I know your insolence and the wickedness of your heart...." Instead of being proud of David's valor, David's brother was angry with him. Unusual as it may seem, David did not stop to argue but "turned away from him." The point is not to turn away from our own people, but we should turn away from the "loser mentality" that refuses to believe that we are able to do great things with God's help. Following David's example, Two-Thirds World Christians in any nation need to embrace a "winner mentality." The time has come to believe that we are able to do things far beyond our own limitations. We need a change of mentality.

The second kind of opposition David faced came from the establishment—from King Saul (vv 33-37). David's offer finally came to Saul's attention. It is remarkable to see David's courage in saying to the King, "Let no man's heart fail on account of him [referring to Goliath]; your servant will go and fight with this Philistine."

Saul's response to this brave declaration clearly indicated his prejudice due to David's appearance. He said to David, "You are not able to go against this Philistine to fight with him, for you are but a youth while he has been a warrior from his youth."

It is easy to discount somebody because of his or her appearance or apparent inexperience. Saul failed to consider David's own resources and experience. According to the text, he did not even remember who David was (see v 55). Some time ago I read a commentary on this passage by a Latin American theologian. He observed that because David's name and record were not in Saul's computer, this did not necessarily mean David did not exist. Like David, the Two-Thirds World missionary movement can be dismissed as "not able" and "too young" to fight the giants of Islam, Hinduism, and other false religious systems.

David's response to Saul's prejudice was not a self-defense or an apology, but it was a reaffirmation of his own principles and experience. David's mind was clear. He did not take time to address Saul's prejudice and fears. Instead, he directly told Saul about his past experiences. "Your servant was tending his father's sheep. When a lion or a bear came and took a lamb from the flock, I went out after him, and attacked him and rescued it from his mouth.... Your servant has killed both the lion and the bear; and this uncircumcised Philistine will be like one of them, since he has taunted the armies of the living God" (vv 35-36).

David understood God's power in his life. He knew he was able to defeat Goliath because God was with him. When we know for sure what we are able to do through the power of the Spirit of God, we do not need to apologize for what God has done through us.

---

1   All references in this section are from NASB.

Here we need to consider the importance of the recent history of Christianity. In the last three decades Christianity has experienced a paradigm shift. While in the past most Christians were in the West, now the great majority are in the non-Western world. The church is growing fastest in countries such as Korea, China, Guatemala, and Brazil. The fact is, many things are different now from before. Churches in many countries have come of age; they have learned their own ways of doing things. God has blessed Two-Thirds World churches in such a way that many churches in the West have begun to learn from them.

The Challenge of Choosing the Right Methods

Like most people, Saul believed it was impossible to fight without proper armor. Therefore, he did what he considered proper; he determined to clothe David with his own armor so David would be able to face the giant. He never thought to ask whether his armor would fit David. He did not consider if, instead of helping David, his armor would hinder him. Saul just thought, since his armor worked for him, it would work for David. Does that sound familiar? It frequently happens when we try to solve problems in other cultural contexts. We assume our own methods must be the best for the people with whom we are working.

Here is a case in which someone with experience on one battlefield tried to impose methods on another person who was new to this kind of fighting, although he had fought his own battles. It is worth noting that David did not refuse to try the armor. He gave it a chance, but he soon found out that it was not the best way for him to enter the battle. Many times, we try methods other than those we are used to. It is good to try, especially when we are in a pre-field situation. Nevertheless, we will find that some methods and strategies will not fit our needs or resources.

We see what happened with David. Verse 39 says, "And David girded [Saul's] sword over his armor and tried to walk, for he had not tested them." Lack of practice with Saul's armor left David unable to use it. In spite of the convenience of advanced methods used by others, if we are not familiar with them, they may not work for us.

Realizing that he could not use Saul's methods (his armor and sword), David "took them off." He then took up his own weapons and used his own strategy to fight. David "chose for himself five smooth stones from the brook, and put them in the shepherd's bag... and his sling was in his hand; and he approached the Philistine" (v 40). David knew what he was able to do with the things that were familiar to him.

What a tremendous message from this passage to the Two-Thirds World missionary movement! We need to remind ourselves that during the past fifty years, we have learned many good things. The church in the Two-Thirds World is growing faster than ever and much faster than in the West. The largest churches are in the Two-Thirds World.

Many wonderful things have been accomplished in what was called the "mission field." Now is the time to use those experiences to enter the battlefield against such giants as Islam, Buddhism, and Hinduism.

There is no better tool than the one we know how to use well. This does not rule out the possibility of being trained in the use of new tools, but even the way training is done should be adapted to the mentality and need of those receiving the training. The question arises, how can those from other contexts pass on valuable experiences without imposing methods that do not fit the needs of the new fighter? How can we apply training experiences and methods that have proven effective in Western countries, but which may not be the best for our particular situation? I will say the answer is contextualization.

We have to learn how to take advantage of tools and methods used in other contexts, taking the core principles and applying them to our own situation. In a sense, David did this when he defeated Goliath. Verse 51 says, "Then David ran and stood over the Philistine and took his sword and drew it out of its sheath and killed him, and cut off his head with it." David used Goliath's sword to finish his task, but he did not depend on it. We need to learn how to take the best things from others and apply them to our need in a contextualized way.

David is a great example to us. While he was experienced and had faith in what he knew God could do through him, he did not refuse to give Saul's methods a try. Nevertheless, he was courageous enough to say, "I cannot go with this. Saul, I cannot do it your way; let me do it my way. God has shown me different methods for fighting the battle, and I trust they will work with this giant." David's goal was to give God the glory and honor. He was not looking for his own exaltation but for God's. When answering Goliath's challenge he said, "I come to you in the name of the LORD of hosts, the God of the armies of Israel, whom you have defied…. This very day the Lord will deliver you into my hand…that all the earth may know that there is a God in Israel" (vv 45-46 RSV). David's ultimate goal was that all the earth would give glory to God—the only one who deserves it!

This is a great example to us; the glory in all we do belongs to God. Sometimes when we do things in a different way, we do not receive recognition. Others may gain credit, but that does not matter since we are seeking God's glory. We are looking at the ultimate goal—that all the earth, all the people on earth, all those unreached with the gospel—may know that there is one God who loves them and sent his Son Jesus Christ to die for them.

What a lesson for us! A youngster, led by the Spirit of God to fight the enemy in an unconventional way, teaches God's people that it is possible to win the battle using methods that fit our realities and resources, and in doing so to give all the glory to God.

The Foundations of Integral Training

Chapter 1

The Integral Ministry Training Journey

Rob Brynjolfson

The Journey

My personal fascination with integral ministry training grew out of developing a missionary training program in Canada from the ground up. At the outset, this was a journey without a map. I had been asked by the directors of WEC International in Canada to start a missionary training program that was "practical." As I considered this challenge, I realized that apart from duplicating the theological education I had received, I really had no idea how to train a missionary. My colleague and partner in the effort, Ken Getty, placed the World Evangelical Alliance (WEA) Mission Commission book, *Internationalising Missionary Training*,[1] into my hands, and reading it convinced me that the specialized needs of missionary training would require different methods than those typically associated with theological education. Later, through a course taught by Bill Taylor, I came across Robert Ferris' book, *Establishing Missionary Training*,[2] and another WEA Mission Commission book by David Harley,[3] which proved to be excellent resources.[4]

Reading these books, I began to understand the concept of integral ministry training—that to ensure a missionary was well trained we had to have a clear idea of who a missionary is (not just what he knows or does). WEC International had developed a missionary profile, and using that as a beginning, my cohorts and I developed a profile of the missionary we wanted to emerge from the center by describing who a missionary should be, along with what he needs to do and know. This profile became the picture for the outcomes of our program. It was to be the foundation to all of the training at our new Gateway Missionary Training Centre. As instructed, we had designed the training by keeping the end in mind—what actually needs to be produced in

---

1   William D. Taylor, *Internationalising Missionary Training*, (UK: Paternoster Press, 1991).
2   Robert Ferris, *Establishing Ministry Training: A manual for programme developers*, (Pasadena: Wm. Carey Library, 1995).
3   David Harley, *Preparing to Serve*, (Pasadena: Wm. Carey Library, 1995).
4   All three books mentioned are available for download at http://www.wearesources.org.

the life of the missionary candidate. Unfortunately, these exciting ideas were easier to discuss than to implement.

As we stumbled forward in implementing our ideas, we suspected that we were learning more than any of our students were. We desperately hoped that we were doing more good than harm along the way. During this time of uncertainty, we had an unexpected encounter with Jonathan Lewis,[5] who provided some much needed advice. The result was greater clarity in *how* to develop a program that provided the attention and the resources needed to produce the desired outcomes in all three areas: *being, doing* and *knowing*. For us, this meant cutting classroom time in half and developing additional programs, such as a three-month structured cross-cultural internship, one-on-one mentoring, a debriefing phase, and more intentional use of our community living experience.

Reflecting on our pilgrimage, we were committed to the values of what we called "hands-on" practical and integral missionary training, but in the beginning we lacked a clear sense of the process to get to where we thought we needed to go. This book, *Integral Ministry Training*, would have helped us immensely in understanding the underpinnings of integral ministry training and would have given us the focus and processes necessary to implement a program with greater confidence and effectiveness. Happily, Gateway did find the help it needed to make the transition and has offered a truly integral program since 1998. (See the integral program descriptions chapter for a fuller description of this and other journeys.)

Mapping Our Course

This book emphasizes the philosophy of integral ministry training first presented by the WEA Mission Commission's 1995 publication, *Establishing Ministry Training: A Manual for Programme Developers*, (Ed. R. Ferris), as well as preserving and enhancing the process focus of the previous work. Ferris' book served the missionary training community well for the past twelve years as is evidenced by the familiarity with the concepts found in various parts of the world.

Two years ago, while translating and using this book as a text for a graduate level course on curriculum design taught in Argentina, Jonathan Lewis and I saw the advantage of updating the material, streamlining the process and supplementing it with needed material on the philosophy of integral training as well as adult education theory. Initially, we believed that this new edition would be limited to a Spanish version, but Bill Taylor strongly urged that this WEA-MC publication be re-edited in English as well.

In this book, the reader will find ten chapters stretched over two sections dividing the theoretical content and the process elements of designing an integral training curriculum. A third section provides additional resources. The first section, titled *The Foundations of Integral Training*, presents the reader with the fundamental elements of integral training. Following this introductory chapter, Jonathan Lewis' chapter *Philosophy of Integral Ministry Training* asks us to consider the important question: "How should we approach education from a Christian worldview perspective?" It suggests a number of principles that should guide our thinking as we design and implement training. The third chapter, *Understanding Integral Ministry Training*, defines what we mean by "integral" and the biblical understanding and education theory that supports this

Chapter Objectives:

This chapter is designed to help you:

- Recognize the need for integral ministry training.
- Create a mental map of the book and its goals.
- Understand the fundamental language and concepts on which the book builds.

---

5   Jonathan Lewis was part of an international team that founded the Center for Cross-Cultural Missionary Training in Córdoba, Argentina in 1995. This center was based on principles of integral ministry training design.

concept. Following this chapter is Lois Fuller's, *Starting a Ministry Training Program*, brought forward from the previous edition. Her chapter is a "must read" for those planning to start a training program, because she addresses many of the basic questions and unexamined assumptions which designers of new training programs will face. The final chapter in this section, Evelyn Hibbert's *Designing Training for Adults*, provides the adult education theory. This chapter is a critical addition to the book. Every integral or holistic training program must not only be familiar with adult education principles, but also be adept at using methods, techniques and interventions that enhance adult learning.

The second section, titled *The Process of Integral Ministry Training Design*[6], organizes the next five chapters in the same way as the previous edition, *Establishing Ministry Training* (R. Ferris). Jonathan Lewis, in *Stakeholders Assumptions and Consensus Building*, leads the reader in a discussion of identifying and involving stakeholders in the training, working through underlying assumptions about the training, and the decision making processes. In the following chapter, *The Outcomes Profiling Process*, Jonathan helps the reader to develop an outcomes profile that is based on a clear description of the task or ministry to be fulfilled. Turning outcomes into well-written and clear learning objectives is the purpose of Steve Hoke's chapter, *Writing Learning Objectives*. Then, in Chapter 9, *Designing Learning Experiences*, Steve helps the reader to move from a learning objective to creating learning experiences that are designed to meet the previously expressed learning objectives. This section concludes with Robert Ferris' chapter, *Evaluating Training Outcomes*. No curriculum design process is complete without an adequate plan to evaluate and improve the whole program.

Following these two sections the reader will find *Additional Resources* in the final section. Two sub-sections are included. The first, *Integral Program Descriptions*, presents a collection of case studies—a rich resource of creative solutions to challenging problems facing training programs in distinct contexts. The second, *Evaluation Tools*, offers unique resources for ministry training and for organization development.

Interpreting the Symbols

Legends are useful devices for every map-reader. How many times do we find ourselves puzzled over a symbol on the map or chart and need to find the legend to explain the meaning behind all the symbols? Words are symbols, and often carry different denotative and connotative meanings to each reader. To ignore this fact may lead to confusion at best, and frustration and suspicion at worst. To offset this problem, this manual uses a number of expressions that need "up front" clarification.

Integral Training

Integral training delivers a learning experience that intentionally addresses the needs of the whole person, including their character and spiritual formation, skill development, and their understanding.

---

6   In this section, the primary difference between the first and second edition is found in Jonathan Lewis' chapter seven, *The Outcomes Profiling Experience*. This chapter clarifies the process, making a simpler five-step plan to help a group of stakeholders develop an outcomes profile describing who a trained person is, and what he or she can do.

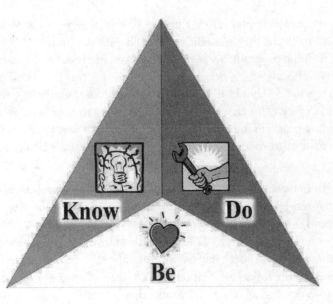

We can use the symbols heart, hands and head to represent these three interrelated aspects or training. The words "be", "do" and "know" are another way of expressing this triad. In fact, triads emerge so prominently in our discussion that we felt it was an appropriate symbol in itself, and became the dominant symbol expressed in the book cover. The educational theory represented by these symbols is found in Chapter 3: *Understanding Integral Ministry Training*. Integral ministry training starts by identifying desired training outcomes—who the trainee must become, be able to do, and understand to be effective in ministry. The program then uses appropriate methods and contexts to produce these outcomes.

The editors of this book chose to use the word "integral" in its title for three reasons. First, it is synonymous with holistic, designating the unification of various separate parts that make up a whole or complete object. Second, something that is integral is necessary, required and incomplete if lacking any part. Ministry training that is not whole-person oriented is definitely incomplete. Third, the ethos of this book emerged from those parts of the world where the English word "holistic" is more precisely translated with the equivalent "integral." It is fitting to indicate the origins of this book in its title. It is important to bear in mind throughout this publication that integral and holistic are used synonymously. Both appear in the text without the intention of any distinction.

Curriculum

This book uses the term *curriculum* to embrace every area of learning and never refers only to the academic or formal learning that takes place in a lecture hall. We refer the reader to Chapter 8 where Steve Hoke aptly defines curriculum saying:

> *We will use the word "curriculum" in its broadest sense, that is, the entire learning environment in which intentional learning takes place. Any time we decide what others should do in order to enable them to become or to do something else, we are planning curriculum.*

In this definition we notice an important qualifying word: curriculum is *intentional*. Informal learning is needed to reinforce proper attitudes and support character and spiritual growth. This happens predominantly in uncontrolled and unplanned learning moments. This is still curriculum, however, because designers of integral ministry training know that it is through interaction with people, experiences and environments that spontaneous informal learning occurs. They cannot be specific about much of the informal learning that takes place, but they can be intentional about providing the context in which trainees will most likely be impacted by other lives, their surroundings, and what is likely to happen. For example, designers of integral ministry training know that just having people live closely together and share common household tasks will likely create self-awareness and generate opportunities for character change and growth.

As the reader progresses through this manual, he or she is encouraged to remember that curriculum is always used in this broadest sense. The word curriculum goes beyond the course of study delivered in a classroom. It includes prayer meetings, chapel services, mentoring sessions, coaching across the table over lunch, as well as evangelistic excursions, leading Bible studies, adjusting to another culture during an overseas internship or learning a new language. A skilled trainer intentionally uses a great variety of methods, processes and contexts in their curriculum to produce the desired effect.

Outcomes-Based

There is another term that needs definition because it can cause suspicion. Some of us have encountered the term "outcomes-based" education in less than agreeable circumstances that may have provoked frustration and annoyance. Such situations occur when an outside authority dictates that a school or training program must be "outcomes-based" to qualify for certification or registration. In such cases, we may find ourselves rejecting a perfectly helpful approach to training because the process of introduction was so flawed. As they say, let us not throw the baby out with the bath water.

Outcomes-based training is an educational approach that identifies the desired end result of the training and systematically develops a program to intentionally develop in the trainee those expressed results. This approach objectifies the training needs by making clear learning outcome statements, which describe the objectives of the training in terms of who a trained person is, should be able to do, and what the person needs to understand in order to be and do those things. Sometimes outcomes are called competencies, but the reader should remember that these words are not exact synonyms. An outcome is more general, whereas, competencies relate to the development of skills and abilities. This term is strongly rooted in the discipline of vocational education.

These learning outcome statements guide the training process so that learning interventions are designed to achieve explicit learning targets. Furthermore, they serve to evaluate the program and provide a criterion to assess the progress of the trainee. The system works well when those responsible for a training program can describe, through a consensus process, who a trained person is, the skills he or she has acquired and the understanding needed to be and do those things. It ensures that the educational process relies not on assumptions, but on a planned process working towards a previously determined level of competence and can objectively define the level of achievement at the conclusion of a course of study.

Outcomes that are generated through a consensus process involving the stakeholders of a training program are normally well received and provide an effective target that can guide the whole design process. The alternative is to design a program based on intuition and trial and error. Yet, experience tells us that when we have a clear goal in mind, it is not only easier to achieve, we can tell with certainty whether our efforts were on target.

Affective Learning

This manual will use a variety of phrases referring to desired learning outcomes in the affective domain. Educators refer to the three areas of learning as cognitive, affective, and psycho-motor. Training for ministry grapples with these three areas, but we prefer to use a different terminology. Instead of cognitive learning, we speak of understanding, because it reflects a higher development than the mere acquisition of knowledge. Instead of psycho-motor learning, we talk about ministry or work skills and abilities. But when it comes to the area of affective learning, we often grasp for an appropriate term.

This manual will frequently refer to learning in the affective domain as character growth and will talk about character traits, qualities or attitudes. In the minds of the writers, the term character refers to who a person is, and includes the area of spiritual formation. Character refers to the "Be" of the "Be, Know, Do" triad.

Character growth is spiritual formation. Christian character begins with spiritual regeneration and renewal. One cannot truly grow in Christian character without a growing relationship with the Triune God. Many training programs will differentiate between character development and spiritual formation, but it is essentially all part of the affective area of learning. The text of this book may primarily use the terms character, or character traits and attitudes, but it should be understood by the reader, that the very important area of spiritual formation is an integral part of character formation.

Who Is This Book For?

This book is designed for anyone interested in or involved in ministry training. Although much of the book is placed in the context of "missionary training," the principles and processes described apply to the design of any kind of ministry training. It is thus useful to leaders of churches, agencies, or any organization that attempts to train persons for Christian service.

> The principles and processes described in this book apply to any kind of ministry training.

As the title suggests, the book is intended both for those who are designing training as well as those who need to evaluate existing training programs. As a design tool, it meets the need of those who are introducing training and are looking for the best way to go about designing or selecting a training program that suits their specific needs. In other cases, the training program already exists, but there is a need to evaluate it with objectified criteria based on performance and outcomes.

Some readers will be administrators of existing training programs or instructors considering how to ensure that the training they provide addresses the needs of the whole person. They may not be convinced that an existing program is effective in its training for a specific ministry. Similarly, an institution or organization may be experiencing transition and the shift in the training mandate requires re-tooling the program of study. Some will be instructors who are not able to change an entire program, but have the opportunity to make certain that the training they do personally addresses the real training needs of ministry students. In some cases, agency administrators are aware of issues relating to attrition and retention in ministry and want to ensure that the orientation or training programs they provide actually impact the longevity and effectiveness of their personnel.

Another group that may find this material useful are instructors or consultants who are responsible to train trainers and need a workable process to put into people's hands that empowers them to design their own training programs. These consultants are frequently called upon to help assess existing programs or facilitate the design of a new program. Using integral ministry training design processes assures a commitment to learning that addresses development of the whole person and their effectiveness in ministry.

Many of you reading these words are students of educational programs or will be attending workshops on how to design ministry training curricula. You come with a burden to equip others for ministry and already suspect that traditional educational methods do not necessarily produce effective people for effective service. You may be seeking a process you can follow that will guide you towards the design and implementation of a whole person training program. We believe this course will help you to fulfill your aspirations and we welcome you as fellow pilgrims.

Because learners may come from a variety of ministry backgrounds and organizations, we encourage you to extract the principles and apply them to the ministry-equipping challenge you face, whether it is training Sunday school teachers, camp counselors, or cross-cultural workers. The exercises in this book are designed to help you address your particular challenge.

Our Commitment

The process described in this book reflects a high commitment to training or equipping people to be *effective* in ministry. Effective ministry means accomplishing ministry goals in a way that honors God and fulfills organizational goals. It is much easier to hit the goal or target when the target is clearly in view. An outcomes-led curriculum design keeps the desired intent clearly in focus. These outcomes also need to address the whole person. This important commitment to effective ministry training recognizes that a significant portion of the desired intent (outcomes) must be expressed in character traits and attitudes—who the person is and how they relate to themselves, God and others.

We also know certain attitudes are important to every ministry because they develop Christ-like character. Developing these attitudes may be a commonly stated objective. Other attitudes are ministry specific, and when articulated as outcomes, can be intentionally addressed in the program. The most difficult kinds of outcomes to intentionally incorporate into traditional training programs are attitude and character outcomes, so they are often overlooked, ignored or assumed to be developed elsewhere or through a "spontaneous" process of trial and error. Ministry-specific skills must also be identified and developed, as well as appropriate levels of understanding achieved in specific areas. Information is used as a tool to achieve desired outcomes, not as something to be accumulated by and stored in overloaded brains.

> This book is based on the training needs of missionaries because there is no greater challenge in ministry preparation than preparing a person to serve cross-culturally.

Addressing the Cross-Cultural Challenge

This book is based on the training needs of missionaries because there is no greater challenge in ministry preparation than preparing a person to serve cross-culturally. It is arguably more complex than other ministry training. By showing how these processes are applied to that which is difficult to achieve, less complex training is also served. Sunday school superintendents can develop a training program using the principles in this book in their context. They too should build consensus amongst the identified stakeholders, create a profile of the ideal Sunday school teacher, write learning objectives, design learning experiences and seek to develop the program in the quest for excellence.

Pastors responsible for the development of home group leaders can follow the same process. Christian summer camps can do the same to train counselors or water sport instructors. The applications are unlimited.

A final justification for the cross-cultural application reflected in this book is the changing context of ministry today. Due to the urbanization of the planet, the cosmopolitan nature of most urban centers and the extent of the postmodernist influence around the world, there are relatively few ministries that legitimately have no need to address the intercultural issues of our day. No seminary, Bible college or institute should train pastors without addressing the intercultural needs of contemporary ministry in a globalized society.

As previously alluded to, the drive to see this book published emerges from the developing world. It is exciting to see many national missionary movements awaken to the need to provide effective cross-cultural training for their workers. Many training programs have been birthed over the last decade with an expressed desire to train the whole person for service. Some attest to satisfactory results, but many struggle as we have struggled. The accumulation of training experience has provided a basis for legitimate reflection and it is time to implement change.

In summary, this book is useful not only for the design of new programs, but in helping existing programs achieve new levels of effectiveness. By utilizing the process described in this book, they can evaluate and improve the training already being delivered. It is a tool to strengthen ministry training in any context.

How to Use This Manual

The end user of this manual, whether a facilitator or learner, will discover many resources scattered throughout the pages of this book. One of the simplest resources available to the reader is the wide margin space that can be utilized to make notes and references. This book is to be used, so do not be afraid to mark it up.

Examples:

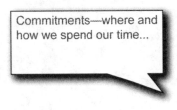

The other resources that readers will find include "callouts" that highlight key content. The callouts are effective summaries of important points and serve as signposts to the reader, and quick references for an instructor. Rely on these to find one's place in the body of the text. This example can be found on page 16.

 What are some of the ways your worldview has shaped .....

The reader will also find a helpful resource in the study questions that are included in the margins. These are designated by the writing hand, indicating that the reader has some work to do here if he or she is to take advantage of this information. This example also comes from page 16.

A different kind of callout can be found at the beginning of the chapters presenting the reader with the chapter objectives. Every reader likes to know where they will be taken at the outset, and the chapter objectives describe this well.

The program descriptions and other resources found in section three are not the only resources included in this manual. There are a number of resources scattered throughout the pages of this manual that readers will benefit from without the need to turn to a reference section at the end of the book. For example, at the end of chapter 6 we discover a list of ten biblical and educational commitments to guide missionary training by Robert Ferris. This table was inserted strategically at this point because it is a resource that a person can use while working on the educational assumptions of a group of stakeholders.

On occasion the reader will discover checklists that serve to guide a process. These are summaries of a procedure and serve a facilitator to quickly review the material, ensure integrity in the process and for use in presentations. This example of a checklist for a profiling exercise can be found on page 85.

Exercises are included in the chapters and these are designed to help readers reflect on the content of a chapter or practice and develop specific skills. This is particularly true of Steve Hoke's chapter on writing learning objectives, a skill easily improved with practice. In this case, the author provides readers with examples and practice sheets, which can be copied and used over and over to ensure the skill is acquired.

A final word of advice regarding the use this manual: "Keep using it!" Those involved in training ministries will continually return to this book because mastering the concepts and learning the process takes time and practice. The best way to ensure that both the philosophy of ministry training and the process are properly learned is for the reader to make three commitments. The first commitment is to an outcomes-based curriculum. When the reader is convinced that this method will ensure that the curriculum is both contextualized and effective, a commitment to this process will give those responsible for the training a degree of assurance that the training will accomplish what they set out to achieve. This is the result of committing to specific end results, and not building a program based on intuition and unexamined assumptions. The second commitment is to follow the process as closely as possible. We are all tempted to take short cuts, but experience dictates that we eventually return and end up following this process because it proves to be both efficient and effective. The final commitment necessary and perhaps the most important, is to an extensive evaluation process using Robert Ferris' key chapter on evaluating outcomes. This will ensure we return to the previous two commitments as we discover flaws, unexpected outcomes, and the subsequent need to change and improve our programs.

Conclusion

Though my journey began without a map, one was soon placed within grasp. Twelve years later, this re-edition of the book (Ferris, 1995) should serve others by providing a well-trodden route, marking a clear path that indicates highlights and pitfalls, as well as providing encouragement through the stories of other travelers. The needed foundational chapters should encourage the reader to trust this map, demonstrating that the route is one borne out of experience and reflection with deep respect for the Word of God and a biblical worldview. The process guides the reader through the practical details of starting or strengthening an outcomes-based curriculum, and the additional resources will provide surprisingly useful material for those of us keen on strengthening missionary training in our quest for excellence.

Example:

Phase 2 Checklist

☐ Brainstorm onto cards, chalkboard or overhead transparency.

- Refer back to the definition until all areas are extracted.
- "Clean-up" list by condensing or amplifying.
- Do not exceed 15 general areas.

☐ Review list with whole group to assure all are satisfied.

- Elicit statements from each participant.
- Build consensus.

Chapter 1: Exercises

Self-evaluation

1. Evaluate yourself based on the "competencies" that a missionary trainer or coach should possess in the following table. This table was developed using the process described in this manual. Carefully review each of the categories and reflect on each of the characteristics described. Rate yourself on a scale from 1-10 with 1 being the lowest rating and 10 being the highest.

2. How fit are you to serve as a trainer? If these were "outcomes" for your own personal training program, how would you go about improving the weakest areas? Identify one or more of the areas where you need the most improvement and create a tentative plan to meet your own needs. Share this with those who are taking this course with you or your ministry team. If you grasp this exercise, you will be well on your way to understanding the philosophy and processes outlined in this book.

Missionary Profile of a Cross-Cultural Mentor/Trainer/Coach

General Outcome Areas	Intended Outcomes					
Spiritual Maturity	Evidences a winsome, growing, obedient, close walk w/ God	Has consistent prayer life; sensitive to God's will	Studies Bible daily; maintains spiritual disciplines, good stewardship	Manifests fruits of the Spirit; demonstrates moral integrity	Practices principles of spiritual warfare & willing to handle biblically	Knows & uses spiritual gifts while not abusing them
Family Life	Has a healthy family life; communicates well	Has no major unresolved conflict within family	Husband & wife can work as a team	Family members are physically fit & emotionally healthy	Maintains balance between family & ministry	Uses home for hospitality & fellowship
Interpersonal Relationships	Positively affirms others; not monopolizing or domineering	Willing to listen, especially when corrected	Builds accountable relationships; respectful of spiritual authority	Relates properly to opposite gender, locals, superiors, employees; not overly-intimate	Experienced in community living; can manage conflict w/out explosion	Relates well w/ people of different personalities & cultural backgrounds
Missionary Experience	Demonstrates effectiveness in cross-cultural ministry	Is accepted by fellow missionaries & national leaders	Has participated in planting a healthy, growing church	Contributes to national church as a team player	Effective in communicating the gospel	Brings specific contribution to training from mission ministry
Discipleship & Ministry Skills	Develops effective disciple & mentor relationships	Has maturity to sustain open & honest relationships	Interacts well w/ others in cross-culturally diverse situations	Manages people & projects w/ sensitivity & wisdom	Enters into coop. relationships w/ diverse peoples	Applies gifts of encouragement as mentor/trainer/ coach
Church Relations	Active member of local church, contributing w/ gifts	Committed to church-based missions outreach	Solid experience in a range of church-based ministries	Recommended by local church	Communicates missions well in the local church	Has a high view of the church in target country & coaches leaders
Teaching & Equipping Skills	Listen responsively & communicates effectively	Assesses learners' needs; sensitive to learning styles	Focuses on practical & relevant instruction	Teaches effectively	Always growing in use of varied educational tools/ resources	Evaluates people accurately & guides them to effectiveness
Facilitating Skills	Establishes a nurturing learning community	Facilitates interactive learning, & stimulates participation	Stimulates inquiry & verbalization	Guides group in information gathering & decision-making	Fosters good interpersonal & team dynamics	Helps groups synthesize, clarify & bring closure
Cross-Cultural Awareness & Skills	Has broad cross-cultural experience; understands inter-cultural principles	Continuing learner of cultures; sees w/ "anthropological eyes"	Adjusts quickly to new culture situations; identifies w/ people easily	Respects & affirms all ethnic backgrounds; teachable spirit	Discerns whether to accept customs or not; finds functional substitutes	Wins acceptance & respect of host culture; has experience in ministry to local religions
Interdisciplinary Knowledge	Relates theological knowledge to mission practice	Familiar w/ local, political, & social situations & organizations	Training & experience appropriate to institution's goals	Keeps current on other missionaries & global missions	Biblical & historical grasp of the local & global church	Effectively helps others integrate & apply the Word into life & ministry
Leadership Skills	Positive track record of followership & servanthood	Apt to be a role model; not controlling	Leads/influences others by character & competence	Willing to listen to new ideas & able to discern priorities	Recruits & trains new trainers; can mentor well	Exhibits good management & administrative skills; delegates

Training for Cross-Cultural Ministry, vol 93, no 2 (August 1993), http://www.wearesources.org/Custom/BulletinCache/assets/93aug.pdf

Chapter 2

Philosophy of Integral Ministry Training

Jonathan Lewis

As with any building, a good foundation is essential to a training program's integrity. A biblical worldview with an understanding of God's purposes for his people should be the foundation that shapes Christian ministry training programs.

Christian training programs can be found around the world based largely on secular and/or humanistic worldviews. They adopt the world's models to equip for ministry because they have bought into the underlying value systems of those secular worldviews. This creates a disjuncture between what Christians say they believe and the actual practices they use to train missionaries and other ministers. Bringing alignment between beliefs and training commitments as Christian trainers is a necessary and essential pursuit for those who shape ministry training programs. For example, Scripture makes it clear that the most important qualifications for ministry are a person's relationship to God and his/her character qualities.

Yet many programs judge people for service by their academic performance and may reward them on the basis of natural abilities, intelligence, and skills. In essence, this is how the world functions.

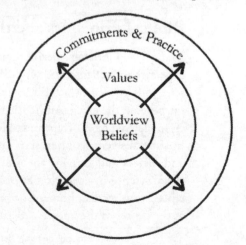

The quest for influence in training design is directional—from worldview to practice—not from practice to worldview. Worldview is largely subconscious, but it can be analyzed and expressed in beliefs about what is real, what is true, and what is important. Beliefs have their more tangible expressions in "idealized" values, such as the importance of relationships over things, moral behavior, the sanctity of life, etc. These values in turn, shape our commitments and practice. In this chapter, we want to reconstruct that process in order to understand its importance in shaping ministry training programs.

The Middle Ground

Mostly, training is shaped by thinking that lies somewhere in the "middle ground"—the dynamic zone between beliefs and commitments. It is dynamic because what is valued is not only influenced by stated beliefs (often expressed as ideals), but by social and cultural pressures (often subconscious and unidentified). To complicate matters, these values are also influenced by our fallen nature with its problematic "cravings of sinful man, the lust of his eyes and the boasting of what he has and does" (I John 2:16). The world's values compete with Christian values. It is out of this dynamic tension that personal and institutional commitments are made—where and how time, money and other resources are invested.

> Commitments—where and how we spend our time, money and other resources.

When it comes to ministry training, it is apparently easier to intellectually grasp and assent to biblical beliefs and articulate them as idealized values, than it is to let them significantly influence training commitments. Somewhere between convictions and training program design, there is a breakdown. Biblical convictions are overwhelmed by social/cultural pressures and personal ambitions. There is a default to what appeals to a sense of social prestige and to norms and standards set by secular institutions. In the pursuit of respectability and social status, many ministry programs subject themselves to secular academic norms in order to gain prestige and acceptance. This is seldom done without sacrificing program integrity. Standards and methods are used that are not conducive to the development of the Christian character or ministry skills that are often touted as the training program's desired outcomes.

 What are some of the ways your worldview has shaped your training principles?

Good ministry training wrestles with this tension and attempts to bring alignment between core beliefs derived from a biblical worldview and the commitments expressed in ministry training programs. Training principles derived from these beliefs must define and support the values that shape training. The journey begins with a conscious attempt to express deeper level Christian convictions about the nature of human beings and their purpose. Then a philosophy of education/training[1] can be articulated through a set of principles and standards that guide commitments in the design and utilization of training programs.

Biblical Principles and the Social Sciences

Evangelical Christians derive their belief system primarily from biblical revelation. They expect these beliefs to be supported by empirical evidence. In this respect, good social science is guided by a biblical understanding of the nature of man and his God-given purpose on the earth. Authentic scientific experimentation often proves long-held principles derived from Scriptures to be true. Good social science is thus useful to Christians. But social scientists often start at the other end of the equation—studying individuals and society and deriving theories and principles from their observations. Too much of social science investigation assumes the absence of God. It forwards theories and principles from secular, humanistic and often atheistic worldviews that put man or society at the center of the universe. Because philosophies of education are formulated without

---

1   A distinction can be made between "formation," "training," and "education" and their correlation to "informal," "non-formal," and "formal" systems of learning. The word, "training" is commonly used to refer to ministry preparation through non-formal as well as formal educational systems.

this biblical understanding of the centrality of God and his purposes, they predictably fall short in providing guiding principles on which to base ministry training programs.

For example, in an address to entering freshman at the prestigious University of Chicago,[2] John Mearsheimer made clear that the institutional goals were: to encourage critical thinking, to broaden intellectual horizons, and to encourage self-awareness. He also made clear that: "Not only is there a powerful imperative at Chicago to stay away from teaching the truth, but the university also makes very little effort to provide you with moral guidance. Indeed it is a remarkably amoral institution. I would say the same thing, by the way, about all other major colleges and universities in this country (USA)." In his address, Mearsheimer seems to taunt the intent of the university's primary patron, Rockefeller, who explicitly stated in reference to the construction of the chapel: "As the spirit of religion should penetrate and control the university, so that building which represents religion ought to be the central and dominant feature of the university group. Thus it will be proclaimed that the University in its ideal is dominated by the spirit of religion, all its departments are inspired by religious feeling, and all its work is directed to the highest ends." This is obviously not current sentiment in public education in much of the Western world.

As trainers grapple with understanding how worldview shapes training practices, it is helpful to look at three secular metaphors of education before arriving at a useful metaphor for ministry training.

Metaphors Used for Education/Training

The discussion of educational philosophy seems to revolve around the question: "Does education primarily serve the individual or society?" Does it focus on students and their potential, or on the production needs of a particular national or social order? The continuum might be drawn as a simple line. This debate often shapes national policies regarding the offering of classical education or vocational education.

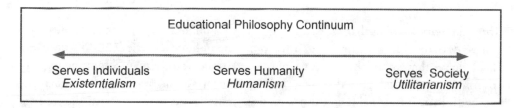

Educational Philosophy Continuum

Serves Individuals — *Existentialism*   Serves Humanity — *Humanism*   Serves Society — *Utilitarianism*

To help us understand this discussion and where we must go as Christian trainers, the following word pictures drafted by educator Herbert M. Kliebard[3] are a helpful starting point.

The Metaphor of Production

The curriculum is the means of production, and the student is the raw material which will be transformed into a finished and useful product under the control of a highly skilled technician. The outcome of the production process is carefully plotted in advance according to rigorous design specifications, and when certain means of production prove to be wasteful, they are discarded in favor of more efficient ones.

---

2   John Mearsheimer, "The Aims of Education Address," *The University of Chicago Record*, Volume 32, Number 1 (October 23, 1997).

3   Herbert M. Kliebard, "Metaphorical Roots of Curriculum Design," *Teachers College Record*, 74, No. 3 (February 1972), pp. 403-404.

Chapter Objectives:

This chapter is designed to help you:

• Understand how worldview shapes our training practices and commitments.

• Present a metaphor for training from a biblical worldview.

• Suggest ten principles that shape integral ministry training

Great care is taken so that raw materials of a particular quality or composition are channeled into the proper production systems and that no potentially useful characteristic of the raw material is wasted.

This particular metaphor fits those who have a utilitarian view and see education as serving societal ends. It draws its core assumptions from behavioral sciences. Training is a "system" where the student moves through a process with a variety of timed "inputs" that will shape and mold him in predictable ways. This approach may see people as "raw materials"—biological machines to be shaped for functional usefulness. In a capitalist system, education and training must be done with great efficiency and at the lowest cost possible for the sake of productivity and the profit line. In totalitarian regimes, people are trained to feed the regime's agenda. This approach at its worst minimizes the value of the individual apart from his or her usefulness to an employer or the state.

> To a certain extent, the high value placed on intentionality, efficiency, and quality can be appreciated.

Christians may be repulsed by this mechanistic and manipulative philosophy, although to a certain extent, the high value placed on intentionality, efficiency, and quality can be appreciated. What can be rescued from this metaphor is a desire to see training be efficient and effective in preparing people for useful ministry. Nevertheless, this cannot be arbitrary and at the sacrifice of individuals' potentiality, gifting, creativity, and uniqueness.

Kliebard's second metaphor is more congenial.

The Metaphor of Growth

The curriculum is the greenhouse where students will grow and develop to their fullest potential under the care of a wise and patient gardener. The plants that grow in the greenhouse are of every variety, but the gardener treats each according to its needs, so that each plant comes to flower. This universal blooming cannot be accomplished by leaving some plants unattended. All plants are nurtured with great solicitude, but no attempt is made to divert the inherent potential of the individual plant from its own metamorphosis or development to the whims and desires of the gardener.

This metaphor assumes that individuals are simply a bundle of "good" potentiality that can be developed through training. This comes in conflict with the biblical worldview that believes that sinful rebellion is deeply rooted in the heart of man. Simply giving way to "inherent potential" runs the risk of helping develop selfish, self-absorbed human beings with little functional usefulness to others. It also seems to assume that the trainers are not training from a higher standard or calling, but rather that they can impose their will capriciously in developing the trainee. This kind of reasoning makes human development an end in itself and allows for arbitrary conduct on the part of the trainee and fickle manipulation by the trainers. This philosophy seems to draw strength from humanism. It does not take into account either the problem of sin and selfishness or an end other than man himself.

There are some good things we can rescue from this approach. The Bible does use "growth" imagery as when the Apostle Paul talks about his "planting" what Apollo "watered" and that "God made it grow" (I Corinthians 3:6). Ephesians 4 uses the image of "growing up into the body of Christ" as the goal of ministry. It is easy to connect with additional planting, weeding, watering, fertilizing, and pruning sorts of analogies: planting—look for the good soil; weeding—pull the sins out while they are little or they'll get out of control; watering—a little each day is better than the occasional flood; fertilizing—fertilize when needed and just enough (it doesn't keep and can't be "banked"); pruning—ouch, that hurts, but it's what makes us grow true, strong and fruitful. This imagery is useful to us if we keep in mind that human development isn't an end in itself. Kliebard's third metaphor tends towards the relational and friendly.

> The metaphor of "growth" fits with biblical imagery if we keep in mind that human development is not an end in itself.

The Metaphor of Travel

The curriculum is a route over which students will travel under the leadership of an experienced guide and companion. Each traveler will be affected differently by the journey since its effect is at least as much a function of the predilections, intelligence, interests, and intent of the traveler as it is of the contours of the route. This variability is not only inevitable, but wondrous and desirable. Therefore, no effort is made to anticipate the exact nature of the effect on the traveler; but a great effort is made to plot the route so that the journey will be as rich, as fascinating, and as memorable as possible.

This metaphor conjures up the age-old image of pilgrims on a pilgrimage. It sees life as a journey accompanied by friends, mentors, and guides. An adventure lies around every turn. Meaning is found in the journey, not in its purpose or destination. On the positive side, there is a great deal to be said about engaging fully in the journey. The idea that meaning is found in the journey resonates with existential philosophy. Seize the day. Live the journey to its fullest for there is no other purpose in life.

> For Christians, the journey does have a destination.

Perhaps the greatest danger of this philosophy, however, is that Christians do believe that the journey has a destination. Further, what happens on that journey affects the destination reached. As humans, it is too easy to let the journey be guided by the voices of human desires, ambition, status, materialism and the baser elements of human nature. This inevitably leads to despair. If the destination of the journey is not aligned with God's purposes, life becomes something other than what God intended it to be. The pilgrimage should be abundant. It should be accompanied. These are elements of the metaphor that are useful. But, this pilgrimage should be guided by a clear vision of the destination.

Failing to examine the underlying assumptions and philosophy of training may lead to reinforcing the wrong attitudes through the training, and leading trainees to an uncertain destination. The "how" of training is arguably more important than the "what" of training because much of the "message" is in the method itself.

The Training Relational Framework

Training always builds on a pre-existing relational framework. This framework is complex because human beings are the product of complex interactions. Integral training programs take into account the trainee's identity, roles and relationships. These are linked in significant ways: a person's *identity* is expressed in *roles,* which in turn are expressed through *relationships and functions.*

Identity answers the question "Who am I?" (The author is a middle-aged male, Caucasian, member of an extended family, follower of Jesus Christ, husband of one wife, father of four children, citizen of two countries, currently residing in a small town in the USA, member of a local church, employee of an international Christian agency, university educated, friend, etc., etc.) Identity is multi-faceted and is expressed in multiple roles.

Roles answer the question "What is expected of me?" Roles are fairly predictable sets of social expectations that let me and others know who I am and what I'm supposed to do. Role expectations are ultimately expressed through a person's relationships.

Relationships answer the question, "What way do I relate with another person or entity in my current role?" Relationships are significantly shaped by attitudes and the skills necessary to function effectively in relation to the person(s) or entities to which the person is related.

Since relationships are strongly shaped by *attitude* and the *skills* to function according to expectations, integral training attempts to create the environment for growth in these two highly related areas. It attempts to accelerate growth and maturity in essential relationships through the formation of right attitudes and the development of personal skills.

Attitudes are the building blocks of *character*, and can be understood as emotionally and spiritually appropriate responses to life's circumstances and interactions with others. Character is the cumulative effect of attitude (right or wrong). A person's character is the evidence of their spiritual and emotional growth. For Christians, this growth is towards Christ-likeness and personal maturity.

Skills are the building blocks of *competence*, which is the ability to perform tasks and functions effectively. Persons come to any function with varying amounts of natural predisposition defined by physical and personality makeup. For example, all adults have achieved some level of skill in basic communication. But most adults are not competent public speakers and not everyone has a natural predisposition for it. In fact, the majority of individuals fear public speaking. Programs can help almost anyone develop skills for public speaking, if that skill is needed to carry out one or more of their roles. They can become competent at it, even though not everyone will become a great public speaker.

A Relational Matrix

Ministry training is about helping people strengthen and mature relationships with others and the entities they serve.

The most fundamental human desire is to relate to oneself. Having a "good" or "healthy" self-image is important to human growth and contentment. This is expressed in the diagram by the stem of a cross.

Important to this first "inner" relationship are intimate relationships, usually with family and close friends. These sources help nurture and grow who we are. This is expressed in the diagram by the left arm of the cross.

External relationships are everything else—social community, workplaces, clubs, government entities, etc. This is expressed in the diagram by the right arm of the cross.

All persons function within these three areas of relationship. But not all function with a fourth and most important relationship—one with God. This is the relationship that changes everything. It is the one that regulates and controls what we do in training and how we do it. It sets our goals and standards. It defines our assumptions and commitments.

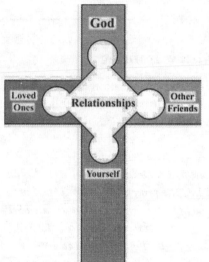

Who Does Christian Training Serve?

Much of the discussion about educational/training philosophy seems to center around the interplay between individuals and their contribution to society. Socialist and totalitarian regimes use schooling to serve their social agendas. Democratic societies tend to lean toward humanistic and existentialist philosophies that focus more on the individual's development as an end in itself.

Our analysis has shown that the missing element in most recognized educational philosophies is God and his purposes. A Christian philosophy begins with God. A God-centered educational/training philosophy intentionally aims at what God wants to accomplish in and through his people. In simplest of terms, its focus is developing people who love and trust God, love others as themselves, and serve in God's mission of extending his sovereign reign over all peoples.

The biblical metaphor that emerges is that of "servant." Servants render service to their Master. They do so in specific roles and functions. Metaphors for servant roles in Scripture include those of "shepherd," "farmer," "athlete," "steward," and "soldier." To function effectively in any of these areas requires training that develops specific character qualities and skill sets. Each servant role requires a different set of conceptual and material equipment. Intentional training greatly increases both the availability and the effective use of this equipment.

Thus, a Christian philosophy of training sees its foremost purpose as developing God's servants—enabling and equipping God's people to engage fully in their "reasonable service" (Romans 12:1, NKJV). The means is a transformational process that requires resisting conformity to the world's standards and attitudes, seeking the infilling of God's

Spirit, and generating right thinking, attitudes and behaviors. It produces a lifestyle that is Kingdom-centered and purposeful in service. The outcome is a "living sacrifice" that is holy, pleasing, and acceptable to God for his service.

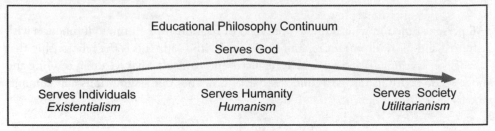

A Metaphor for Ministry Training

We have examined three metaphors of education that reflect existential, humanistic, and utilitarian worldviews. Using Kliebard's format, the following metaphor is suggested as one that reflects a Christian worldview:

A Metaphor of Service

The curriculum is a process by which those who pledge allegiance to Christ become useful to him in his service. The process counts on experienced servants who have oversight for the equipping of fellow servants, and use a variety of means, methods and contexts in so doing. These mentor-guides recognize God's design in the individual's vocation, personality, abilities, gifting, and interests, and work with that design to develop trainees for specific roles and functions in God's work. Trainees learn and grow together as they obey their Master's instructions for their lives and are diligent in developing their vocational gifts and abilities. Instruction, discipline, interaction with their fellow servants, life experience, and lots of practice are used to produce character growth and service competence. The goal is to grow more like the Master and to serve him well. Mentor-trainers know they are managing the process of developing God's servants well if their trainees are developing into grace-filled, mature persons who render effective service to God.

Ten Principles of Integral Training

Imbedded in this metaphor are some key concepts that can be tested against the high standard of biblical worldview. There are at least ten corresponding principles as suggested below:

1. The goal of the curricular process is to motivate and help believers grow in the likeness of Christ, and increase their effectiveness in serving him and his purposes.

2. The training program encompasses an integrated, intentional, and culturally appropriate process that contributes to health and growth in every area of life.

3. The training process understands and employs a broad range of different methods, means, and contexts that cater to learners' learning styles and the achievement of specified learning outcomes.

4. Learning outcomes include specific skills, attitudes, and understanding needed for life and ministry competence.

5. Trainers and trainees assume mutual responsibility for learning outcomes.

6. Trainers are mentors—fellow servants personally committed to the trainees' growth—who guide the training process based on their experience, moral authority and competence to do so.

7. God has a unique design for each individual (calling, gifting, personality, intelligence, etc.) that trainees, trainers and others perceive and help develop.

8. Learning happens in community and is equally dependent on interaction with fellow trainees, learning contexts (environments, situations, relationships, etc.), and the conceptual input of mentors/teachers/guides.

9. Knowledge is not a goal in itself, but combined with obedience and diligent practice, will lead to understanding, maturity, and competence.

10. The training program and skill of the mentor-trainers is evaluated by the faithfulness and success of their trainees in every area of their lives and ministry.

A Model for Ministry Training

The above list provides support for developing a model of ministry that is based on sound biblical worldview concepts and principles. Since the goal of training is to develop effective people for effective service, the two aspects of this goal should not be separated. Effective ministry flows out of effective lives. Training that attempts to place a balanced emphasis on developing the person's character, their understanding, and their skills is "integral" ministry training.

> Effective ministry grows out of effective lives.

The aim of training is growth in service to God. Growth is an inherent characteristic of human beings. God designed them to grow. But training programs can't cause growth. They can only set the environment and conditions for growth. Responsibility for growth is primarily vested in each adult. Although trainers help trainees grasp their responsibility, guide their learning, and set conditions for growth, God causes the growth.

Everyone is motivated to grow to some extent, even though that motivation may come indirectly through a felt need. Biologically, a child may not "feel like growing," but hunger will motivate him to eat, which in turn allows natural growth to take place. In this case, hunger motivates the action that fulfills one of the conditions for growth. Emotional and spiritual growth is also inherent in humans, but growth does not always occur. (In fact, spiritual growth is not possible without spiritual birth.) Emotional and spiritual hunger motivates a person to feed these parts of their being. There are other motivators, such as the desire to do things well. Discipline and practice are essential to growth in many areas, not just understanding. In all these areas, there is a shared responsibility for growth between trainers (parents, authorities, teachers, coaches, etc.), and individuals.

Human growth happens through a complex interaction between information and action, and the context in which these take place. Accelerated growth is achieved when appropriate information is applied in meaningful ways at the right time and in environments that favor growth (hothouse effect). Integral training programs try to achieve this in a balanced way.

Training is a science. Relevant information is provided in measured doses and sequences at the correct time, using appropriate learning techniques and methods in the best learning environment possible. But training is also an art that understands that not all learning can be programmed, and not all learners are the same. Good training requires skilled and practiced trainers.

How can you (or how have you) encourage(d) the student's responsibility for training in your program?

When the underlying principles for integral ministry training are adopted, they can be applied to some degree to almost any training effort. Training should address the whole person even when it is somewhat compartmentalized, as when it is aimed at developing a specific skill. A skilled individual who does not have the maturity for a role or is not living a godly life will only hamper God's purposes and thus defeat the purpose of ministry training. A godly individual that is inept in morally "neutral" areas such as interpersonal relationships, communications, ability to adapt or contextualize, etc., may also be unsuccessful in their useful service to God. Integral training sees all three elements—personal godliness, personal maturity, and skills as indispensable in serving God well. Servants must be both "holy" and "pleasing" in their service to God (Romans 12:1).

Integral ministry training is done in a way that connects different aspects of the person's life. This can only be achieved through dynamic community—not simply through information transfer or intellectual development, valuable as these are. Jesus formed a community of learners and employed dialogue, experience and reflection to transform their attitudes. He used "learning moments" masterfully. He showed them how to minister—demonstrating first the skills he wanted them to develop and then sending them out to practice them. He helped them evaluate their experience through reflection and debriefing. He knew that a disciple would not be greater than his master and that he had to model the whole of life and ministry if he expected his disciples to practice what he taught.

Is this model too much to ask of our trainers and training programs? Perhaps... life seems to be made up of any number of concessions to practicality. Yet unless ministry training is solidly based on biblical worldview, it will defeat the purpose for which it is being offered. The ten principles of integral ministry training are derived from a Christian worldview. Their use may allow trainers the opportunities to modify or incorporate aspects of whole person training into their training programs that produce servants that can truly render service to their Master.

Conclusion

Examining the secular approaches to education reveals that they don't take God into account. It is no surprise to find that ministry training based on these models often doesn't develop effective people for effective ministry service. A sound ministry training program requires a solid biblical foundation. The most appropriate metaphor to guide the development of training is the metaphor of service. Service is played out in any number of roles and ministries, but it is the basic framework for the trainee, the trainer, and the training design. From the metaphor of service can be derived principles to guide training development. Adopting this servant metaphor and its principles can help trainers design training that achieves godly character and competence in worshipful ministry that renders glory to God.

Chapter 2: Exercises

Examine Your Organizational Commitments

1. If you are doing this course in an organizational setting, with others in your ministry team, carefully examine documents that express your organization's mission and values. These documents should clearly state the purpose of your organization, why it exists, and to what it is committed. Then:

    *   Evaluate your organization's training program in light of its commitment of resources. Where are most of the resources being spent? Do program priorities and expenditures line up with the program's values and mission statement?

    *   How do you know if you are actually fulfilling your purpose as an organization? How do you measure "success"? Is this measure linked to your trainees' success as people and in ministry?

    *   Is your program flexible enough to allow for the uniqueness of each trainee in terms of calling, gifting, abilities and interests? Do you use assessments and inventories to help your trainees understand themselves and each other better?

    *   Do your trainers model the kind of character qualities and skills expected of trainees?

    *   Does your program keep a careful watch on trainees' personal struggles and character growth issues? How does it do this?

2. With a group of your fellow students or ministry team members, examine each of the Ten Principles of Integral Training described on pages 22-23 in this chapter. Do you understand each principle? Do you agree with it? How is it fleshed out in your context of ministry training?

Chapter 3

Understanding Integral Ministry Training

Rob Brynjolfson

The old bridge spanning a broad river could not keep up with traffic volume, but building a new span was cost prohibitive; adding a lane seemed to be the wisest solution. However, adding a lane to an existing bridge required a complete re-engineering and strengthening of all the arches, columns, and girders. The whole bridge needed to be modified to add one extra lane. Logic prevails: it would be perilous to just simply add a lane without taking into consideration the added stress and load factors to the entire bridge.

When Christian workers, especially missionaries, find themselves bridging cultures and adding the "cross-cultural" component to their ministerial job description, they would do well to seek out training for ministry that addresses the whole person. Adding cross-cultural issues to ministry doesn't just require another layer of knowledge to learn before going to a new environment; cross-cultural issues place stress on many areas in missionaries' lives, including their character, their ability to perform skills and their interpretation and transferal of knowledge. Therefore, ministry training in isolation of the whole person needlessly places at risk the individual and the enterprise.

Whole person training, or integral ministry training, addresses the training needs of the entire person. It is training that focuses on who the person is (body, soul and spirit), what they must be able to do, and the understanding needed for effective personal and skill development. It is a challenging approach but one that reaps desired benefits not only in the life of the vocational Christian worker, but for others who have an important interest in the success of the Christian worker; that is, the stakeholders—the churches and agencies who benefit from the services of these workers and those who have invested in their ministry work.

Integral Ministry Training Impact

Apart from knowing intuitively that integral ministry training is the right approach, there are real world reasons why agencies and sending churches should require holistic training, particularly in regard to their missionary candidates. Though the nature of cross-cultural change for a missionary is different from stress factors that impact other types of church ministers, the study of missionary success as it relates to their training can bring insight to all areas of ministry training.

Evidence strongly supports the added benefits of integral ministry training for both the endurance and effectiveness of a missionary. For example, the "Reducing Missionary Attrition Project" (ReMAP I) published in *Too Valuable to Lose*,[1] indicated that missionary training that includes holistic principles is one of the three contributing factors reducing attrition (leaving the missionary field prematurely) in career missionaries.

The ReMAP II project focuses on why missionaries choose to remain as career missionaries. Detlef Bloecher produced a pre-sampling of the analysis of reasons missionaries remain in the field that relate to missionary training to demonstrate the correlation between significant pre-field training and missionary longevity.[2] This study shows marked improvement in missionary retention as related to the duration of training in general.

How does integral ministry training contribute to the reasons missionaries stay in the field? How does the lack of integral ministry training contribute to the reasons missionaries leave the field prematurely? First, one needs to understand the factors contributing to why missionaries return prematurely from the mission field. In the first study pertaining to attrition (ReMAP I), "Inappropriate Training" was listed as the first of 26 reasons for leaving missionary service. Among the old sending countries this was ranked as the 20th reason but in newer sending countries it figures as 9th.[3] It would seem that newer sending countries perceive a greater need for appropriate training. However, Bill Taylor reaches a different conclusion upon closer examination:

> *Perhaps a better way to state the case for training is to address the top five causes of OSC (Old Sending Countries) "preventable" attrition and realize that these causes have to do primarily with issues of character and relationships. Then we can ask the question: In what ways do our formal and nonformal training equip missionaries in these two crucial dimensions?*[4]

These two crucial dimensions (character and relationships) are not easily taught. The formation of character and attitude traits is a task difficult to achieve in the context of the formal classroom. Integral ministry training seeks to address the needs of the whole person and therefore attempts to develop growth in these "crucial dimensions." This sentiment appears to be echoed amongst missionary trainers in general. During the International Missionary Training Network Canada 2003, consultation trainers from around the world expressed their common concern to seek improved methods for addressing the need of character development.

---

1   William D. Taylor, ed., *Too Valuable to Lose*, (Pasadena: William Carey Library, 1997).

2   Detlef Bloecher, "Missionary Training Makes Missionaries Resilient – Lessons from ReMAP II", (http://www.wearesources.org, ReMAP I & II Articles and Files, cited 18 December, 2003), pp. 4-5.

3   Peter Brierley, "The ReMAP Research Report," *Too Valuable to Lose*, William Taylor, ed., (Pasadena: William Carey Library, 1997), p. 92.

4   William Taylor, "Examining an Iceberg Called Attrition," *Too Valuable to Lose,* William Taylor, ed., (Pasadena: William Carey Library, 1997), p. 13.

Training for Endurance

The dark side of missionary attrition is the enormous cost to the missionary enterprise. Multinational corporations calculate the financial loss of unsuccessful mid-level personnel returning early from overseas assignments in the hundreds of thousands of dollars per individual. This takes into consideration the costs related to training, setup, overseas moves, settling, and later the transfer and retraining of replacement personnel. We can expect that the cost to the missionary enterprise might not scale as high when comparing missionary salaries, but even if it were fifty percent, our costs in missionary attrition would reach millions of dollars per year.

More significantly, we concern ourselves with the human loss, which is, as Bill Taylor puts it, "staggering and incalculable."[5] The problem of preventable attrition is the escalating expansion of impact. The individual suffers and may never recover from the disappointment of failure. Anecdotal evidence abounds in support of the difficulty returning missionaries have to re-order their lives and become effective servants in their homeland. Churches become the victims of severe attrition problems, finding themselves investing counseling and resources into the lives of failed missionaries. The worst impact, unfortunately, is the potential loss of missionary vision in the lives of other individuals or in the home church. The pastor responsible for missions in a large church recently expressed commitment to short-term missions, and disfavored sending career missionaries, because of the recent experiences the church had with three families who returned from the field. Instead of questioning and seeking to improve the pre-field training they required, he was "throwing in the towel."

Training for Effectiveness

When considering the importance of integral ministry training, attrition or retention is only part of the equation. It serves no purpose to increase the longevity of ineffective servants. Integral ministry training seeks to increase the effectiveness of cross-cultural workers, providing the skills and character traits that are essential to success on the field. Demonstrating field effectiveness is a difficult affair. First, how should one define effectiveness? Longevity is not an end in itself. Some of the hardest people to get along with are the ones who outlast all co-workers on the field. Their longevity contributes to the problem of attrition. Furthermore, longevity is not indicative of suitable adaptation, or successful language acquisition. Effectiveness must include success in cultural adaptation and language acquisition, interpersonal relationships and communication skills, conflict resolution, and the transference of gifting and ministry skills into the new cultural context.

> Effectiveness must include success in:
> - Cultural adaptation and language acquisition
> - Interpersonal relationships and communication skills
> - Conflict resolution
> - The transference of gifting and ministry skills into the new cultural context

Integral Ministry Training Addresses the Whole Person

Integral ministry training is defined as focusing on who the person is, what they must be able to do, and the understanding needed for effective personal and skill development. The importance of the body, soul and spirit is paramount. Integral training intentionally provides learning interventions to develop understanding, skills and traits or qualities deemed necessary for effective overseas service using different contexts and diverse methodologies.

---

5   Taylor, *Too Valuable to Lose*, p. 14.

During the Canada 2003 consultation, the International Missionary Training Network met and discussed core values and current needs in missionary training around the world. The area of character development continually emerged as the most important aspect for successful missionary training. Integral ministry training recognizes the importance of this particular area, along with the development of needed cross-cultural skills and knowledge. Holistic training aims at achieving growth in every area of the trainee's life, with particular attention on those issues known to impede missionary field effectiveness.

The process to developing a ministry training program is:

- Work together with other vested leaders.
- Develop a picture of what an effective missionary or minister should be, do and know.
- Design learning objectives and experiences.
- Continually evaluate the training against the desired outcome.

There is a process to developing integral ministry training. First, training needs are identified by determining what a trained missionary or minister looks like: what an effective missionary should be, do and know. It begins with the end in mind, and is developed through a consensual process including sending church, agency and receiving field and, if possible, the national church. The list of training goals becomes what trainers call the *outcomes profile*: this is a snapshot inventory of the ideal missionary at various stages of their development. All of the learning objectives and learning activities will grow from this profile. Any specific learning objective or activity will be able to point to the outcome that it is intended to fulfill. A planned program of evaluation to measure the training against the original desired outcome completes and refines the process.

Frequently, outcomes are referred to as competencies. Trainers will measure skill development by qualifying *skill competencies*. However, integral ministry training seeks to produce growth in every area of need. As such, missionaries need to develop cross-cultural competencies but they also need to grow in *character and attitude qualities*.

Integral Ministry Training Emphasizes Skills and Character Formation

Outcomes-based training programs identify the character/attitude traits, the skills and the required knowledge a missionary needs to become effective. These three areas of emphasis have been called the training triad and are often described metaphorically as the heart, the hands and the head.

Figure 3.1. The Three Areas of Training

The question of how to train a missionary holistically depends on a commitment to addressing each of these three areas. In traditional educational models the emphasis is on the acquisition of knowledge or understanding. The word "education" conjures up images of rows of uncomfortable desks, black or white boards behind the teacher's cluttered desk, dusty libraries with threadbare carpets, stacks of books that beg the inquisitive to blow some dust off the cover, and the usual educational methods associated with these places or things. In fact, our academic learning centers excel at producing certain outcomes like the acquisition of knowledge or understanding, and facilitate the development of skills like critical analysis, and research. Integral ministry training is not anti-academic, but it does attempt to correct the over-dependency on intellectual training.

Character Growth

Not ignoring the head, but recognizing the importance of the heart and the hands, integral ministry training intentionally allocates more training resources to address needed skills and character growth. The essence of biblical leadership has always placed a unique emphasis on the importance of character and spiritual formation as qualifications for ministry. Look at this list of the characteristics of elders and deacons fit for service in the New Testament church taken from 1 Timothy 3:1-15 and Titus 1:5-9:

Leadership Qualifications (Elders and Deacons)
1 Timothy 3:1-15 and Titus 1:5-9 (Adapted from the NIV)

1. Above reproach (blameless) (1 Tim. 3:2; Titus 1:6)
2. The husband of but one wife (1 Tim. 3:2; Titus 1:6)
3. Temperate (1 Tim. 3:2)
4. Self-controlled (I Timothy 1:8; Titus 3:2)
5. Hospitable (1 Tim. 3:2; Titus 1:8)
6. Able to teach (1 Tim. 3:2)
7. Not given to drunkenness (1 Tim. 3:3; Titus 1:7)
8. Not violent, but gentle (1 Tim. 3:3)
9. Not quarrelsome (1 Tim. 3:3)
10. Not a lover of money (1 Tim. 3:3)
11. One who manages his own family well with children obeying and respecting him (1 Tim. 3:4; Titus 1:6)
12. Not a recent convert (1 Tim. 3:6)
13. Having a good reputation with those outside the church (1 Tim. 3:7)
14. Worthy of respect (1 Tim. 3:8)
15. Sincere (1 Tim. 3:8)
16. Not pursuing dishonest gain (1 Tim. 3:8; Titus 1:7)
17. A man whose children believe (Titus 1:6)
18. Holding firmly to the trustworthy message (Titus 1:9)
19. Able to encourage others by sound doctrine (Titus 1:9)
20. Able to refute those who oppose it (sound doctrine) (Titus 1:9)
21. Not over-bearing (Titus 1:7)
22. Not quick-tempered (Titus 1:7)
23. One who loves what is good (Titus 1:8)
24. One who is upright (Titus 1:8)
25. One who is disciplined (Titus 1:8)

Four characteristics from this list do not relate to character qualities or attitudes, because they are ministry skills. These skills can be developed, and do not describe who a person is, but what that person can do. From this list we can extract four ministry skills that the Apostle Paul mentions. These are:

1. Able to teach (1 Tim. 3:2)
2. Manages his own family well (1 Tim. 3:4; Titus 1:6)
3. Able to encourage others by sound doctrine (Titus 1:9), and its twin,
4. Able to refute those who oppose it (Titus 1:9)

Biblical leadership is founded upon an overwhelming commitment to the formation of character and spiritual qualities and the development of ministry skills and not upon a mere understanding of the Scripture or theology. If biblical leadership is based on the formation of needed character and spiritual qualities, how much more so, for the missionary who is heading into a more challenging ministry than leadership to one's own culture? Missionary profiles that objectify the training needs of missionaries repeatedly recognize the critical significance of character formation for effective service.

The only way that these areas of critical need will be addressed in the training goals is at the sacrifice of other well intentioned but less urgent training outcomes. As a missionary begins his or her career, it is more important that he or she be mature spiritually, exuding character qualities and attitudes that will facilitate years of continued growth and development. A good Christian character, humility and a learning attitude are more urgently needed at the start of the missionary career than finely honed theological positions and philosophical understanding.

Skills Development

In a similar fashion, the new missionary urgently needs skills to adapt to another culture and to learn the language. The skill set of the overseas worker is critical to speedy adaptation and long-term effectiveness. These too are more urgently needed than academic and professional degrees.

Knowledge and Understanding

Nevertheless, knowledge is instrumental in the acquisition of ministry skills or in the growth of character. To become adept at skills or even to grow in the other twenty-two character and spiritual qualities, a person needs to develop a level of understanding. One cannot teach without understanding, or "encourage others by sound doctrine" (Titus 1:9) without it. This implicit concern that leaders develop adequate understanding is very important. A preceding theoretical understanding enhances the practice of skills. Likewise, awareness and subsequent understanding is needed before a trainee will begin to model the desired trait or attitude. The character quality of humility or having a learning attitude needs to be taught, then modeled and practiced before it can be caught.

Three Domains of Education

The three distinct approaches or domains of education are formal, nonformal and informal. Though we easily recognize formal education with its structures, and familiar icons such as the graded school systems, classrooms, staffing, curricula, and learning resources, it is important to note other characteristics of formal education. For example, formal education is hierarchical or graduated, and it benefits the society by reinforcing cultural values and traditions. Formal education is usually defined as learning that is intentional, staffed, funded and measured (usually leading to a diploma).

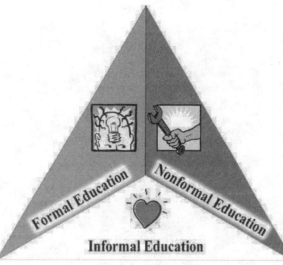

Figure 3:2. The Three Domains of Education

Nonformal education tends to be less dependent on structures, and advancement is frequently determined by competence as opposed to tested knowledge. It too is intentional, staffed, funded and measured (though usually leading to a certificate). Much of the professional development that takes place in the workplace is nonformal education. This kind of education does not have the same ability to reinforce values or traditions. It is more flexible and by nature is more accessible.

Informal education is where the bulk of learning happens. Though we often do not recognize it, informal education accounts for the majority of our learning over a life span. Informal education is sometimes called socialization, and our families and friends are the teachers who have the greatest impact on our lives. Our first language was acquired through this kind of learning. We rose up into our home culture through informal education. The manners we were taught around the dinner table were learned through informal education. By definition, it is not staffed, planned, funded or intentional. By nature it is spontaneous, yet no other domain has the same life changing impact as informal education. It surpasses the others with respect to reinforcing cultural values and traditions.

Integral ministry training will make use of all three domains. Formal education is used to develop the theoretical knowledge necessary to acquire desired outcomes. The familiar classroom and lecture, with hours of reading and study will be part of an integral ministry training program. Nonformal education, the learn-on-the-job approach, is needed to develop and refine cross-cultural skills or interpersonal relationship skills. These are intentional, planned learning experiences directed more to producing skill outcomes or competencies in ministry and life overseas. Informal education must also be part of an integral ministry training program because it has the greatest potential to address character and attitude issues. The question is, how will these be achieved?

Holistic training, with its emphasis on all three domains of education, recognizes the important contexts in which learning takes place. The following figure portrays three common contexts in which learning occurs. The school is the best known of these and is relied upon heavily when ministry training programs are initiated. Eventually, ministry trainers discover that this context excels in the outcomes relating to the transfer of information or achieving understanding. This context is less than satisfactory at developing character attributes and skills.

Figure 3:3. The Three Contexts of Training

Other contexts for ministry training need to be added to the formula of ministry training. The working environment is quite suitable for the development of needed skills. Surgeons learn their operating skills in the operating room. Missionaries will only acquire cross-cultural and language acquisition skills in the working context of ministry overseas or in a cross-cultural environment. Integral ministry training values the development of these skills and provides both the time and resources needed to assist the trainees in moving into a cross-cultural ministry context. When resources are limited, the cross-cultural ministry context can be developed without costly overseas travel. A missionary training centre in Argentina requires trainees to relocate to a northern province with a high native or aboriginal population, where trainees not only must adapt to another culture, but also are required to begin language learning in order to refine and hone these skills. It is not the same as an immersion experience in the target culture, but the learning objectives can be achieved without travel overseas.

One of the commonalities that integral ministry training centers share is the use of training in communities. When students are required to join a training community, this additional context serves to provide informal education that will help to achieve the formation of character and attitude traits needed for the field. The nature of these training communities will vary depending on the ethos of the institution and the resources available. In some cases, trainees and trainers will live together. In other instances, trainees will share living accommodations. Frequently, trainees are required to work and maintain the needs of the community by cooking, cleaning and building or fixing. It is in the daily grind of the community that many lessons of character and attitude are learned.

 How has community impacted your Christian character?

Educators struggle to value this kind of learning that happens informally because it is not easily planned and measured. This is a well-known distinction between domains; i.e., nonformal and formal are planned lessons, whereas informal is spontaneous learning that is not pre-planned. It is not uncommon to perceive in both students and trainers the attitude that affective learning is not as significant or important as cognitive learning or skill development. The desire to measure outcomes leads to siphoning off time and resources dedicated to informal learning. Success on the field, however, relies heavily on the affective domain.

On the other hand, the context of community can become more effective as a learning tool when more intentional interventions are utilized. Many training communities develop mentoring programs or cohort groups to increase the likelihood of achieving the learning objectives for this domain. Community meetings, chapel and prayer times all contribute in an organized fashion to the informal learning that cannot be planned or measured, but can be reasonably calculated (given adequate time in the community) that trainees will form the intended outcomes.

The integral training model, therefore, will reflect an attempt to balance the kind of learning that takes place in the cognitive, affective and psychomotor areas. It utilizes the three approaches of informal, nonformal and formal education, making use of distinct contexts that are malleable to achieving the needed outcomes. Time and resources are directed to each of these areas without greater consideration of one over the other.

Figure 3:4. Synergistic Integral Ministry Training

Integral Ministry Training Is Synergistic

Unfortunately, the above model—utilizing three distinct contexts for training—is costly and difficult to provide. The notion of training the whole person requires access to resources and opportunities that few institutions can afford or have at their disposition. Many training centers struggle just to maintain their "in-house" training, let alone develop a field representation where cultural immersion experiences can be gained.

Integral ministry training is most effective when developed through synergistic partnerships combining skills, allocating training resources and providing key contexts in which the training may occur. When asking, "Who does the training?" the answer should be, "All of us," including voices from churches, agencies, fields of service and institutions. When training partners come together in recognition of the potential each contributes towards the training of a Christian worker, a wealth of experiences and resources are made available that individually would simply be impossible to provide. Centers cannot provide the kind of character formation given through a well-developed discipleship program in a local church. Ministry opportunities are made available through local churches where ministry skills can be developed. Seminaries and schools of higher learning will provide the needed philosophical and analytical understanding that underpins the missiological concepts of the trainee. Agencies and fields can provide

List some of the potential local resources in your area for synergistic training opportunities:

the kaleidoscope of cross-cultural ministry experiences where skills are learned, the rudiments of language learning achieved and theoretical understanding is tested.

Conclusion

The concept of integral ministry training may seem intuitive, and a natural approach to take. Although its design appears simple, implementation is complex. As someone remarked, "After all is said and done, much more is said than done." To be integral, a training program must be intentional about whole person outcomes. And the program can't be effective unless it is accompanied by a commitment to excellence. Integral ministry training centers will find in this book much more than just a process for initiating ministry training programs. More importantly, trainers will discover a reusable resource so that yearly the programs of training can be revisited, evaluated, refined and improved.

Chapter 3: Exercises
Understanding Integral Ministry Training

Analyze your program's commitments to different kinds of learning through the following exercises:

1. Find a comprehensive description of a learning program (curriculum) and try to determine what the true learning priority of the program is by comparing the three areas of learning.

    a. What percentage of the student's time and energy is dedicated to each of the three areas of learning?

        i.   Understanding

        ii. Character/spiritual formation

        iii. Ministry/work skills

    b. Give examples where character/spiritual formation and ministry/work skills are targeted.

2. If you were designing a learning program that included outcomes relating to character/spiritual formation, what kinds of learning experiences would you include in your program to address these learning needs? In what ways would you adapt the context in order to ensure that these outcomes were achieved?

3. If you were designing a learning program that included outcomes relating to the development of ministry/work skills, what kinds of learning experiences would you include in your program to address these learning needs? In what ways would you adapt the context in order to ensure that these outcomes were achieved?

Chapter 4

___

Starting a Ministry Training Program

Lois Fuller

As the church around the world awakens to its global responsibility to fulfill the Great Commission, missionaries are volunteering for service from countries that have not had missionary training programs in the past. Often the first missionaries have struggled and even failed because of problems that good training might have enabled them to avoid or resolve. Likewise, many church and ministry workers "burn-out" because they do not have the proper tools to deal with the tough situations and spiritual battles that they face. Now, ministry training programs are being started in many countries around the world. This book raises considerations and presents information needed by people leading ministry training programs. The proceeding chapters address issues related to creating ownership to a ministry training program, curriculum planning, and evaluation. This chapter will look at matters of planning and administration. We hope this manual will be useful both to those starting new ministry training programs and to those evaluating and improving existing programs.

Before You Start

Everyone on the training committee was sure that a missionary training school was a terrific idea. They asked around to find out how such schools were run in other places. Then they tried to do the same in their own area. Six months later, when the training program closed in failure, no one could understand why. They were sure they had provided thorough publicity, a great curriculum, and wonderful resources, but they just could not seem to attract enough students. What could the training committee have done differently to assure that their program would meet the training needs of the greatest number of students?

1. Determine Who Is Responsible for Training

The Great Commission was given to the church. The task of making disciples of all nations belongs to the church. Therefore, training personnel for the task of world evangelization and ministry also belongs to the church. While God may use an individual or a small group of individuals to excite others with a vision for ministry training, it is important to recognize that successful ministry training never can be a private project.

When God lays a burden for ministry training on the heart of one or more believers, it is important for them, first of all, to seek to win others to that vision. Those in leadership roles within the church, and in local and global ministries, should be among the first to be challenged with the need for effective ministry training.

Two things are needed in order to implement a successful ministry training program. First, the project must be the fruit of incessant prayer. "The prayer of a righteous man is powerful and effective" (James 5:16)! Second, those who challenge others to share their vision for ministry training must be well informed about the task they expect to undertake. Some initial research may be needed in order to identify clearly the need that exists. Great care should be taken, however, since research always begins with assumptions and leads to decisions. The earlier that leaders join in this process, the greater their sense of *participation* and *ownership* will be. As the ministry training program is shaped by the collective wisdom of many godly men and women, the viability and effectiveness of the program will be enhanced. More about how to organize and vitalize such a group will be covered in the second section of this book.

2. Establish the Need for a Ministry Training Program

In the commercial world, when a company wants to launch a new product, they do market research to predict whether people will buy the product. A commercial company exists to make money, so research is designed to find out if a new product will bring a profit. The aim of ministry training, in contrast, is to see many unreached individuals and people groups evangelized and people everywhere discipled as followers of Jesus Christ. Training will not be successful if trainees are not gifted and called to ministry service, if too few are trained, or if training does not equip people to be effective in their area of service.

If there are other ministry training programs available in your area, find out more about them. What are their training goals? For what level of involvement in ministry are they preparing people? Where do they get students? How are they run? How well are they serving the church of Jesus Christ and its agents? Can you combine efforts, in order to avoid expensive duplication of resources and to strengthen the ministry of other programs?

Are there groups of people who would be interested in Christian service but who, for some reason, cannot take advantage of existing training? Perhaps a certain kind of training is not available. If a new program is needed, it should aim at meeting the training needs of a neglected group.

The missionary training of Youth With a Mission (YWAM) is an example of this philosophy. YWAM targets people without formal theological training, perhaps without the means or time to go through the long preparation required by most Western missions, people who are nonetheless interested in missionary service. By providing short, segmented training without heavy academic prerequisites, YWAM has recruited and trained a vast army for the evangelization of the world. They could never have done this if they had just started another Bible college.

People come to a ministry training program because they, or their sponsoring agencies, recognize a need for training. They will come, however, only if the costs in time, opportunity, and money are affordable. They might not finish the training if it does not

Chapter Objectives:

This chapter is designed to help you:

- Understand the complexities of starting and maintaining a viable training program.
- Discuss the important administrative functions of a ministry training program.
- Introduce missionary training into an existing school context.

   List the ministry training programs available in your area:

hold their interest or meet their needs. Research should be designed to answer two questions:

- Who are the people who recognize a need (or should and could be taught to recognize a need) for ministry training?

- How can training be offered so that potential trainees are able and willing to take advantage of it?

If your research reveals that ministry training programs that are currently available are serving the church well and are meeting the training needs which exist, perhaps your training committee should concentrate its efforts on strengthening one of the existing programs, rather than trying to amass the resources to start something new.

3. Determine the Type of Training Needed

There are various aspects to ministry education, including pre-candidate missionary training programs, training for overseas and local missionaries, training for ministry in the city, training for church outreach programs, training for care, counseling and discipleship. The following questions can help focus on the type of training needed.

Who are the people to be trained?

Do they already have some theological training? What is their theological orientation (pentecostal, fundamentalist)? What is their secular educational background? From what ethnic group or groups are they? What are their cultural values and economic levels? Will families be involved as well as individuals? Men as well as women? What will be their age range? What skills and occupations do they already have? What will the trainees expect to gain from the program? Will they be satisfied with the outcomes?

> Brainstorm about people, circumstances and organizations that correspond to each of the questions proposed.

Often, until trainees appear, we cannot be sure of the answers to all of these questions, but we can try to predict. The answers will affect some of the informal training that will take place outside class whether we like it or not (for example, trainees may try to influence each other theologically). Sometimes we will have to plan how to minimize any undesirable results. For example, if ethnic groups with traditional animosity are to be mixed, how can love be fostered? The characteristics of the trainees will also determine in part how effective certain teaching methods will be and how necessary it will be to include some things in the curriculum while other things can be assumed to be already understood.

What kind of co-workers will the trainees likely have?

In some parts of the world, missionaries work with international sending organizations, where their missionary co-workers may have a different culture and mother tongue. These students will need help in coping with the cross-cultural element inside the mission. Other programs will train missionaries and ministers whose co-workers all share their own background. All trainees need skills in getting along with their colleagues.

In what ministry areas are the trainees likely to work?

Especially at the beginning, our program will not likely be able to train students for every potential opportunity. It may be that the missionaries we train will work mainly with unreached groups in our own part of the world. We might not need to teach Hinduism in a training program in West Africa, for instance, if the students will be targeting unreached African tribes. Training for those who will work in remote rural areas should include practical things that may not be needed by urban missionaries and vice versa. The necessary survival and health skills for those reaching Eskimos in the cold north will be somewhat different from those needed by people working in the tropics. Language learning techniques needed for various fields may be different. Some countries are strict about letting in only missionaries who are perceived as academically or professionally "qualified." Should missionary training help them gain that status? If yes, how? Is there a receiving church whose voice should be heard about the kind of missionaries that would be of most help to them?

What churches, receiving ministries or sending organizations will be served by the training?

Churches, receiving ministries and sending groups must be taken into consideration. How does their administrative structure affect their relationship to the program? Do they agree with the philosophy and curriculum of the program? If several sending organizations are to use the program together, will some be afraid of trainees switching over from one organization to another? Can the organizations trust the training staff theologically? Will they, in the end, be willing to employ our trainees? How will sending organizations be represented in the decision-making processes of the program? How committed will they be to helping the program? Are there parts of the training task they will be asked to look after? If the training is for a single agency or denomination, will the training fit into the overall strategy of the organization?

In what country is the training program located?

Are there legal or economic limitations on how the program can function? Are there cultural expectations about how a training program operates or the awards that should be given to those who complete it? If so, do these expectations conflict with attitudes the program wants to inculcate? What should be done about this conflict?

Who is available to staff the training program?

What individuals are qualified to serve as administrators and teachers? Are any of these people available to work with the program full time? If not, what are their schedules? Could they help part time? Who is available but not yet qualified? What could be done to train these potential staff members?

Staff selection is the single most important factor in the effectiveness of any ministry training program. If the staff themselves are experienced ministers of the gospel whose lives are marked by personal holiness and a zeal for the Lord, these qualities will be communicated to trainees as well. Experience teaches us, however, that any staff member who lacks these qualities or who is oriented toward scholarly recognition or toward personal power and esteem, despite many other positive qualifications, will diminish the effectiveness of ministry training and may become an instrument to turn the program away from its original training objectives.

What outside partners or sponsors will have an interest in the program?

Should foreign donors and staff be used for the program? If so, who are they and how can they be contacted and interested? What are their expectations? Are there strings attached to their help that need to be considered? Does the program need to conform to some standards set elsewhere?

The potential for foreign funding is understandably attractive to many who consider starting new ministry training programs, but it can be a dangerous snare. From many parts of the world we receive reports about training programs that lose the support of their national church when they are perceived as funded from abroad. In other cases, leaders of training programs who look abroad for financial support seem to develop an independence from their local Christian brothers and sisters, which is both unattractive and unhealthy. Whenever funding for a training program comes from the churches it serves, on the other hand, natural accountability structures exist. In addition, the involvement of the national church is developed through its participation in the ministry training program.

4. Pray!

The ultimate reason for ministry training is to make disciples of all nations, filling heaven with worshippers, in obedience to our Lord's command. We must have no other agenda than this. It is his work, and it becomes ours only because we have joined ourselves to him. All our plans and research are auxiliaries to prayer. We ask the Lord for his direction about ministry training in our situation. He leads us to information sources and shows us the significance of our research findings. He gives us his vision for what should be done, and wisdom for all the decisions that must be made along the way. It must be supernatural work from first to last.

> All our plans and research are auxiliaries to prayer.

Making the Administrative Plans

We previously noted that starting a ministry training program cannot and must not be the personal project of a single individual. Nevertheless, such a project needs at least one person with vision, drive, and commitment to see the dream come true. Unless someone expresses this vision, shares it with others, and rallies others who are prepared to explore ministry training opportunities and needs, nothing will happen.

So many people need to cooperate for a ministry training program to succeed that unless they all "own" the project, progress will be hindered. Key people whose cooperation is needed must take part in making decisions about the program very early on. We have referred to this group as a *training committee*.

Once it is clear that a ministry training program is needed and once the type of people who are likely to use the program is defined, decisions must be made. It is wise at this point to assemble a *working decision-making group*. This group may consist of the training committee plus church leaders and representatives of the missionary sending organizations or ministries to be served. Having a number of people involved in decision-making brings wider expertise to the plans.

> Successive administrative planning groups:
>
> - Training committee
> - Working decision-making group
> - Board

As the project continues and administrative policies are drawn up, however, a *board* can be formally constituted. All those who ought to have a say in how the program is run should be represented on the board, including all cooperating sending organizations in the case of missionary training. The board sets policies and oversees the work of the training program. It usually makes sure that the money is handled properly and that the policies it approves are carried out. It meets from time to time to hear and deliberate on reports by those delegated to carry out decisions. These delegates eventually include the administrative staff.

As soon as the board is formed, some kind of constitution or set of regulations for conducting the business of the program should be drawn up to clarify the authority structure. Under the board, some programs have a person who oversees the daily work, such as a principal. Other programs are run by a committee of leaders or rotate leadership among the staff.

The way authority is handled and the structures for handling it will affect the atmosphere and learning experience in the program. If we want to inculcate a servant spirit among the ministers we are producing, the leaders of the program need to model a servant leadership style. These issues need to be intentionally addressed, but are part of the informal curriculum discussed in Chapter 3.

The board plans how to accumulate the spiritual, human, physical, and financial resources needed for the ministry training program. It makes decisions about how to get staff and students. It also looks for finances and other physical resources. It promotes the program with publicity and raises up prayer support. Three important questions that need to be considered by the board relate to setting admission standards for admitting trainees, procuring and handling funds, and raising public awareness and prayer support.

Three Important Functions of the Board

1. Selection of Trainees

Trainee selection policies should reflect the purpose of the training program. If the training program is aimed at pre-candidates, the selection criteria may not be too stringent. Programs for missionary candidates need clearly stated selection criteria.

> Clearly stated admission policies will assist in determining when candidates are most likely to benefit from the training program.

There is little debate that missionary candidates and people committed to full time ministry must be committed Christians who feel called to Christian service. They need to be emotionally mature and otherwise personally suitable. It is difficult to find out these things just from a single personal interview. Recommendations from the church and from other spiritual mentors of the candidate need to be obtained. Missionary programs that take only trainees sent by a missionary sending organization allow the organization to screen the candidates. Even then, clearly stated admission policies will help the sending organization staff determine when candidates are most likely to benefit from the training the program provides.

In-service training programs for people who are experienced missionaries or already serving in ministry should require recommendation from the ministry organization in which they serve. While admission qualifications may not be so important, clearly stated program purposes and objectives are essential.

Some training programs insist that when considering married candidates, both husband and wife must qualify as students and come as a couple. This is less common for non-residential training programs or short seminars. Attention needs to be paid to training couples, however, since they will work as a team on the mission field. Both the husband and the wife need to understand what missionary life and ministry are all about.

Is there any question about the applicant's proficiency in the language in which training is conducted? If so, that needs to be tested. Are applicants expected to have a certain level of Bible knowledge? Then some evidence of their attainment in this area is required.

Is the program being run for trainees who have attained a certain educational level? People of varied educational backgrounds can be mixed profitably in informal and nonformal learning situations, but this is more difficult in formal settings. If a certain academic attainment level is expected before admission to our program, how does this affect the recognition and perceived qualification of our graduates? How does it affect teaching styles?

2. Funding and Accounting

Few training program leaders feel they have no worries about funding. Most ministry trainers rely on the Lord and need to pray for the resources to run their programs. Often the programs that do the best in this regard are those sponsored by an established denomination or by an independent mission agency with a reasonable support base. Even a denominational training center can face problems, however, if the churches of the denomination have not caught the ministry vision. Often one of the tasks of a ministry training program is to spread awareness and vision among its constituency. People do not give to programs or projects that do not catch their interest and zeal. The program as a whole, from the board to the trainees, needs to make funding a constant matter of prayer.

> One of the tasks of a ministry training program is to spread awareness and vision among its constituency.

Programs run jointly by several missionary sending organizations experience more problems. Unless all the partners are committed to owning and providing for the program, everybody's business tends to become nobody's business. Sending organizations may wonder if they would not be better able to bond trainees to their home and field staff if they did all the training themselves. They find it difficult to squeeze from their meager resources money and manpower to support a program that is not fully their own. They may feel that other partners are not putting in their own share, so why should they? They may find that the program is not meeting their organizational needs adequately and so hold back from fuller involvement. This may lead to a situation where the program staff must win greater commitment from partner organizations, must restructure the program, or must close the missionary training center.

Joint programs, however, can make good sense in stewardship of resources, since together, organizations can afford what individually they cannot. Trainees gain by exposure to other organizations, and the pool of trainers is larger. If a joint effort is being considered, it is important to get very firm commitments from the partners before beginning. This requires whole-hearted agreement about the aims and policies of the program.

Training programs of small, less established organizations seem to suffer the most financially. Sometimes training does not have the glamour of missionary work or Christian service to attract donors. The program may be unrecognized by any government or official body, so trainees are unwilling to pay large fees. These programs need to align themselves with specific missionary sending organizations or join some kind of fellowship, which can bring them to the attention of donors and provide input for their improvement.

There are two main sources of funding for ministry training programs:

- Fees paid by trainees or by the organizations sponsoring them.

- Donations from the Christian community, including both local and foreign donations.

Fees need to be set to meet as much of the expenses of running the program as the trainees can reasonably be expected to pay, given their financial background. In a few cases this could be 100%, but this is rare even in affluent countries. Awareness and publicity also are needed to attract local donations. Encourage visits to your program or to your graduates in their fields. Take presentations to churches and fellowships.

Foreign donors usually are most interested in giving for one-time capital expenses (like buying equipment and facilities) rather than recurrent expenses (like salaries and office supplies). They also usually want a lot of reports, pictures, etc. They may specify how the donated money may be spent. Sometimes these restrictions are due to government regulations about charitable giving in their own country. Whether you appreciate their attitude or not, if you want these donations you must respect the conditions under which they are given. Many recipients from the Two-Thirds World resent what is perceived as a paternalistic attitude on the part of Western donors. Whenever you accept large amounts from anyone, however, the factor of donor control comes into play, no matter who the donor may be. If you don't like this situation, avoid these donations. In any case, only accept donations for projects that are in line with your own priorities.

As noted above, large donations from abroad also can make local donors lax about supporting the ministry training program. There may be quarrels about how the money should be spent. Staff and students may have raised expectations about what they are entitled to, financially. For these reasons, experience indicates that cultivation of local donations is safer and wiser. If foreign donations are accepted, the more people who are involved in planning how outside aid will be used, the better. The whole situation needs to be bathed in prayer.

Sometimes staff can be funded by personal support-raising, just as many missionaries do. At other times staff may be seconded and paid by a cooperating organization. They model dependence on the Lord for their own support to the students, who may have to do the same. It is important, however, that sponsors of a training program should not purposely under-support the staff. Whenever this occurs, the sponsors are communicating something about their attitude toward the worth of ministry training work!

Some ministry training programs have had success in adding to their income by practical projects done by the students, such as a dairy project which sells milk or an agricultural project which helps feed the students. Proper arrangements need to be made for keeping the accounts of the program. If the accounts can be audited regularly, this will increase the confidence of people who want to give and will provide a good example to the trainees of financial honesty and accountability.

3. Publicity and Prayer Support

A ministry training program needs prayer support as much as missionaries and ministers on the field. So much of what needs to be accomplished in the lives of trainees has to be done, in the final analysis, by the Holy Spirit. We cannot neglect doing something, therefore, to generate intercession on our behalf. Most programs have a newsletter or a column in a ministry publication to make known information about the program. This also may be an avenue to raise finances and recruit students. Specific prayer points should be given for the program, along with news of answers to prayer.

> Ministry training programs should train students to present the work of their training, and provide opportunities for students to do so.

Besides using printed publicity, ministry training programs should train students to present the work of their training, and they should provide opportunities for students to do so in churches and fellowships. In addition, a program that goes out of its way to serve missionary-sending organizations, ministries and churches in promoting the outreach work they do will be noticed and appreciated. This means ministry leaders should be ready to help others with their own training programs, especially with literature and visiting teachers.

A training program also can organize prayer seminars and can encourage the setting up of support groups who pray for and help with the program.

Starting a Missionary Training Program in an Established Theological Institution

An established institution has traditions of administration, curriculum, and ethos which can seldom be changed overnight. If missions have never been a noticeable part of the program, any effort to introduce them must overcome considerable institutional inertia.

The first step often is to convince those who shape the curriculum that mission studies are important. These people should be the targets of mission awareness efforts through personal conversation, presentations, survey trips, student requests, encouragement from larger movements such as the AD 2000 Movement, and missions literature. If the institution's leadership is ready to promote missionary training, a lot can be accomplished in a short time.

If support for missionary training is weak, however, those trying to get missions into the theological school may have to be content to work gradually. The contagiousness of their own passionate commitment to world evangelization and their on-going involvement in missionary outreach, local and remote, may be their most powerful strategy. At the same time, however, they can work toward the introduction of core missions courses, one by one, into the existing curriculum. They can identify courses already being taught which would be part of a missions curriculum (such as World Religions or Church Planting), and they can pass on resources to the teachers of these courses to give more missiological content. As time goes on and demand increases, they can ask for a missions minor and finally a missions major to be offered in the school. Some schools are used to the idea of departments, and a missions department can be proposed. In other schools, departments are not used, so it may be harder to know the status of the missions courses. This may be an opportunity to infuse missions into the entire curriculum, rather than isolate it in a department.

The people interested in teaching missions also need to keep looking for materials giving a missiological perspective, that they can pass on to teachers in other departments, such as Bible, theology, or Christian education.

Barbara Burns lists the advantages and disadvantages of missionary training in a theological school in her article "Missionary Training Centers and Their Relationship to Theological Education Institutions" in *Internationalizing Missionary Training*.[1] Students in theological schools are exposed to a broader range of Christian studies as a context for the study of missions. They also can develop more in-depth Bible knowledge, and they have time to digest what they are learning. The school benefits as well by having mission insights added to balance other disciplines. The Great Commission stands at the heart of the Christian faith and, strange as it may seem, schools which separate biblical and theological studies from missions are irresistibly drawn toward a scholastic orthodoxy and an impotent faith. It may take time before teachers desire and understand how to integrate the mission insights into other disciplines, but when they catch the vision for missions they will become great allies in preparing good missionaries.

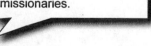

When they catch the vision for missions, teachers will become great allies in preparing good missionaries.

Some theological schools are better than others at the kind of lifestyle training that comes from the informal educational experiences of school life. Usually, as the push for a large enrollment increases (often for economic reasons), the harder it is to maintain

---

1   William D. Taylor, "Missionary Training Centers and Their Relationship to Theological Education Institutions," *Internationalising Missionary Training*, (Exeter, UK: Paternoster Press, 1991), pp. 251-264.

the community life and devotional atmosphere of the school. It may be that only the missions teachers consciously model a missionary zeal and lifestyle; if so, some missions students may be carried away by other ambitions. When the student-to-teacher ratio is high, missions teachers also have less impact per individual student. The length of a school's program also gives time for missionary zeal to ebb.

Some schools do internship and field work well, and this emphasis can provide an opportunity for mission internships. Other schools concentrate on classroom work, so major adjustments need to be made for missions students. Since missions internships often entail travel, which costs money, special fund-raising efforts may be needed to cover these expenses.

Once a theological school has established a missions department or major, the focus can shift to developing a missionary training program using steps similar to those listed previously.

Conclusion

People devoted to missions and service to the Lord are needed in the world today if finishing Jesus' last command is to be realized. This probably means that more ministry training programs will be needed. One of our most serious limitations, however, is the availability of qualified trainers. We must not be discouraged by this shortage, because training that is less than ideal is better than no training at all. When Jesus told his followers to pray laborers into the field, surely he also meant laborers who would train the others. As we face the challenge in ministry training around the world, let us commit ourselves to prayer that God will see his program accomplished in the earth.

Chapter 4: Exercises

Determine the Type of Training Needed

The following fundamental questions not only need to be answered when starting a missionary training program, but should be reviewed regularly by existing programs. If you are involved in a training program or are starting one, answer these to the best of your ability to do so.

1. Who are the people to be trained?

2. What kind of co-workers will the trainees likely have?

3. In what ministry areas are the trainees likely to work?

4. What churches, receiving ministries or sending organizations will be served by the training?

5. In what country is the training program located?

6. Who is available to staff the training program?

7. What outside partners or sponsors will have an interest in the program?

Chapter 5

Designing Training for Adults

Evelyn Hibbert

Everyone reading this book has probably completed school and also some level of tertiary education. In most cases, this will have meant at least ten years in child-orientated education and about three in an institution for adult students. If your experience is anything like mine, the style of education in the tertiary context was little different to the style in primary and secondary education. This means that our view of education is likely to be highly biased towards a model which focuses on the education of children. Adults have different needs, characteristics and expectations than children. This chapter explores these differences and the way trainers need to adjust their approach to facilitate learning in adults.

Adults are different from children. They are capable and responsible. This is necessary in order to survive in the world and to rear the next generation. Adults deserve respect. Adults know what the world is like and have some idea of what kind of problems they encounter and need help dealing with. If they are entering ministry training, they have made a decision to give up other things which the world values in order to serve God and His people. They do have an idea of what Christian ministry involves and want help in learning how to be prepared to become effective. It is our responsibility as trainers of adults to *listen* to trainees, to understand them and to help them to grow in understanding, attitudes and skills which will help them to work with God and His people to extend God's Kingdom on this earth.

Cross-Cultural Considerations in Adult Education

Learning Is More Than Decontextualized Knowledge

The pre-eminence of the view that knowledge is an end in itself has profoundly affected western culture and education, including theological education. Unfortunately, the West has also done a good job of exporting this unbalanced view of education around the world. In this view,

Chapter Objectives:

This chapter is designed to help you:

- Understand the principles of adult education.
- Analyze your own program in light of these principles.
- Apply adult learning methods and techniques.

 Are there things which you are doing which might lead trainees to think that truth can be learned in isolation from life experience?

 Are there other ways of learning the Bible apart from reading it? Can theology be learned without reading text books?

knowledge is perceived as being an entity sufficient to itself. This is referred to as the *decontextualization* of knowledge (isolating knowledge from the rest of life) (Fenwick 2000). The problem that this causes in ministry training is that truth is defined solely in terms of right doctrine, forgetting that Truth is embodied in the *person* of Jesus. This view has also encouraged the development of the learning of knowledge in institutions which are cut off from the world. Obviously this has serious implications for the training of Christian workers whose work is very much involved in relating to and interacting with the day-to-day problems of normal life. In order to be effective, the discipline of adult education must be associated with a re-discovery of other dimensions of human experience and the parts that the learner, the group, other sources of authority (including tradition) and other aspects of context play in learning.

Consider: what is truth? What is knowledge? How are they related? Reflect on what you could be doing to help trainees integrate knowledge and truth with daily life and ministry experience.

Learning Is Not Solely Dependent on the Written Word

Many educational approaches are characterized by the primacy of the written word. Literacy is viewed as an index of talent, skill and intelligence. So dominant is literacy in western thinking that some now talk about the *text* of life. Although literacy is important, there are other ways of learning apart from the written text. This is an area that theological education has been slow to discover.

What kinds of learning apart from reading and writing are you aware of? What ways of learning are valued in your culture? Have you considered experimenting with some different ways of learning that are found in your culture? In your opinion, is any one way of learning more important than any other?

Learning to Value Other Viewpoints

In any situation where one group of people dominates another, educators have to be particularly careful to examine their own assumptions, avoid the marginalization and invalidation of non-dominant group members and to ensure that all participants truly have an equal voice. Domination is not necessarily determined by having a majority in terms of numbers; it can equally occur when a teacher represents a group which has a cultural dominance in relation to the other cultures represented in the learning group. It is especially important for educators to remember that inclusion does not guarantee equity. Simply being included in the learning group does not ensure that a person from a non-dominant group has an equal voice in group discussions.

In cross-cultural and multicultural learning contexts, these are extremely important issues. It is too easy for any one of us to adopt ethnocentric views of knowledge and education. Incongruously, we can often adopt quite reasonable levels of cross-cultural sensitivity in communication outside the classroom and then, especially in theological areas, continue to assume that our cultural heritage (or what we have learned, including the way we learned it) has the monopoly on the interpretation of truth. A classic example of this is Hiebert's[1] anthropological observation on the West's "excluded middle" in which western Christianity and its teacher/trainers have difficulty providing adequate answers to questions and training in skills related to dealing with the realm of spirits and non-material reality.

---

1   Paul G. Hiebert, "The Flaw of the Exclude Middle," *Missiology: An International Review*, 10 (1), (1982), pp. 35-47.

In a multicultural or cross-cultural learning context where only one cultural view is expressed, people from other cultures feel ignored and devalued. This can inadvertently happen where any aspect of history, language or culture is denied or ignored. To deny cultural heritage and reality is to deny identity.

Are you aware of all the different cultures in your training context? Are non-native speakers of the language of training freely able to express themselves? How certain are you that the way you are teaching and the content is right? Consider asking an independent observer to assess your training sessions to evaluate how much each person or group has an equal voice and to ask you difficult questions about any unconscious cultural assumptions you might have.

Creating a Healthy Multicultural Learning Context

Cross-cultural issues are difficult to resolve, not least because they are deeply rooted in unconscious assumptions about truth. We are not aware of our unconscious assumptions until they are challenged. Because they are so deeply held, it is natural to react defensively when confronted about them. For learning to occur, it is critical for the trainer to overcome defensiveness and communicate openness to ideas and ways of doing things which are different from what the trainer is used to.

In a learning context including adults from other cultures it is vital that the trainer actively affirms *all* members of the learning group and ensures that everyone has equal opportunity to speak. Lack of equal opportunity to speak is often compounded when not everyone is fully fluent in the language of instruction. If this is not countered, it is easy for native speakers to unconsciously act as if the less fluent speakers are less mature. It is the teacher's responsibility to ensure that *all* members see each other as mature adults with an equally valuable contribution to give to everyone's learning.

Where the trainers are from a different culture than the trainees, trainers also need to make an extra effort to examine their unconscious assumptions concerning education and course content. The curriculum needs to be carefully examined according to the cultures of the students and a holistic view of the world. Leaders from the students' culture must be consulted on content and assumptions, even on issues that seem very obvious to the expatriate trainer.

It may seem as if I am overemphasizing these issues. Too often, I have seen trainers from one culture treating trainees from another as if they are children who know nothing, when often the trainees are older and have more life experience than the trainer. I have also personally seen the damaging results of the devaluation of culture, history and viewpoint concerning truth in the lives of many mature Christian adults taught by people from other cultures. The results are confusion of identity and depression. This must stop! Adult education is about valuing difference. Culture is a too-often neglected dimension of human difference in adult education contexts.

How familiar are you with the different cultures represented in your training program?

The following box outlines some principles and values that are critical for effective adult learning in cross-cultural situations.

Hints for Those Setting Up Training Programs for Adults

- Make sure your curriculum and approach is focused on the whole person, not just on developing the mind.

- Actively counter any tendency to isolate knowledge from the rest of life and human experience.

- Ensure that all cultures and heritages are valued and affirmed. Ensure that trainers do not think their way is the best or only way.

- Explore other paradigms of learning and put what you learn into practice.

What Do Good Adult Educators Do?

Focus on the Learners

The key to being an effective teacher of adults in any context, including ministry training, is to be *learner-focused* rather than focused on information transfer. It is a great temptation to put our own needs and desires, including the need to get through *our* content and to provide learning experiences that are comfortable for us, over the needs of the learners.

Some people, including many ministry trainers, are afraid of being learner-focused. They may be concerned about loss of control and resulting chaos. If they have any self-doubts, they are also concerned that allowing trainees more freedom means an increased risk of the trainer's lack of knowledge or competence being exposed with a subsequent loss of face or status. These are valid fears. But adult students are not subordinate to teachers in the same way that children are. We are not all-knowing as teacher/trainers. Sometimes trainees might have better ideas than we do and may even come up with new insights which challenge the ways we think and do things. This should be viewed positively. The starting place for becoming an effective teacher of adults is recognizing that we are all learning together.

How does your attitude about your trainees affect your practice?

Do you think you need to change your attitude or practice?

Examine your attitude towards your trainees. Do you view them as adults, or as if they are immature young people or children? In honesty, consider how much you think they know in comparison to yourself. Do you think they have anything to teach you? Are you afraid of your trainees in any way? Why? What could you do to overcome your fears?

Empower

Teaching, like all human social activity, is a complex task. It is often very difficult to identify the dynamics in a learning experience, but one of the most significant is the teacher's hidden agenda in the process. This is the underlying, often unexpressed philosophy governing a teacher's approach. A hidden agenda can be positive or negative or a mixture of both.

There are many reasons why people teach: a desire to help people grow in understanding, skills, or character, to help them meet new challenges, or to help individuals resolve issues. But teachers can also teach out of a need for significance, status, power or control. In adult education, a teacher's need to be in charge or to feel significant can be a major obstacle to learning. Adults are responsible members of society who want to be consulted on matters relating to themselves and who expect education to help them to achieve *their* goals. A teacher of adults needs to be able to empower others to achieve learning objectives.

Can you identify your hidden agenda? What is it? Whose needs does your agenda serve (yours, your trainees, the denominational leaders, others?)? Where is the balance of power in your training context? Draw a diagram or build a model illustrating this. Think through the implications for your practice. Does anything need to change?

Develop Positive Learning Contexts

Learning is a social process. Sometimes it seems as if teachers think that learning will occur through the passive acquisition of transmitted knowledge. Learning occurs in a social context. Human interaction, even when it is only minimally relational, is always affected by social and emotional dimensions. There are many different players and dimensions to the social milieu: the learner, other learners, the teacher, the organizational context of the teacher and the learner, the extended family and other influences on both the teacher and the learner. All these relationships affect the way the learner and teacher relate to each other and the way they interpret the communication between each other. Often this influence is unconscious as its origin is in unexpressed thoughts and attitudes.

Characteristics of Adult Learners

Adults Are Self-determining and Capable Human Beings

The hardest thing for trainers of adults to come to terms with is that their students are adults. This includes *all* students in Bible Colleges and other Christian ministry training programs. It is a common mistake to view Christians-in-training as immature and therefore like children. Adults are self-determining and capable human beings. They marry, have children, manage families, jobs and other responsibilities and do not appreciate being patronized. Adults are already shaping their own destinies and seek help to achieve this. They are not empty bottles waiting for the all-knowing teacher to fill them up. This view of teaching was very well exposed and critiqued by the Brazilian educator, Paulo Freire,[2] who referred to it as the "banking concept of education". Freire talks about the need to move away from the concept that the teacher is all-knowing and offering the gift of knowledge to those who know nothing, to a situation where students and teacher are *both* simultaneously learning and teaching.

Malcolm Knowles, the widely recognized "father" of adult learning theory, describes four characteristics of adult learners :[3]

> 1. Adults need to know why they need to learn something before they will go to the effort to learn it.
>
>   You can do this by a number of methods including:

Margin notes

 How does your hidden agenda affect your practice?

Can you identify your trainees' needs? Have you asked them what they think?

Draw a diagram illustrating the power relationships in your school or classroom.

Identify the hidden agendas of all groups. Evaluate the hidden agendas.

Does anything need to change? How could you help it to change?

How well are you communicating why your trainees need to learn what you are trying to teach them?

---

2   Paulo Freire, *Pedagogy of the Oppressed,* (New York: Continuum, 1994), p. 53.
3   Malcolm Knowles, *The Adult Learner: A Neglected Species,* (Houston, TX: Gulf Publishing, 1990), pp. 57-63.

- Getting trainees to identify their own needs and showing how the learning experience will help them to fulfil these

- Demonstrating a competency gap between what the trainees need to be able to do and what they are currently able to do

- Doing a role play to evoke inappropriate attitudes and/or emotional responses which trainees will need to learn to overcome

- Using case studies or stories which help trainees to understand why what they are going to learn will be helpful to them or others

2. Adults are self-directing and have a deep psychological need to be respected for this.

   The main principle in dealing with this area is to provide valid choices and alternative routes of learning towards the same learning outcomes, giving the adult learner control over those choices and routes. In the event of an adult learner needing to do something he would not naturally choose, the trainer has to provide a reasonable rationale and convince the trainee of the benefits of participating, rather than attempting to force the trainee to comply. Ways of providing choice are:

   - For different learning objectives, provide several alternative activities for their achievement and allow the trainees to choose the activity which suits them best.

   - Use learning contracts. These are more likely to apply for a whole course, but could be used for projects or assignments. In this method, the trainee and trainer negotiate what learning objectives will be worked towards, how the trainee will achieve the learning objectives, the time frame in which the trainee will achieve it and the way in which the trainer holds the trainee accountable.

   - Clearly communicate why a particular learning activity is being used in order to achieve learning objectives, but be flexible enough to listen to trainees' views and be ready to adjust or change if trainees offer a better approach.

3. Adults bring life experience to the learning experience. This can be both positive and negative in terms of further learning.

   - A principle I use is that I try not to teach anything that someone in the group already knows – especially if that person is better qualified than me in that area! Hand over the teaching of different areas to trainees who have experience in those areas.

   - Use the life experience of the trainees as the illustrative starting point for learning. This can be elicited by questions or stimulated through the use of stories or case studies relating to what is being examined. Remember to use these as springboards to discussing trainees' experience rather than as abstract cases in their own right.

   - Sometimes, especially if learning skills, or working on attitudes, it may be necessary to create a real or simulated life experience to help trainees to relate to what they are learning.

   - Sometimes the most difficult things to deal with are negative life experiences which adversely affect a trainee's reactions in the learning

How much control are you allowing trainees to have over their learning?

How well do you know your trainees? What is their life experience?

context. It is helpful to enable the trainee to deconstruct the negative experience through discussion, role play or simulation.

4. Adults come ready to learn the things they need to cope with life experiences *now*.

    This area is perhaps the most difficult for institution-based training programs. Where training is situated in the learners' context it is much easier to relate the training to real life problems. Ways in which institutional training can adapt to meet this need are:

    - Provide modularized training organized around real-life ministry issues, and allow trainees to do the training when they feel the need for it, rather than according to a pre-set order or timeline.

    - If the program cannot be reorganized in the above way, simulate real experience in the institutional training setting or send the students out to receive an authentic experience, in the hope that this will evoke a felt need to learn whatever is required.

    - In some cases, careful selection of trainees will ensure that they have the required experience and felt need relevant to the training being offered.

> Is your basic intention in training to place knowledge in the "bank" of your trainees' minds for future reference? Can you see any problems with this approach? What proportion of your training is related to the lived experience of your trainees?

How Do Adults Learn?

Adults Have Different Learning Styles

Adults learn in different ways and adult educators need to adjust their styles of teaching in order to cater the needs of *all* adults in the group. Three major learning styles have been identified—audio, visual and kinaesthetic[4]—but there is no reason why this list should be exhaustive, nor is each style mutually exclusive (each adult employs a combination of the styles, and may change according to the nature of what is being studied).

Auditory Learners
Auditory learners prefer to learn by *listening*. They love to listen, are attracted by sound and distracted by noise. They prefer to hear things rather than to read them. They learn best using questions and answers, lectures, stories, discussion pairs or groups and other auditory approaches including music.

Visual Learners
Visual learners prefer reading, watching television and looking at photographs, plans and cartoons. They are attracted to words such as: see, look, appear, picture, make clear, overview. They may have strong spelling and writing skills. They may not talk much, dislike listening for too long, and may be distracted by untidiness or movement. Visual learners learn through posters, charts, graphs, visual displays, booklets, brochures and handouts, and a variety of color and shape.

Kinesthetic Learners
Kinaesthetic or tactile learners prefer learning by *doing*. They move around a lot, tap their pens, shift in their seats, want lots of breaks, enjoy games and don't like reading. You can train a kinaesthetic learner best by team activities, hands-on experience, role plays, simulations, note taking, and emotional discussions.

4   Rita Dunn and Kenneth Dunn, *Teaching Students Through Their Individual Learning Styles: A practical approach*, (Englewood Cliffs, NJ: Prentice Hall, 1978).

What is your learning style? Does your teaching approach use sufficient variety so that all learning styles are equally catered for?

All adults like variety. It is not realistic to meet everyone's individual preferences all the time, but by using a number of different teaching methods in each session, preferably emphasizing the same points in different ways, each learner will experience something which suits them, as well as providing an interesting and stimulating learning experience for all involved. This means the trainer has to do more work in preparation and use a wider variety of educational tools, contexts, approaches, and methods.

Adults Like to Have Control of Their Learning

Adults will resist being forced to do things they dislike or disagree with. They need to feel in control of their lives. This requires instructional strategies to be made clear so that adult learners can either choose alternative routes to achieving learning objectives or, where a method they dislike is being used, they can choose to engage in it for the sake of learning. Learners can often be greatly helped to see the value of learning tasks they dislike when trainers explicitly explain their purpose. The role play is an educational technique that provides a good example of this. Role plays are particularly important for learning about attitudes and feelings, and helping a trainee to experience another person's perspective. Most people don't enjoy being moved out of their comfort zones and indeed, role plays can generate very real feelings of frustration, anger and discomfort. The following dialogue illustrates how a trainer could help a reluctant trainee choose to be involved in this type of learning.

I hate doing role plays. I feel so stupid and unnatural when I act.

Many people hate doing role plays as it makes them feel uncomfortable, but what we are trying to understand is how people feel when they encounter prejudice in the classroom. This is a feeling thing, not a cognitive activity. If we experience the unpleasant feeling ourselves in a role play, we are more likely to be sensitive to people experiencing it in a training context and therefore try to prevent it. Another thing we could do is to deliberately put ourselves in a situation where we are a disempowered minority.

That could be a bit risky, couldn't it? What if they decided I was the enemy and wanted to make an example of me?

Well yes, that's very possible and that's often how people from minority backgrounds feel in our classrooms. That is one reason why we use role plays—they are a bit more controllable, and therefore safer for the participants. We could also have a discussion about when we might have felt devalued or uncomfortable in a group situation, but that is not quite so powerful as experiencing the feeling and then working out how to handle it…

Okay, I'm willing to try a role play. Then, if I'm really feeling brave maybe we could go to the local slum together…

Adults Learn by Solving Real-life Problems

Knowles[5] reminds us that adults come to learning with life experience. They come with questions and opinions. Adults like to solve problems. Starting from problems in real life, adults bring questions to the learning experience and expect to find answers to those questions through the process of learning. The study of theory brings insight and suggests solutions to the questions and problems. These solutions then need to be tried in real life. This concept of learning is often referred to as "top rail – bottom rail," using a railway track as the metaphor (cf. Plueddemann[6]). The top rail represents theory, the bottom rail, practice in real life and the railway sleepers between the rails represent reflection between the two. Reflection is the process of evaluating theory in the light of practice, and practice in the light of theory. Without reflection, theory or practice does not change. The following diagram describes this process.

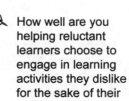

How well are you helping reluctant learners choose to engage in learning activities they dislike for the sake of their learning?

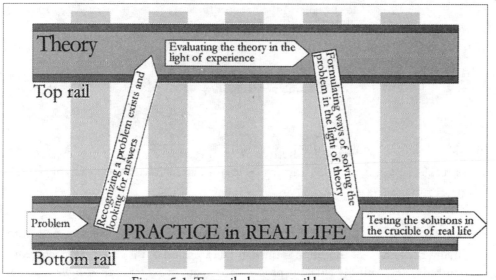

Figure 5:1. Top rail - bottom rail learning
Source: Adaptation of Plueddemann's top rail – bottom rail concept

Many people add another step to this picture and make it an ongoing cycle or spiral. Sometimes this is called action learning or research. Kolb[7] gave perhaps the earliest description of this model. An adaptation of Kemmis'[8] action research cycle follows.

---

5   Knowles, 1990.

6   James Plueddemann, "The Real Disease of Sunday School," *Evangelical Missions Quarterly* 9 (2), (1972), pp. 88-92.

7   David A. Kolb, *Experiential Learning: Experience as the source of learning and development,* (Englewood Cliffs, NJ: Prentice - Hall, 1984).

8   Stephen Kemmis and Robin McTaggert, *The Action Research Planner,* (Geelong, Victoria: Deakin University Press, 1998).

Plot your school's own specific teaching/training on each of these diagrams. How well are you doing?

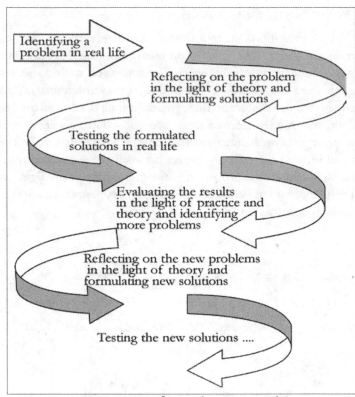

Identifying a problem in real life

Reflecting on the problem in the light of theory and formulating solutions

Testing the formulated solutions in real life

Evaluating the results in the light of practice and theory and identifying more problems

Reflecting on the new problems in the light of theory and formulating new solutions

Testing the new solutions ....

Figure 5:2. Reflective learning spiral

Source: Adaptation of Kolb's learning cycle and Kemmis' action research spiral

For many, the aim of all education is the natural extension of the above cycle where it is recognized that learning is a lifelong process carried out by *reflective practitioners*. Schön[9] explains how the development of professional skills requires a communal, interactive, reflective process between trainers and learners. He explores the difficulty of identifying exactly what is being transferred in the learning process and how those trainees who are unwilling to reflect on their own practice or to explore approaches or ideas outside their comfort zone are unlikely to learn.

 Would you describe yourself as a reflective practitioner?

Daloz[10] emphasizes the importance of both individual and group mentoring in helping adult learners grow and develop as people and in their area of study. Reflection on life and application of what is being studied to the learner's personal and social context is a major part of mentoring.

> Learning = reflecting on experience, changing and then putting that change into practice

---

9   Donald A. Schön, *Educating the Reflective Practitioner*, (San Francisco, CA: Jossey-Bass, 1987).
10   Laurent A. Daloz, *Effective Teaching and Mentoring*, (San Francisco, CA: Jossey-Bass, 1986).

Adults Learn When New Concepts Are Congruent with the Way They Already View the World

Unlike children, adults already have established ideas about the way the world works. Mezirow[11] explained this in terms of their internal structures, or perspectives of meaning. These are often referred to as *meaning frames*. Where new experience or information doesn't easily match the internal structure, it is either approximated to the nearest equivalent or totally rejected. In an educational context this means it is important to try and match new concepts and ways of doing things to established, understood patterns. If the concept is completely new, it may be necessary to build bridges of meaning.

Adults Have Differing Motivations

Unlike children, adults can choose whether or not they will participate in a learning experience. This means that understanding adults' motivation in learning is very important. Motivation is a complex area. For learners who are achievement-oriented, there is a need to provide challenges, whilst for those who are afraid of failure, the trainer needs to provide an encouraging, supportive learning environment. Some learners are primarily motivated by the interpersonal interaction within a group. The main thing to realize is that different trainees will be motivated by different things and, as is the case with learning styles, it is good to provide a variety of learning activities which suit the different motivational needs of the trainees.

Adults Appreciate Different Methods of Teaching

If formal schooling is the only recognized learning experience adults have had, some adults will be confused by a less formal, interactive and more creative approach. The trainer also needs to set the tone of the learning experience as a dialogue among peers and explain why different instructional methods are being used. Just because prior learning experiences have taught adults to expect a particular format of learning, does not mean they are not open to and appreciative of other ways of learning.

Hints for Those Setting Up Training Programs for Adults

- Use as much variety in training methods as possible, making sure equal emphasis is given to visual, auditory and kinesthetic learning styles. Where possible, allow alternatives of learning activity matching each style and give trainees the opportunity to choose the method of learning which suits them best.
- Relate training to real life situations. Start with life experience, explain the theory and then move to application in real life.
- Use an approach which encourages continual reflection, evaluation, experimentation and improvement.
- Reflection is often done best with other people who can help to provide alternative perspectives on the same situation. This can be done one-to-one or in groups.
- Do your best to understand the meaning frames of the trainees and then to build bridges from their frames to new concepts.
- Do not ignore the emotional, physical and spiritual dimensions of meaning.
- Gently use physical and emotional discomfort to help trainees be more open to learn.

---

11   J. Mezirow, "How Critical Reflection Triggers Transformative Learning," *Fostering Critical Reflection in Adulthood*, (San Francisco, CA: Jossey-Bass, 1991), pp. 1-20.

Draw two pairs of scales. On the first, show the relative balance of your institution's agenda versus the trainees' agenda. On the second, show the relative balance between your agenda and your trainees' agenda. Do you think the balance you have drawn is right and good? Why?

Can Learners' and Trainers' Agendas Be Balanced?

As became clear in the examination of how adults learn, the learning context for adults cannot be static or monochromatic in terms of a singular teaching approach. The trainer of adults must cater for the needs of *all* the learners. To do this effectively requires a very different approach than the traditional teacher-focused, presentation-heavy style of teaching. It requires a more chaotic, interactive approach in which learning objectives are clear but the routes to achieving them are negotiable.

So far this chapter has emphasized the importance of allowing adults to control their own learning and making sure the course meets the felt needs of the learners. But this may not be sufficient. If trainers provide only what students want, they might cause students to miss out on some essentials that they need. The wider experience of the curriculum designers and requirements of stakeholders will inevitably result in the course having elements which go beyond what the trainee feels they need or want to learn. This provides a significant challenge to the trainer.

Balancing the needs of the learners with the demands of the curriculum can only be achieved through communication and negotiation. The clearer the learning objectives are and the more clearly the trainer can explain the rationale for particular training approaches, the easier this will be. Clear learning objectives help the trainee to understand the difference between their current status of knowing, being or doing, and what is expected in a qualified graduate. If the trainee disagrees with the description of "qualified," it is much more difficult. It may be possible to start with the trainee's felt needs and attempt to evoke a desire for further achievement in line with the objectives in the course.

Another way of looking at this is to see the trainer as needing to build bridges from the felt needs of the trainees to the place where they need to end up. This means that the trainer has to make an effort to understand the trainees well. If this cannot be done, it is not possible to force adults to do things they do not want to. To attempt to do this can be damaging to both student and teacher and, in the worst cases, even emotionally and spiritually abusive.

The trainer of adults has to be flexible. It may well be that an adult trainee could achieve the learning objectives by a means or method other than the way a teacher desires. In this case, why should the teacher's method have to be used? It is very important to be conscious of power-play issues between teachers and adult students. Often a teacher's insistence on doing things a particular way is simply a desire to be in charge of or to control the students. Adult teachers need to be self-aware, humble and ready to learn from their students.

Conclusion

By the age of 30, Alexander the Great had conquered the known world. In many cultures of the world, young teenagers marry, have children and set up house. In the last two centuries people in their teens and early twenties were sent out to other countries to start churches among peoples who were without any experience or knowledge of Christianity. Many of the trainees in Christian ministry training across the world today are the same age or much older than their trainers. They are adults and capable of doing great things. The greatest mistake an adult educator can make is to forget that his trainees are adults.

If the adult educator respects his trainees as mature individuals, he has to let go of exclusive control of the education process. Using the learning objectives as a guiding foundation for the learning, the trainer and trainees enter into an interactive journey towards the accomplishment of the objectives. While the trainer may understand the nature of the objectives and various training techniques which might help the trainees to achieve them, the trainees are the ones who know themselves, how they learn best and how what is being learned can be applied in their own contexts.

For some trainers, adult education theory seems to promise a frightening descent into chaos. Others are concerned that the curriculum requirements will not be achieved or that the mass of information they have to share will not be transferred. The focus in adult learning is on the learner. Can we trust and respect our trainees enough to believe that they will want to work with us to achieve the purpose of the training?

There are many dimensions to human experience. These include social interactions and context, personal history, emotions, spirituality, personality, cultural background and experience, learning style and motivation. All these affect how a person will interact with a learning experience and how well they will be able to learn within it. No trainer can expect to meet all the needs and orientations of his trainees, even on a one-to-one basis; but all trainers should provide a variable learning situation which has the potential of meeting most of the needs of learners most of the time.

If you are choosing to be an educator of adults, you are choosing a demanding but also highly rewarding task. In making the effort to interact with adult learners, to understand them and to meet their needs, you will have to spend as much time or more listening to them as you spend talking or leading. Sometimes you will feel vulnerable, sometimes as if things are totally out of control, but you will also have the great privilege of seeing people empowered to go out and achieve what is on their hearts.

Summary

- Adults want to be in control of their own learning.
  - They know what they want to learn,
  - They want to be able to choose how to learn,
  - They want to use what they learn *now*, and
  - They want their trainers to be able to do with them what they talk about.

- Different adults learn in different ways and all adults like variety.

- Instruction should be designed according to a process which starts with real life problems, reflects on these in the light of theory and then ensures the testing of derived solutions in real life.

- New ideas will be adopted more readily if they can be related to structures of meaning which already exist.

- Adults live in a social and physical context. Learning and teaching needs to actively interact with these contexts.

Chapter 5: Exercises

Analyzing Adult Learning Elements in Your Program

Consider your program and answer the following:

1. Who is in control of the learning? Why?

2. How much do you value difference? What dimensions of difference are there? How exactly do you demonstrate that you value difference?

3. Plot your program and/or courses on the figures on pages 59 and 60. Note that the "problem" in the figures is the learners' experienced problem prior to or during the learning.

4. What dimensions of the social context are you interacting with? Especially consider the affective, power, cross-cultural and multicultural dimensions.

5. What messages does your physical context communicate?

Section 2

The Process of Integral Training Design

Chapter 6

Stakeholder Assumptions and Consensus Building

Jonathan Lewis

A well executed ministry training program may have a wonderful design, but falter significantly in its operation because of a lack of support by key leaders. If these influential people are not involved in the process of designing the training, they will not fully understand the program or value it, particularly if it is innovative and aims at the outcomes of integral training rather than more traditional values they are used to. If they are not convinced of the value of the training, they will not require ministry candidates to undergo the training, even though some may recommend it on an optional basis.

The key leaders of groups that are involved in the support of and deployment of the candidate in the ministry are referred to as "stakeholders." When considering the training of missionaries, this group includes the sending church, the sending agency, and the receiving field team and/or church. Because the program serves each one of these groups, it is useful to picture these stakeholders as our "clients." In the case of other ministries, stakeholders could include churches, denominational leaders, leaders of parachurch agencies and ministry trainers.

Trainers often think primarily of students as their clients because in many cases, they are the ones who will decide whether or not to take their training. But if we think of training as developing human resources to be deployed in the work of the church or agency, then the "client," would be the institutions whose ministry goals are being achieved by these persons. The sending and receiving church, and the ministry or mission agency and field team are the direct beneficiaries of these human resources. Yet in many cases, broad, generalized guidelines about training requirements (usually focused on biblical and theological studies) leave the candidate to choose from a variety of schooling options, many of which are not aimed at developing ministry specific competence.

Chapter Objectives:

This chapter is designed to help you:

- Identify key stakeholders and engage them in training program design and/or evaluation.

- Draw out stakeholder assumptions and values and clarify these as a group.

- Use consensus as a means to generate stakeholder ownership for a program.

This reinforces the notion that the candidate is the program's client and must be the center of a training program's recruitment efforts.

In order for training programs to succeed, they need trainees. If the direct beneficiaries, the "clients," make ministry specific training optional or leave it up to the trainee, trainees will tend to take the shortest and least costly route into service. In the case of missionaries, this often leaves them without adequately developed skills and attitudes to cross linguistic and culture barriers that will enable them to succeed. Major international studies on missionary attrition and retention demonstrate that specific, pre-field cross-cultural training is significant in keeping missionaries on the field. [1]

This chapter will help you identify your "stakeholders," and encourage you to convene these individuals for a "profiling process" (Chapter 7). You will learn how to facilitate a consensus-based activity that will surface training needs and create genuine ownership for the program.

The Role of Formal Biblical Training

Before identifying stakeholders, it is useful to understand the role of formal Bible training—including Bible institutes or colleges—in ministry training. Two to four-year Bible institute programs have been a widely accepted standard of ministry training during much of the 20th Century. This standard created a symbiotic relationship between the sending church, the agency or denomination, and the training institutions. With a supportive stakeholder environment, Bible institutes prospered and multiplied.

Candidates also acknowledged and accepted this standard. Many young people went into this training straight from high school. They needed not only the biblical and theological training to become ministers of the Gospel, but time to mature and become responsible adults. The Bible school community was an important setting to develop and mature Christian attitudes and character. It was so successful, that it is not surprising that missionaries also established Bible institutes throughout the world as they went out.

While this model served its purpose particularly well during much of the 20th Century, demographic shifts from farm to city and other sociological factors forced many of these institutes into decline. A better-educated population in North America preferred candidates with college and/or seminary degrees. Many Bible schools accommodated to this pressure by pursuing academic accreditation with a subsequent shift from basic ministry vocational training to general education.

In places where formal Bible training was reproduced, Bible schools have also undergone various kinds of pressures. Residential schools are costly to maintain and mission agencies have been reticent to continue to support ongoing campus and personnel costs. Single young people—the ones most able to study in residential Bible schools—were often not acceptable by their societies for leadership in churches or other ministries. Furthermore, few churches could afford to support their pastors. Thus ministerial training in many cases appears to be an occupational dead-end. In other cases, Bible schools have simply become an affordable educational stepping stone for Christian young people

---

1   The World Evangelical Alliance Mission Commission conducted a fourteen-nation study on missionary attrition from 1994-1997 (W. Taylor. *Too Valuable to Lose.* (Pasadena, Wm. Carey Library 1997)). Pre-field training was found to be a significant variable in reducing missionary attrition. A second study was conducted from 2002-2004 on missionary retention. Focused missionary training was again found to be an important variable in missionary, long-term retention (D. Bloecher., *Missionary Training Makes Missionaries Resilient – Lessons from ReMAP II.* e-article, www.wearesources.org, 2003).

seeking greater secular employment opportunities. Many Bible schools have eliminated their residential component in order to cut costs, and are offering night school or modular programs. Out of necessity, these programs focus principally on knowledge transfer.

Traditional Bible institutes have further been weakened by the trend toward "in-house" institutes sponsored by local churches. This is a popular alternative since it supports institutional needs for control of the ministry ethos and doctrinal content, as well as keeping costs contained. While the quality of these institutes varies from church to church, the training is usually effective in supporting primary values of the church (e.g., loyalty, internal leadership needs, organizational growth).

With cross-cultural missionary training, the pressure to train "in house" is also strong. Yet if training is to be effective, it needs to provide essential elements that are often beyond the means of local churches and smaller agencies. Effective programs need experienced resource people (i.e., missionaries, pastors, and expert trainers), and the community context that produces character growth through example, practice, and high accountability. In addition, missionary training must also include supervised internships where candidates can focus on developing essential cross-cultural skills needed for effectiveness. These elements may be beyond the abilities or resources of many local churches and of formal Bible institutes that have had to dismantle their residential components or are primarily pursuing formal academic learning.

In spite of these problems, the Bible institute model still holds a prominent place in the ministry training paradigm. But if churches and Bible institutes cannot incorporate essential accountability elements and supervised internship opportunities into their training programs, they should seriously consider partnering with programs that can offer these elements in complementary ways. Dedicated missionary training programs that offer integral missionary training are increasingly available in many parts of the world. Great synergy and efficiency can be created through partnership arrangements.

Training Is Always a Shared Activity

The strongest partnerships are created when all of the major stakeholders are involved in designing the process and implementing training programs needed for getting well-equipped candidates into ministry. When this is done, training is seen as a shared responsibility and each component of the triad—church, trainers, agency—can assume responsibility for specific parts of candidate training. It also creates the commitment necessary to the program's effectiveness.

One of the challenges that program developers face in working with stakeholders is that their potential clients may have an incomplete understanding of what training is really needed for missionary or ministry effectiveness. Even once these needs are acknowledged, they may still command a low commitment because of the time and cost involved. Clients operate with assumptions, biases and prior obligations that can be significant barriers in creating program commitment. Thus the program developer is left with the challenge of creating understanding of the need for holistic training and turning clients into partners that will commit the resources needed to meet effective training standards.

One of the best ways to both create an awareness of the real training needs and to create partners of potential clients is to involve them thoroughly in the discussion of the program and its development. This involves discussing relevant issues as well as getting them drawn in to the curricular design process by conducting an "outcomes profiling" session, defining the understanding, qualities and skills their ministry candidates need in order to succeed.[2] This exercise creates a profile that clearly shows the complexity and scope of training needed, and is useful for either creating a new program or revising an existing program that is genuinely seeking to become more effective.

Identify and Convene

Stakeholders must:
- Recognize a need for training.
- Be in a position to influence commitment to a program.

✎ List potential stakeholders for your ministry training program:

As Lois Fuller suggests in *Starting a Ministry Training Program*,[3] the first step is to personally research the needs and context. During that research, you will have identified the key stakeholders—potential clients that recognize a need for training and are in a position to influence commitment to a program that is created or modified to meet their organizations' needs.

If you are creating an in-house program for your own agency, church or denomination, this will be a different list than for someone who is offering training to the general Christian community. For an in-house program, primary stakeholders would be executive leaders, heads of related departments, and ministry field leaders. It would also include ministry candidates as well as training staff. For a program serving a broader group, stakeholders would include influential pastors and/or denominational leaders, agency leaders, and ministry field leaders as well as candidates and trainers.

As you think through this list, *plan to convene 12-15 of these key individuals for a day or more of reflection and planning*. You are inviting them to influence the design of a new or ongoing program. Assure them of the importance of their participation.

Examining Educational Values and Assumptions

Once the stakeholder group comes together, one of your goals will be to surface and examine closely held values and assumptions about the nature of the training and its goals. Most ministry trainers are keenly interested in providing training that will help candidates be *effective* in ministry. Some of your stakeholders, however, may be products of educational systems and practices that may have had little to do with creating ministry effectiveness. Yet these clients may hold on to these as the norm because it is what they've experienced. For example, many leaders may have been products of a particular Bible school or seminary that offered little in the way of integral ministry training. They may assume that what they received in training is all a missionary really needs—biblical and doctrinal understanding and, perhaps, instruction on how to preach or teach. In creating an integral and effective training program, these assumptions may be challenged and unless they are persuaded to see the need for cross-cultural adaptation skills and attitude/character formation, they are unlikely to support the program.

Educational systems are not always focused on training for effectiveness.

Educational systems are not always focused on training for effectiveness. They often sustain institutional agendas or are simply grounded in tradition. We are all products of educational systems that create support for cultural and/or national agendas. To be "well-educated" or the graduate of a certain school often brings with it social status. A frank discussion with clients should surface these less obvious, but closely held values and preferences. These need to be acknowledged and dealt with; otherwise, they will hamper or defeat efforts to get client support for the program.

---

2   How to conduct a profiling exercise is explained in "The Outcomes Profiling Process," Chapter 7.
3   "Starting a Ministry Training Program," Chapter 4.

Pragmatic considerations also drive educational systems and form traditions. In North America, for example, the school calendar was originally created to accommodate the need to free children to work on farms during the summer when the workload was heaviest. Although most North Americans no longer live on farms and machinery replaces much of the need for hand labor, this calendar continues. Educators have challenged this calendar, but the tradition is hard to break. In designing ministry training, established patterns may need to be broken and clients must participate in these decisions in order to support them.

> In many parts of the world, the cost of education is the greatest over-arching factor in determining its quality and availability.

In many parts of the world, the cost of education is the greatest over-arching factor in determining its quality and availability. In some cases, training is not offered or is qualitatively poor because of the expense. It is a tough assignment to design a high quality program on a low budget. Many trainers are willing to take on this challenge, but the cost of training must be acknowledged and accepted by stakeholders as well.

In order to discover stakeholders' assumptions and values, it is important to discuss some of the following topics with them:

> What are some of the assumptions and values you hold in regard to education?

- What are the specific goals of missionary (or other ministry) training?

- What methods should be used to achieve these goals?

- In what setting or settings should this training be provided?

- What relationship does this training have to existing organizations such as the local church, the agency or denomination, and the national church?

- Who do we intend to train and what should be their qualifications?

- Who should do the training and what should be their qualifications?

- Who should pay for the training?

The discussion of these questions will help program developers understand their clients' values and what will be needed to create or alter a program to meet their expectations.

Assuming the Role of Facilitator

Once the stakeholder group is convened, the program developer's mission is to help them capture the scope of ministry training, to understand the need for it, and to create commitment to the program. The program must meet real needs, and that is why stakeholder opinion is essential to its design. The program developer will need to be prepared to let this group significantly shape the program.

A facilitator[4] manages this process towards defined ends. During that process, all participants will be encouraged to express their opinions and values. These opinions will differ and the facilitator must wisely steer the discussions toward points of consensus. Consensus does not mean everyone agrees 100% with a decision. Consensus requires a generous spirit that acknowledges the validity of different points of view and recognizes that there is wisdom in taking counsel from a broad spectrum of leadership. Consensus-building is a biblical model for decision-making that may not always feel comfortable, but is worth the effort.

---

4   Ideally, a skilled consultant who is not a stakeholder should lead the facilitation process. This person should be well acquainted with the issues surrounding ministry training, how to conduct the profiling process, and clearly understand the goals of the meeting. Since this material is being used to train facilitators, we will assume that the program developer is also the person who will facilitate the process.

Decision-Making by Consensus

Consensus-building is the art of helping a group come to collective agreements. Effectively employed, all group members share in the decision and agree to support it. No one reserves the right to disown the decision, even if it incorporates aspects that don't match all their preferences. The underlying assumption is that, guided by the Holy Spirit and through a process of give and take, the best decision will be made in light of insights, wisdom, and values shared. When organizing a new training program or evaluating one for change, decisions are being made that will impact all of the stakeholders. Consensus-building helps leaders come together to make these decisions as a group, and is of critical importance.

Decision-making is often patterned after cultural norms. People in democratic societies are probably more democratic in decision-making. Those in autocratic societies may lean toward autocratic decision-making. This raises a legitimate question as to whether there is a biblical method or pattern to making decisions. While we could criticize some of the methods used in the Bible, like casting lots (Acts 1:26; 1 Samuel 14:41) or consulting Urim and Thummim (Numbers 27:21; Deuteronomy 33:8), we can still affirm that Christians believe in Divine guidance and when we subject important matters to the Lord, we can expect him to guide the decision-making process. We can also affirm that in the counsel of many, there is safety (Proverbs 11:14), and that councils of all kinds have been instruments that God has used to provide leadership and direction throughout the centuries.

Christ is the Head of the Church. When leaders come together and seek the mind of the Lord, he can and will provide wisdom and insight that assists the group to make good decisions and right choices (Matthew 18:18-20). But this can only happen in an atmosphere of mutual respect and trust. Such an atmosphere happens when each participant recognizes the gifting and experience of every other participant in the group.

What are some of the challenges and solutions to fostering a culture of humility in your group of stakeholders?

Through consensus, we work together to build up the body (Ephesians 4:15-16). When a group really seeks the mind of Christ, the Holy Spirit can guide the decisions and He will impart gentle wisdom (James 1:5;3:13-18). Consensus takes humility as we defer to others. Their experience can inform our opinions. Discussion around key biblical texts may be needed to convince all of the value of this process, perhaps done in the context of a devotional to start the meetings.

Steps to Consensus-Building

1. Present the Issue (not the solution)

Your research will have informed you of the need for the training program. It is not helpful, however, to show up at your team meeting with the answer or solution already on your mind. Consensus should be a creative, open process. Avoid the desire to come up with solutions prior to the meeting. Once a conclusion is reached, you may find it hard to let it go. Consensus requires that everyone keep an open mind, even the program developer. Sincerely seek the mind of the Lord through group prayer.

A meeting of training directors of institutions was convened to grapple with common issues and problems. After two days of opening up their hearts to each other and defining the issues, the final session was to generate a joint proposal for a way forward. Much to everyone's surprise, the convener of the meeting unveiled a full color chart that he had developed before the meetings, revealing the solution to the problem with his program squarely in the middle. Participants felt betrayed by the process and the trust that had been developed was broken.

2. Define the Issue

As issues are presented, participants will reveal their assumptions, biases and preferences. Try to get the group to hold these lightly and focus on issues. This is critical because teams have problems reaching agreement when members focus on preferences rather than real issues.

During a stakeholder meeting, the director of a Bible school insisted that the proposed program be run at his facility since it was currently underutilized. There were a number of reasons why his was not a great suggestion, but others hesitated to confront this strong personality. The discussion began heading in an unproductive direction as further discussions stumbled around this suggestion. The facilitator steered the discussion towards more productive channels by graciously acknowledging the "offer" and clarifying that the meeting was not trying to determine which facility to use, but rather what training methods and context might be most appropriate to reach the training goals. One of these contexts might be the facility that was offered, and that option would be discussed at a later time.

3. Listen

Reaching consensus is about listening to each other and hearing together from the Lord. Listening is the best way to show respect and fully understand and appreciate each other. This creates an atmosphere of trust and collaboration. As different perspectives and views are generated, the group will come to good solutions that would not have appeared otherwise. The facilitator can deploy active listening techniques—such as repeating back to the participant what they heard without embellishment—in order to acknowledge and affirm each person's contribution.

A consultant was contracted to facilitate a group process that would lead to an integrated training program. As the meeting progressed, people were encouraged to express their opinions. As they did, the facilitator reinterpreted the comments to suit a particular direction in which he was steering the discussion. As the meeting progressed further, people felt they were not being listened to and fewer participated in the discussion. This caused the facilitator to explode with frustration as the meetings became less participative and it became obvious that there was little buy-in to the process and his intended outcome.

4. Generate Options

Different techniques can be used to generate opinions and comments such as "brainstorming" or "go arounds."[5] During these sessions, opinions are not to be judged or discussed, just recorded. The purpose of these sessions is to generate ideas that can be evaluated once there are a number of options to consider.

> A program director was facilitating a discussion with a group of stakeholders in order to review her program for possible modification. As the first issue of training goals was raised, a client commented on the lack of practicality of what was offered and that the goal should be to produce missionaries with evangelistic skills. Another client immediately put the comment "in its place" by making the point that not all missionaries will be evangelists. The facilitator skillfully acknowledged both comments but reminded the group that she was only looking for suggestions at this point. The first comment was synthesized and the group secretary recorded it as other suggestions were forwarded.

5. Process Options

The consensus-building process involves generating a wide scope of options and then narrowing those through convergent thinking. Ideas and options generated through the brain-storming sessions should be posted and examined systematically. It is often useful to group similar kinds of options and discuss them together. For each one, pros and cons should be listed. The goal of the exercise is to narrow the number of options and evaluate them on the basis of whether they will actually meet the need effectively and efficiently.

> Following a good brain-storming session on the context for the training, suggestions seemed to be grouped into three areas—using the existing Bible school program, a field internship with an experienced mentor, and training using local ministry opportunities. The pros and cons for each of these was discussed and listed. As the discussion proceeded, it became clear that all three contexts were needed to produce the desired results. A strong proposal emerged for designing an effective program using all three elements.

6. Arriving at Consensus

More often that not, the solution will be a creative combination of elements from different options—a weaving of good components into a strong solution. When no solution is forthcoming or opposing opinions are stalemating the process, the facilitator can make the suggestion that a question be delegated to a sub-committee. If need be, it can also be

---

5   A "brain-storming" exercise solicits random ideas on an issue from the whole group. A "go around" allows each member in turn to speak to an issue. In both cases, ideas are not judged for their merit or discussed until all the suggestions are made. As each person speaks, the facilitator should try to repeat the idea back to the person and a meeting secretary should be recording a synthesized version of the comment on block paper so that the whole range of suggestions can later be displayed on these sheets of paper by taping them to a wall or other surface.

deferred to another meeting when more thought and perhaps research can be conducted that sheds light on the issue.

> The meeting was running overtime and the facilitator was pressing for a decision on an important matter before dismissing the participants for the night. The complexity of the issue and tired brains were making it hard to bring matters to a "vote." One stakeholder suggested that the decision be deferred to the morning session, but this would take valuable time from a packed, final meeting. Someone added the suggestion that a smaller group might continue to meet and bring their recommendation to the meeting the following morning. The suggestions were followed and a small group presented a solution the following morning, with which everyone felt comfortable. This set the stage for the final session, which produced an excellent initial program draft.

Test for Consensus

It is important to test for consensus because members of the group may have felt pressured to agree with the proposal when they really did not. These reservations are often masked by a desire to "go along" with the group or by a sense of withdrawal that occurred somewhere along the process. A good technique for testing for consensus is to ask participants to write out their answers to a few questions on a slip of paper. The facilitator then collects the papers and the group secretary writes out the answers for all to see. This gives an opportunity for a truer evaluation of the outcome. Questions that might be asked are:

1. Can you support the decision or proposal made?

2. What part of the proposal is the most important to you?

3. What elements of the decision or proposal would need to change for you to fully endorse this proposal?

> A three-day meeting with a large and diverse group of stakeholders from a newer sending region of the world was drawing to an end. An exciting profile of an entry-level missionary had been produced and everyone was convinced of the importance of creating better training opportunities. A list of four suggestions for developing better training in the region had emerged. To create a strong conclusion, the facilitator placed all four options on a black board and asked each participant to rank them in order of importance. The option to partner in creating a regional training program received 75% of the participants' highest rankings and became the basis for starting a new center with involved partners.

Conclusion

In such a complex context, it is difficult to imagine how a program can be designed to meet not only the program developer's goal of ministry effectiveness, but also accommodate a variety of clients' biases and values. It is easier to do with a group of stakeholders that are from the same organization who share the same history, ethos, doctrinal bent and church practices. When a number of churches, agencies and fields are involved, reaching agreement is more difficult—but not impossible. In both of these scenarios, a consensus-building process will help to surface the critical issues, provide clarity to task, and help create client commitment.

The definition of issues and their subsequent discussion is an important preliminary step in helping the program developer get a sense for the variety of concerns and opportunities. At the end of such a session, there may be less clarity than hoped for, but the next part of the process—generating an outcomes profile (Chapter 7)—should bring focus. When the profile is created, participants will be able to step back and measure their commitments against a desired outcome that they have helped define. The outcome is one that is not shaped by assumptions and preferences, but by a picture of what is needed. This provides the stage for training specialists to then design a program with the freedom needed to achieve the desired results.

Chapter 6: Exercises

Stakeholders, Commitments and Decision Making

1. Who are the real stakeholders in your training program? In forming a stakeholder group for designing or evaluating a program, you should invite an influential member of each of these stakeholder groups to attend. Who are these people? List them to the extent possible.

2. Examine each of the educational commitments that Robert Ferris suggests in the following table. Comment on whether or not you agree with these precepts and how you demonstrate your commitment in your current program or how you would plan to do so in a program you design.

Biblical-Educational Commitments to Guide Missionary Training

1. Training objectives should be determined by the understandings, skills, and qualities required for effective service.

2. Training is Church related; learning occurs best in the context of community.

3. Training structures and relationships must be consistent with training goals.

4. Training strategies should be appropriate to the learner's ways of thinking and learning.

5. Training strategies should incorporate and build upon the learner's experience.

6. Theory should be validated by Scripture and by general revelation.

7. Information should be appropriated and obeyed.

8. Skills-learning should include instruction, demonstration, and guided practice.

9. Character qualities and values are effectively communicated only when teaching includes modeling and reflection.

10. Training equips the learner for effective ministry and continuing growth.

Source: Robert Ferris, ed. *Establishing Ministry Training*, (Pasadena: William Carey Library, 1995), p. 145.

2. What decision making style do you or the leader(s) of your organization employ? In light of the information in this chapter, which style is the most effective in your organizational and social structure? Is consensus based decision making a good option?

Chapter 7

The Outcomes Profiling Process

Jonathan Lewis

The outcomes profiling process requires integrity. It asks participants to describe the outcomes of training that are truly needed for ministry effectiveness. It assumes that effective ministry is done by people who are effective in all areas of life. It assumes that character development and skills are more important than simply what the student knows at the end of the training. Thus, a profile is not just a definition (or redefinition) of content (knowledge) areas, but focuses primarily on what typically gets left out of intentional training—the needed personal qualities and ministry skills.

Curriculum will eventually look like a series of courses with objectives, learning activities, lesson plans, and assignments. But the knowledge implicit in a curriculum is not an end in itself, rather a means to an end intended to fuel a process. To generate the desired outcomes, a strong commitment to the internalization and application of this information is required. Thus, the effectiveness of the training is measured not by what trainees know, but by how much the trainees have grown and to what degree they are equipped to be more effective at what they are doing. Seldom is information retention a good measure of these outcomes.

The profile helps objectify these outcomes and becomes a primary tool for both the design of a program and its evaluation. It is an idealized profile, but it need not be larger-than-life. In fact, it should be very realistic. Every competency described should pass the test of being absolutely essential to ministry effectiveness. There is no room for things that would be "nice" or "might be" important. Efficiency is a very high value in training design. Thus, the comprehensive outcomes profile helps a training program define both what it does and does not address through its training.

The outcomes profile is a verbal picture. It uses action verbs to describe, in succinct phrases, the character and/or attitudes to be developed through the training, as well as desired skills and/

Chapter Objectives:

This chapter is designed to help you:

- Understand the importance of an outcomes profile to integral ministry training and its design.
- Conduct a process that leads to creating a training outcomes profile.
- Be able to use the profile in the design and evaluation of training programs.

or competencies. Knowledge is essential to the development of these, but as we have pointed out, it is not an end in itself. However, being "knowledgeable" in an area of specialization is often deemed to be important to vocational effectiveness. For example, both biblical and theological knowledge are generally thought to be essential for those who are pursuing a vocation in Christian service. This knowledge provides the theoretical framework for ministry.

More important than biblical and theological knowledge itself is the fruit of that knowledge, expressed tangibly both in who that person is and how he goes about life and ministry. So an outcomes profile may list "Bible Knowledge" and "Theological Knowledge" as *areas* requiring attention, but will go on to describe them in terms of *competencies*, such as, "Accurately exegetes Scripture," or an attitude, such as, "Is devoted to the study of Scripture," rather than "Can list the books of the Bible."

Planning the Profiling Exercise

The purpose of this section is to enable you to develop an outcomes profile in your own institutional training context. This will require some planning and an outline of the procedures to use. First, you will need to answer some basic questions:

1. How long will the profiling process take?

Experience has demonstrated that a thorough discussion of underlying assumptions along with a well-organized profiling workshop will take two to three days if it is conducted with a relatively small, homogeneous group (eight to twelve people[1]). The more time allowed for reflection and dialogue, the more complete and satisfying a profile can be developed. When the workshop is spread over at least three days, greater depth will be achieved, and participants generally will become more committed to what is produced. In some cases, initial profiling can be done with a larger group the first day, and a smaller, more committed group can carry the process to completion—refining underlying assumptions, finishing the profile, and beginning to develop the curricular plan. A retreat environment will generally be the most focused and productive.

2. Who should be involved?

Profiling depends on information given by expert practitioners. In the case of missionary training, experienced and effective missionaries should be the most important source of information regarding the qualities and skills missionaries should possess. But our other stakeholders need to be involved as well. This includes leaders of mission agencies, pastors of sending churches, the missionary candidates themselves, and possibly leaders from receiving national churches. It also includes those who will be responsible to design and implement the training programs.

> Without the commitment created from a consensus approach, even a great training program will struggle for lack of support.

Wise, respected, and representative members of each of these groups should be invited to participate in the profiling workshop. This group will identify the knowledge (or understanding), skills, and character qualities a training program should seek to develop. This consensus approach is critical in creating widespread commitment to implementation of or change in a training program. Without this commitment, even a great training program will struggle for lack of support.

---

1   If more people are involved and they are from a wide range of constituencies, the process will take more time. Limit participants to those who are most influential and representative, and those who are involved in designing and implementing the program and/or any changes.

3. What size group should be involved?

Ideally, a missionary profile should be developed by a small group (eight to twelve participants) of representative stakeholders. A small group allows for good interaction. If the group is too small, it may not be representative enough and thus miss valuable perspectives and subsequent buy-in. If it is much larger, the size will complicate the management of the process.

Some profiling workshops conducted in Latin America and Asia have been performed with as many as 70 international representatives from many different denominations, mission agencies, and training programs. These workshops divided the large group into smaller working groups for the most interactive phases. Small group coordinators were selected and oriented before the workshops. They were given assignments to work on in their own small groups, and then report back to the group of coordinators, thus bringing cohesion to the process. While these initial workshops were important in creating understanding of outcomes-based training, as a rule, it is not recommended that the profiling process be conducted with a large group, and when necessary, only by an experienced facilitator.

4. Who should conduct the process?

A *facilitator* leads the profiling workshop. The facilitator is not necessarily an expert on missionary training, but must understand the profiling process and assure that it results in a completed outcomes profile. He or she must manage the time and agenda, and solicit participation from all. A facilitator must not be domineering. Ideally, this person is not a principle stakeholder, and thus is freed from any need, personal or official, to influence the outcome of the process. Younger persons may perform best for a number of reasons. They quickly capture the concept of engaging group members in the process, they are less likely to be authoritarian, and they usually exhibit the mental agility needed to keep the group focused on an assigned task.

A *secretary* assists the facilitator. This person's main function is writing comments and thoughts, generated as part of the process, on poster paper or other appropriate media. It is important to have the skill to listen carefully and fairly record the comments generated. The secretary will also be available to assist the facilitator in other duties related to conducting the workshop process.

5. Where should a profiling workshop be held?

The usual location for a profiling workshop is a classroom or conference facility. The room should have one or more blank walls where cards listing ministry qualifications can be posted. Seating should be arranged in a circle or semi-circle. Good lighting, ventilation, and acoustics also are important.

6. What is needed to conduct the sessions?

There are several simple items that are necessary to conduct the profiling workshop. These include:

- 150-200 cards or pieces of paper (cardstock, or half of a standard sheet of paper works well).

- Some way to affix these on the wall or bulletin board (non-greasy sticky putty can be used; tape can be used if it will not damage the wall paint, push pins or tacks).

- Narrow-tipped marking pens.

A *"group memory"* consists of large sheets of paper on which important opinions, salient points, and consensual agreements are recorded during a group discussion. These are then posted on a wall or around the room as the meetings progress. Reference can be made to previous discussions when need be. This keeps the meeting moving along and prevents, to some extent, visiting and revisiting the same issues.

- An easel with blank paper to help generate a "group memory." Definitions and other important group products can be put on a wall for ready reference. (A chalkboard, overhead or video projector can also be useful.)

Conducting the Profiling Workshop

In order to help you conduct the profiling workshop, we have listed each phase of the exercise, step by step. First-time profiling facilitators will want to rehearse these steps and assure their own understanding of the process. It will give you a feel for timing and other factors critical to the success of the exercise. You don't want to disappoint participants by transmitting confusion and lack of personal understanding of the steps in developing a ministry or missionary profile.

The facilitator will lead the workshop group through five steps:

Phase 1 – Identify the ministry to be carried out in a *job description or definition*, and specify what kind of person *(minister)* is needed to carry out the work.

Phase 2 – From the above *description*, extrapolate the *general areas* that the training will need to address in order for the worker to perform effectively. These can be relational, developmental, skill sets, or bodies of knowledge.

Phase 3 – For each of the general areas identified, specify competencies, attitudes and comprehension needed, using phrases with action verbs.

Phase 4 – Arrange the work into a *profile chart* by ranking or ordering them.

Phase 5 – Review and endorse the *profile chart* with the whole group.

When your workshop group is small, each of the above phases will be carried out with the whole group. If the workshop is large (more than 12 people) and/or the time is short, the large group should be divided into smaller groups for some of the phases.[2]

Profiling Exercise Orientation

Facilitator: Create a sense of anticipation about the profiling process. It is important for participants to know why they are involved in the workshop and what outcome is expected. Schedules and other administrative matters should be explained. Questions regarding the process should be answered before the brainstorming sessions begin.

---

2   In a large group the work may be divided as follows:

Pre-session – Anticipate the number of small groups that will be needed. Recruit and train one coordinator for each small group. The coordinators will also function within the group in Phases 2, 4, and 5.

Orientation– Facilitator leads large group; coordinators lead introductions in small groups.

Phase 1 – Facilitator leads coordinator group and presents recommendation to the large group to be adjusted, as needed, and approved.

Phase 2– Facilitator leads large group.

Phase 3– Coordinators lead small groups. Coordinator group collates lists generated by the small groups. Facilitator presents the collated list to the large group to be adjusted, as needed, and approved.

Phase 4– Facilitator leads coordinator group.

Phase 5 - Facilitator leads large group.

Introduce participants: Workshop participants should be helped to view one another as colleagues, working toward a common goal. When participants do not know each other, they should be given opportunity to introduce themselves. It may be valuable to conduct an "ice breaker," an activity that helps the group to relax and to begin to participate. There are many ways to do this.

Group Work: Ask each person to share a "nick-name" they have (or have had) and how they received it. These (or first names) should be written on cards that are visible to the group so others can use these names in ensuing discussions. During these introductions the facilitator should highlight the potential contribution of each individual, to encourage all to participate. When a workshop is large, introductions and the icebreaker should be conducted in the small groups. Once the group is oriented and comfortable with each other, begin the profiling process.

Facilitator: Before beginning with the next phase, review all the phases of the profiling exercise with the participants and what you can expect from each one.

Phase 1 - Describe the Occupational Role and Ministry

The world of Christian service is complex. There are some common areas of character and competence that cut across all ministries. Some profiling exercises attempt to describe only these broad, general areas of competence. But training for effectiveness in ministry must go well beyond these common elements to work on competencies needed for specific ministries.

To begin the profiling exercise, we first want to generate a discussion that will lead to consensus on the description of the ministry with a focus on occupational roles, expectations, and relationships. These roles and expectations are often influenced by variables such as potential length of service, cultural distance (in the case of missionary work), and means of support. The purpose of this discussion is to set the parameters for the profiling exercise. Because many ministries require people who carry out very different roles, the group will have to agree on which one of potentially several different roles they will want to profile.

Group Work: Generate a discussion using the following questions:

1. What is the work that needs to be done? How does it resemble other kinds of ministries? In what ways is it specialized? What kinds of primary relationships are involved with supervisors and constituents? What kinds of roles will be needed to accomplish this work?

2. How is each of these roles supported (volunteer, paid staff, self-supported)? Do they need special areas of competence to meet the support model?

3. How long are these persons expected to stay in this ministry?

4. Does the ministry require inter-cultural or cross-cultural interaction? How much and what will this require of each kind of worker?

When there are significantly different occupational roles that emerge from this discussion, you will want to create separate profiles for each one. When the discussion has matured sufficiently, a descriptive definition should be written on the board or on a sheet of poster paper in light of a distinct occupational role associated with the work (i.e. cross-cultural field worker, home support staff, administrative leader, etc.).

Profiling Exercise Orientation Checklist

☐ Set expectations:

- Establish "desired outcomes" of a ministry training program.

- Build backwards to determine the *resources, methods and context* needed to reach the training goal.

- Create a verbal picture of the character, skills and understanding needed.

- Work together as colleagues toward a common goal.

☐ Let participants know why are they involved.

☐ Ice Breaker (e.g., share a "nick-name").

Phase 1 Checklist

☐ Create a clear title for the type of missionary to be profiled. Consider:

  • Cultural distance

  • Occupational role

  • Financial support

  • Term of service

☐ Create a detailed definition of the type of missionary, who they are and what they do. This could include:

  • How they come to the mission field.

  • Detail on where they are sent.

  • How they will share the gospel.

  • Expected or desired outcomes.

  • What they will teach or model.

  • What new believers will do or go on to do.

  • Etc.

Specifying the job to be done and the type of missionary to be profiled sets the limits of the profiling exercise. If these things are made clear, consensus usually develops rather quickly, even in a large group. Profiles can be quite general or very specific. If several types of missionaries are needed, individual profiles should be developed for each one. To avoid duplication of effort, a core set of characteristics may be identified which are common to all types of missionaries. Then build upon this core set to create specific profiles for each of the occupational roles (church planter, home administration, literature work, etc.).

Phase 2 - Identify the General Areas of Qualifications

The task before the group at this point is to list the major areas of qualification needed for effective missionary service. The process entails using deductive reasoning to extract the general areas from the description of the ministry role to be profiled. For example, in Figure 7.1, we can deduce that since the person is involved in cross-cultural church planting, they should gain some competence in learning another language, and in understanding what culture is and how it affects the missionary enterprise (along with other suggestions from the group). The group might then conclude that two of the general areas for training would be *Language Acquisition* and *Culture Learning*. Since the missionary is involved in church planting, after due deliberation, the group might conclude that trainees should have some developed competence in church planting in a same or near culture context. Hence, another general area might be defined that is titled *Church Planting*.

> **Description of a Cross-Cultural Church Planting Missionary**
> (Denominationally supported, career workers)
>
> Cross-cultural church planting missionaries are messengers sent by their respective churches to places where there is little or no Christian witness. They live an exemplary life as witnesses for Christ, and communicate the gospel in ways their new neighbors can understand its personal implications. Their aim is to see families become followers of Jesus Christ. They do this through proclamation, leading to repentance and baptism. They teach believers to obey all of Christ's commandments. The final goal of their missionary activity is a multiplying body of obedient Christian disciples who are able to carry on the work of evangelism and discipleship among their own people and who are eager and able to reach other peoples also.

Figure 7:1. Example of a "Job Description"

The most efficient way to create this list is to facilitate a "green light" or "brain-storming" session. Suggestions are taken from the group and the secretary writes them on cards, a chalkboard, or an overhead transparency. The assistant should list areas proposed by the group, while the facilitator works to elicit additional responses. As each area of the definition is discussed, the facilitator should seek to accurately synthesize the discussion and have the secretary list these for all to see.

The facilitator should continually refer back to the description until all the potential areas are extracted. Once these are listed, the group should clean up the list by condensing or amplifying areas as needed. The number of general areas should not normally exceed fifteen. Too many areas make the curricular development process unwieldy. With a little work, the group will find ways of creating a workable list.

Phase 2 Checklist

☐ Brainstorm onto cards, chalkboard or overhead transparency.

   • Refer back to the description until all areas are extracted.

   • "Clean-up" list by condensing or amplifying.

   • Do not exceed 15 general areas.

☐ Review list with whole group to assure all are satisfied.

   • Elicit statements from each participant.

   • Build consensus.

Sample List of Missionary Areas

- Language acquisition
- Culture learning
- Church planting
- Home church relationships
- Pure and simple lifestyle
- Good family relationships
- Evangelism
- Cross-cultural communication
- Spiritual disciplines
- Discipleship
- Leadership development

Figure 7:2. Sample List of General Areas Extracted from Job Description

When the list has been compiled, review this list with the whole group to assure that all are satisfied with it. The facilitator should elicit statements of support—or residual concerns—from each participant. Building consensus will require concessions on the part of all. It is important, however, to make sure that everyone stays with the process and that individuals don't withdraw because they feel their opinion is being ignored. At this stage, it is not too late to make adjustments that would help create fuller consensus.

Phase 3 - Identify Specific Ministry Character Qualities, Skills and Knowledge Competencies

This is the heart of the process. For each of the general areas, character qualities, skills, and personal competencies essential to that area must be identified and articulated in succinct statements. Ultimately, these will be arranged in a profile chart with the general areas in a vertical row on the left and the qualification statements extending in horizontal rows to the right from each area.[3] This phase involves four distinct steps:

1. *Choose a general area to work on.* There is no specific order in which the general areas need to be treated. An area that seems simple and straightforward may be best to start with. Each area may take more than an hour to discuss.[4]

2. *Conduct a "green light" session.* Encourage everyone in the group to think of specific character qualities,[5] skills or personal competencies that a person effectively carrying out the defined role needs to develop in the area selected. This is a similar exercise to that conducted for identifying the general areas, but now the focus is on specific at-

---

3   Due to the difficulty in reading columns of tiny print, this format has been modified in most of the examples in this manual. See the end of the chapter for a picture of the complete chart.

4   In some cultural contexts, it may be more appropriate to open up the discussion to all the identified areas. As each quality and competency is discussed, list it in the appropriate area.

5   Character qualities are difficult to measure. It may be more useful to specify character qualities in terms of attitudes as these reflect character and are more easily demonstrated and observed. For example, "steadfastness" may be a desirable character trait and be demonstrated in part by an attitude of "persistence." Or a "loving" character may be observed in acts of "kindness." Both persistence and kindness can be easily observed and also "taught" through admonition, demonstration, and modeling.

Phase 3 Checklist

☐ Choose a general area to work on.

☐ Brainstorm specific qualities or skills in the general area selected.

☐ Discuss and refine the list to 8-10 per area.

  • Express in measurable or observable behavior.

  • Use action verbs.

  • Character qualities are best observed by specific behaviors.

☐ Review list of character qualities and skill competencies.

  • Remove duplicates.

  • Reword to express a more specific concept.

  • Add character areas and skills that have been overlooked.

titudes and skills that will be required in that area. Figure 7:3 illustrates this process in the general area of "Language Acquisition."

General Area	Specific Qualities or Skills
Language acquisition	• Shows skill in techniques for learning words and phrases in another language. • Understands principles of phonetics helpful in learning his target language. • Eager to practice language learning at every opportunity.

Figure 7:3. Identifying Specific Qualities and Skills
Required for Each General Area

It is best to brain-storm and try to cover the entire area first, rather than discuss each character quality or skill competency as it is suggested. Avoid listing courses or using verbs that indicate knowledge components. These will eventually be covered and be listed as learning objectives when courses and lesson plans are created. Encourage participation by all until no more suggestions are forthcoming. It is not unusual for this original list to have twenty or twenty-five suggestions for a single general area.

3. *Discuss the character qualities and skills listed.* Once a fairly comprehensive list of items has been compiled, begin discussing these to ascertain their appropriateness to the area. Some items may be compressed into one.

Each item should be expressed in succinct statements of measurable or observable behavior. This will require the use of a verb, preferably an action verb. To the extent possible, items need to be observable and/or measurable; without a verb, this is impossible. As you examine each item, you will want to ask: Is this observable? If so, how? Asking these questions will help the group sharpen each item in such a way that it will be useful in the eventual design of a curriculum that recognizes or develops the quality or skill. Figure 7:4 illustrates this principle.

> This rewording moves the qualification from a passive skill to an activity that demonstrates the skill.

> Under the area "Home Church Relationships" a qualification may be identified:
>
> *Knows how to inform the church about the missionary task.*
>
> This competency might be stated more strongly as:
>
> *Successfully informs the church about mission efforts.*
>
> This rewording moves the qualification from a passive skill to an activity that demonstrates the skill.

Figure 7:4. Expressing Competencies in Terms of
Measurable and/or Observable Behaviors

It is important to note that most character qualities will be difficult to articulate in directly observable terms, but that attitudes and specific behaviors can indicate a presence of these character qualities and may be more easily identified. ("By their fruit you will recognize them..." Matthew 7:20.) The item, "Christ-like in character," is difficult to observe, but behaviors reflecting Christ-likeness, such as, "Considerate of others," or, "Serves others readily," are more specific and observable. A skillful facilitator or coordinator will help the group come up with the right verb and phrasing for each item.

The product of this phase should be a list of succinct statements under each general qualification area that expresses in terms of observable characteristics the qualities or skills that are required for effective missionary service. Each area may have up to eight or ten of these succinct statements. If there are many more, however, it is likely the area is too broad and, under analysis, a natural division will be apparent.

Whenever possible, state qualifications in terms of demonstrable skills or attitudes rather than more passive "knowledge" statements.

4. *Review lists of character qualities and skill competencies.* Once the specific character qualities and skills for all the areas have been identified and listed, they should be reviewed together to assure appropriate completeness. A quality or competency might be removed from an area if duplication occurs, or it may be reworded to express a more specific concept. Likewise, qualities or competencies that have been overlooked may come to light.

Phase 4 - Create the Profile Chart

Once the qualities and competencies for each area are identified, attempt to order or prioritize them. Skill competencies should be arranged in sequential order of development. Likewise, character qualities may be ordered by complexity of the concept or difficulty in achievement. It is helpful to think of a teaching/learning sequence. This exercise is only intended to make it easier to review and elaborate on the profile chart, as it creates a logical order.

General Area:	
Minimal Qualification for Entrance into Field Ministry	
Pre-Field Training Outcomes ↓	On-field Training Outcomes
1.	4.
2.	5.
3.	6.
	7.

Figure 7:5. Competency Continuum

Phase 4 Checklist

☐ Use diagram of Figure 7:5 to arrange skill competencies and character qualities in sequential order of development or order of priority.

☐ Create profile chart.

• General areas are placed vertically along the left hand side of the workspace.

• Qualifications are placed to the right of area name.

• Measurable/observable behaviors are placed to the right of qualifications.

To assist in this process, draw a horizontal line with a vertical mark near its mid-point, as in Figure 7:5. Let the vertical mark represent minimal qualification for entrance into field ministry. The line extending to the left will represent goals for pre-field ministry training, while the line to the right will represent goals for in-ministry professional development. This simple tool will help place the defined qualification in an appropriate training sequence. For example, under the general area of *Language Acquisition*, if the competency of "Shows skills in techniques for learning words and phrases" is a pre-field requirement (Fig 7:3), then additional characteristics such as, "Speaks the target language fluently," or, "Reads and understands local newspapers," would be placed to the right of the vertical line in the "On-field" side of the continuum. The continuum is useful for setting standards for learning as well as knowing the order of desired outcomes and where to place them in a comprehensive, progressive training plan.

Next, order character qualities in ascending order of priority, and skill competencies in ascending order of complexity. Thus, the most basic quality or competence for each area will appear first, at the left end of the line, with the highest or most developed evidence of each area indicated on the right end.

Now create the profile chart. Place the general areas vertically along the left hand side of the wall or workspace. Array the prioritized list of qualifications for each area immediately to the right of the area name.

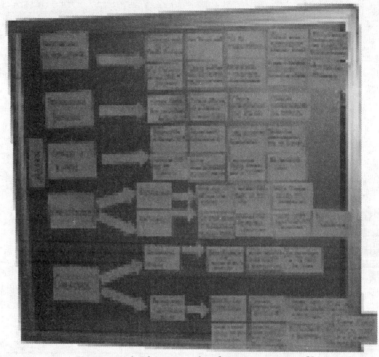

Figure 7:6. Photograph of Outcomes Profile

Phase 5 Checklist

- ☐ Ask for modifications.
- ☐ All participants should verbally or symbolically endorse the profile chart.
- ☐ Give all participants a finished copy of the profile to share with their constituencies.
- ☐ Discuss who is responsible to train for specific areas in the outcomes profile.

Phase 5 - Review and Endorse the Profile Chart

The participants should review the completed profile chart. Any modifications called for should be made to the satisfaction of the group as a whole. Again, it is useful to call for verbal or symbolic (e.g., standing, signing) endorsement of the profile chart by each participant.

Once the profile chart is endorsed, the profiling exercise is over. All participants should receive a finished copy of the ministry profile to share with their constituencies. In most cases, however, you will want to engage the group in a discussion of who is responsible for the training for specific areas in the outcomes profile.

Use of the Ministry Profile

An outcomes-based profile may have several applications. It may be employed in the internal evaluation of existing ministry training programs. By comparing current outcomes with those listed in the profile, programs can determine whether they are on track with their goals and where to make appropriate adjustments.

An outcomes-based profile also may be used by candidates, pastors, mission administrators, and trainers to evaluate a candidate's readiness for ministry work at each stage of his/her development. Each item can be rated by those involved in the evaluation, and expectations clarified in terms of standards to be achieved.

When developing individualized curricula, participants should set a target level of function, or standard of achievement, for each qualification. Some standards regarding emotional, spiritual, or other personal traits may need to be based on the subjective evaluation of trainers or mentors who observe and monitor the candidate's life and ministry over a period of time. Individualized training can then be implemented to address specific strengths and weaknesses.

Finally, a ministry profile may become the basis for developing new ministry training programs. This is the primary use envisioned in this manual. New ministry training programs can be organized and implemented to develop the outcomes identified by the profile chart. Translating qualities and competencies into curricula involves developing appropriate learning objectives and teaching-learning strategies.

Conclusion

Those who have worked together to develop ministry training profiles consistently affirm that the task of creating an outcomes profile is much more complex than it appears at first sight! The formal classroom experience, which traditionally has been emphasized, seems but a small part of the equipping process. For a minister to function successfully, much depends on critical character qualities, attitudes, relational skills, and ability for ministry.

The outcomes profile affords a means for understanding the scope of this training task. It also provides a ministry-based beginning point for curriculum development and for allocating training responsibilities. Understanding our task gives us greater confidence that we can hit the training target.

Figure 7:7 Photograph of Outcomes Profile in Nigeria

Chapter 7: Exercises
Creating a Ministry Profile

1. Use the suggested process to create an outcomes profile of a ministry. Limit this to a project that you can manage in a few hours with a group who are taking this course with you, or are a part of that ministry. Smaller projects might include creating the profile of a short-term missionary, a Sunday school teacher, or a small group leader. To the extent possible, select your group using the criteria suggested in the previous chapter and expect the profile to be useful to evaluate existing training or to design new training.

2. With a group of your fellow students or ministry colleagues, validate the profile of a Cross-Cultural Church Planter that follows. Do this by examining each of the characteristics described in each area and ranking each one from 1-5 with 1 being the lowest value and 5 being the highest. Any significant discrepancies among those ranking the items should be discussed and clarified. Look for characteristics that may be missing as well and add them to the list.

Training Profile of a Cross-Cultural Church Planter

General Outcome Areas:	Intended Outcomes					
Spiritual Maturity	Knows & loves God & exhibits fruit of Spirit	Spontaneously worships God; growing in personal & corporate worship	Responsive to God's guidance; exhibits endurance	Recognizes God's lordship & leadership; evidences obedience submission	Committed to World evangelization; has a clear vocational calling	Growing exercise of spiritual gifts and spiritual disciplines, especially the Word & prayer
Family Wholeness	Both spouses practice mutual submission & loving service	Freely expresses feelings & empathizes w/ others	Nurtures & trains children lovingly	Protects planned time & recreation for family	Encourages each family member in spirit & ministry growth	Relates to the larger mission family/ community
Servanthood	Accepts God's love & forgiveness; growing in grace	Submits to Christ's Lordship in trust & obedience	Puts others above self; actively serves to meet needs of others	Serves others w/ diligence, faithfulness & joy	Gravitates to the needy	Models the example of Christ
Adaptability	Recognizes God's sovereignty	Accepts w/ gladness difficult circumstances	Adapts flexibly to new situations & is resilient	Appreciates various personalities & styles of leadership	Evidences contentment in various settings	Distinguishes between judging what is "wrong" or "different"
Cultural Sensitivity	Appreciates & values aspects of the host culture	Sensitive to host culture's expectations & mores	Sensitive to host culture's models of learning & leading	Recognizes the importance of language learning as ministry	Takes responsibility for life-long language learning	Appreciates appropriate technologies
Commitment to the Church	Active in a local congregation	Reflects Christ's love for the Church	Partners w/ & serves the national church	Stewards relationships & activities for maximum long-term impact on planting a reproducing church	Values the heritage of a people & church, & learns from their past	
Language Acquisition	Recognizes the importance of language learning	Listens actively & discerns language sounds & patterns	Develops "bonding" relationships, disciplines self to regular practice	Takes responsibility for life-long language learning	Accepts small failures & learns to laugh at mistakes	Uses language in living, learning & ministry
Cultural Adaptation & Contextualization	Appreciates & values aspects of the host culture;	Copes w/ cultural differences; lives incarnationally	Exegetes cities, cultures & communities	Conversant with needs & concerns of target group	Collects relevant data; analyzes & interprets findings accurately	Adapts own behavior & "contextualizes" appropriately

Evangelism & Discipleship	Shares Christ in culturally appropriate ways	Leads people to Christ; actively involved in local church	Disciples new believers in Word, prayer, witness & fellowship	Equips believers to reproduce & have a heart for lost in local communities	Motivates others to use their spiritual gifts; engages in spiritual warfare	Models active participation in a local church
Church Planting & Development	Prays strategically	Analyzes the social environment	Builds relationships; can grow cell groups of new believers	Develops an effective evangelistic strategy	Trains small group leaders to train others	Establishes a reproducing congregation; empowers & releases members
Leadership Development	Identifies, nurtures & equips potential leaders	Helps believers interpret & apply the Word in their context	Equips believers in appropriate Bible study methods	Empowers & entrusts others for responsibility	Plans & equips for transitions in partnership w/ national leaders	Plants churches that contextualize biblical leadership styles
(Leadership Development continued)	Envisions new ministries; enlists others in vision	Uses historical insights to teach churches	Motivates, recognizes & celebrates others' contributions	Matches appropriate biblical leadership style w/ situation	Functions as team player & servant-leader	Ministers in Word, deed & power of the triune God

Chapter 8

Writing Learning Objectives

Stephen Hoke

Rev. Owandere had been a missionary for twelve years in West Africa, and he was thrilled with the invitation to help train the next generation of missionaries going out from his country. But as he sat in the shade planning his "Introduction to Missions" course, he grew increasingly anxious. He had so much he wanted to say, and so little time. He had experienced so much, and he wondered how best to put his experiences into communicable form. He wanted to share his heart with these young candidates, but he couldn't see a way to organize all he had learned and experienced into a coherent *course plan*.

Half the globe away in Manila, Rosa Macagba grappled with the same frustration in planning a lesson at the newly established missionary training center. After two terms among an unreached people group in Southeast Asia, she was asked by her mission to become a lecturer and mentor for missionary interns. She could clearly visualize the ideal missionary needed, and she had stacks of notes and ideas she wanted to mold into courses and presentations. But how to shape her first *lesson*? How could she be sure that what she wanted to say would actually be helpful in moving the candidates toward the established goals? How should she focus her thoughts into a process that would be educationally effective?

These two trainers are facing a typical problem—how to transform their commitments and goals into a training plan, into curriculum. In this chapter we will outline a step-by-step process for trainers to translate their ideas into learning objectives. Chapter 9 will help you turn these objectives into meaningful learning experiences. Whether you are working at the macro-level in planning *courses* or at the micro-level in planning particular *lessons* within a longer course, the principles you apply in the process are the same.

Defining Learning Objectives and Their Role in Ministry Training

Defining Curriculum

To begin, it may be helpful to clarify how we use the word curriculum. The word literally means a pre-determined path along which a race is run, a "racecourse." Traditionally, the curriculum was considered the *content* that a student was expected to master before moving on. More recently, the term connotes the *activity of the student* as she moves through a variety of experiences which involve content, skills, and character issues.[1] We are using an even broader definition which reflects our assumptions and values.

Various definitions and approaches to curriculum development have been suggested which reflect distinctive value orientations and commitments in the field. Consider the following:

1. Curriculum is the content that is made available to the students.

2. Curriculum is the planned and guided learning experiences of students.

3. Curriculum is the actual experiences of a student or participant.

4. Generally, curriculum includes both the materials and the experiences for learning. Specifically, curriculum is the written courses for study used for Christian education.

5. Curriculum is the organization of learning activities guided by a teacher with the intent of changing behavior.

6. Curriculum is the interface between intentions and operations—between the why and the what/how of an educational activity .

7. Curriculum is the entire set of processes used to identify learner needs and cooperate with the learner in meeting those needs.[2]

We will use the word "curriculum" in its broadest sense, that is, the entire learning environment in which intentional learning takes place. Any time we decide what others should do in order to enable them to become or to do something else, we are planning curriculum. Here are some examples of curriculum:

*   A missionary and his twenty-two year-old disciple are having lunch together. They talk about work, family, and pressures of the day. They read the Bible and pray. The missionary embraces the young man before he has to hurry off to catch the bus back to work.

*   Later, the missionary's wife reads a bed-time Bible story to two preschool children. They talk about Jesus stilling the storm. The mother listens to the children's fears about bad dreams and talks about Jesus' care all through the night.

These are planned activities that seek to bring both the new convert and the missionaries' children a step nearer to maturity in Christ. Curriculum includes the setting or context

> Any time we decide what others should do in order to enable them to become or to do something else, we are planning curriculum.

---

1   Lois E. LeBar and James E. Plueddemann, *Education That Is Christian*, (Wheaton, IL: Victor Books, 1989), p. 254.

2   Definitions 1-5 are from Robert W. Pasmino, "Curriculum Foundations," *Christian Education Journal*, Vol. 8 no. 1 (Autumn, 1987), p. 31; Definition 6 is from Ted Ward, Unpublished notes, College of Education Doctoral Seminary (East Lansing, MI: Michigan State University, 1979), p. 1; Definition 7 is from Rodney McKean, Unpublished notes, College of Education Doctoral Seminar, (East Lansing MI: Michigan State University, 1977), p. 1.

in which the learning takes place—whether inside or outside, whether at home or the workplace; the content that is made available to students; and the actual learning experiences guided by a trainer, mentor, or helper.

Shared Responsibility

This definition of curriculum implies that the trainer and the trainee share responsibility for the learning process. The trainer assumes responsibility for planning and implementing content and experiences, while the trainee assumes responsibility for actively and intentionally participating in the learning process.[3]

Another helpful way to understand curriculum is as "the educational planning that leads to the actual teaching experience."[4] Essentially, a curriculum is an educational plan. It is a road map for how to get where you want to go and what you will do to get there. Plueddemann suggests that the curriculum plan includes three major components: the assumed teaching-learning context, the intended outcomes in the life of the student (what we are calling the "profile"), and the intended educational activities. To determine the effectiveness of ministry training, therefore, it is not enough only to evaluate learning outcomes; we also must evaluate the educational activities, including the appropriateness of intended outcomes and learning activities in the teaching-learning context. (See Chapter 10 for a procedure which applies this insight.)

> The trainer and the trainee share responsibility for the learning process.

Training as Science and Art

Training is a science, an art, and a gift. As a science, effective training is based on principles that emerge from research that can be learned by study and enhanced by skillful implementation. Educators tend to talk about this aspect of training quite a lot, because the "science" of training can be taught.

As an art, training calls for relational sensitivity, intuition, flexibility in uncertainty, and timing. These artistic people-skills are largely natural talents but can be developed by training and practice. Donald Schon[5] suggests that the skill of an effective teacher-artist depends on putting what one knows into action in day-to-day practice. The art is finely tuned by consciously thinking about (reflecting on) what one is doing, often while doing it. "Stimulated by surprise, [effective teachers] turn thought back on action and on the learning which is implicit in action." As a teacher-trainer tries to make sense of what is happening in the midst of the teaching-learning process, he or she "also reflects on the understandings which have been implicit in his action, understandings which he surfaces, criticizes, restructures, and includes in further action." Schon concludes: "It is this entire process of reflection-in-action which is central to the `art' by which practitioners sometimes deal well with situations of uncertainty, instability, uniqueness, and value conflict."

In addition, the Apostle Paul names teaching as one of the equipping spiritual gifts (Eph 4:11-12; Rom 12:7; 1 Cor 12:28). Teaching involves a special spiritual empowerment or enabling by the Holy Spirit to equip or train Christians toward maturity in Jesus Christ or effectiveness in ministry. Science can be taught, art can be developed, but a gift only can be exercised.

---

3   LeBar and Plueddemann, 1989, p. 280.

4   James Plueddemann, "Curriculum Improvement Through Evaluation," *Christian Education Journal*, Vol. 8 No. 1 (Autumn, 1987), pp. 56-57.

5   Donald A. Schon, *The Reflective Practioner*, (New York: Basic Books, Inc, 1983).

The Flow of Curriculum Planning

A cascading waterfall provides a useful image to visualize the process of curriculum planning (see Figure 8:1). Although not all educational plans proceed so neatly in such a linear fashion, the analogy is helpful in illustrating the relationship of the component elements in the process.

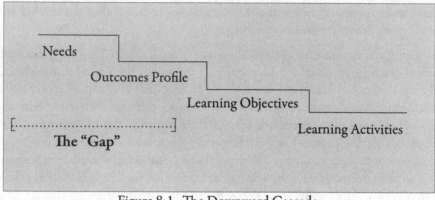

Figure 8:1. The Downward Cascade

- Learning **objectives** flow from the "gap" between where a trainee is and the outcomes profile.

- Learning **activities** are strategies for accomplishing the instructional objectives.

Since learning starts where the trainee is, then course and lesson planning must begin with the needs of the trainees. What do they already know? What skills have they developed? What skills and character traits do they possess? This is the starting or entry point of the learning process. Determining *entry level* characteristics in understanding (knowledge), skills, and character is one way to control the level at which courses will be taught. This can be done by setting entry qualifications or requirements, by measuring incoming trainees and adapting training to their needs, or by a combination of both. When entry qualifications are set, incoming students that meet all requirements should be able to move into training without difficulty. Students who do not meet entry requirements, however, may require special tutoring to acquire basic understandings and skills, as well as individualized mentoring to address character deficiencies. Brian Massey (see Figure 8:2) suggests another creative way to measure incoming trainees vis-à-vis the training goal.

The next stage in the progressive planning flow is to compare the trainees' entry level characteristics with the outcomes profile (see Chapter 7). When you measure the trainees against the outcomes profile, you identify a "gap" between where they are now and where they need to be upon completion of training.

Stating clear learning objectives in terms of the "gap" is the third stage. Learning objectives are tools which break the larger, more comprehensive learning goals into smaller, more attainable steps. Learning objectives flow from the profile and point the way in which the trainee will grow.

Finally, appropriate learning activities are designed to "close the gap." Learning activities help bridge the gap between the trainee's present status and the desired goal. They are *strategies for accomplishing* the instructional objectives. Learning activities should flow naturally from the needs, outcomes, and learning objectives you have identified. They answer the question, *"What kinds of experiences do we need to provide to help trainees become who they need to be and to do what they need to be able to do?"*

The Australia/New Zealand Experiment

A working group of nine missionary trainers representing eight organizations met in Australia and New Zealand in mid-1994 to develop an inter-mission Pre-Departure Orientation (PDO) program. Their profiling exercise led them to an issue not addressed in the Pasadena seminar – how to adequately assess the participant on entry to an existing training course. They recognized that the "gap" between the entry point and exit point defines what needs to be taught, but how the entry and end points are determined needed to be designed.

They borrowed the idea of a "Competency Continuum" from the training department of a leading manufacturer. This continuum had been designed to provide attainment levels within each competency for workers. Examples of low, mid, and high levels are given on a continuum, and each person is able to assess his or her current level and plot it appropriately. PDO participants arrive having plotted on each of the continuum lines their assessment of their level of competency. This exercise builds a profile of each participant on entry to the program. The participant, together with the course coordinator, uses this self-assessment to develop a set of learning objectives for the course. These are recorded on a learning contract. When the course is complete, the personal learning objectives are reviewed, and competencies are replotted along the continuum, again by self-assessment. The result is a profile of the participant on exit. The following three examples illustrate the PDO competency assessment levels:

Adaptation:	Low	Mid	High
Identification:	Low	Mid	High
Communication:	Low	Mid	High

Several guidelines should be noted. First, the competency continuum levels, especially at the high end, are not expected to be achieved solely as a result of the course. Many will only be developed through cross-cultural living experience, and therefore the continuum will be of assistance to the missionary as a personal review aid.

Second, it is possible that participants may discover that their initial assessment of a competency level was too high, and therefore on exit they actually see themselves as less competent. But that is OK; that is what is needed – a realistic understanding of where they are now. The course will have given them growth skills to enable them to develop in that area, along with all the others.

Third, this concept is firmly based on the principles of both Adult Education and Competency–Based Education – the learner is the focus and is responsible for the learning. Hence the decision to allow the participants to set their own learning objectives, rather than set them ourselves for the course curriculum elements.

Figure 8:2. Measuring Incoming Trainees Vis-a-Vis the Training Goal
Source: Brian Massey, Personal letter to William D. Taylor, August 8, 1994.

The waterfall image also illustrates the natural flow from the general content of a course to the specific content of a particular lesson (see Figure 8:3). A *course* (sometimes called a *subject*) in "Missionary Life," for example, might include *units* on Bible study, Christian character, culture adaptation, and cross-cultural communication. These units, in turn, will be broken down into *lessons* on such topics as Developing Holy Habits, Living the Spirit-Filled Life, Coping with Culture Shock, and Following Jesus' Model of Communication. Notice how a particular *lesson* cascades naturally from one or several *units*, which flow out of the selected *course* content. The flow should be logical, natural, and interrelated, not forced or disconnected.

```
Course
        Unit
             Lesson
```

Figure 8:3. The Natural (Logical) Integration of Content

Balanced Learning

We are committed to balanced learning that includes knowledge (*understanding*), being (*character qualities*), and doing (*ministry skills*) (see Figure 8:4). Whenever we talk about writing objectives, our intention is objectives that promote learning in all three dimensions, although certain activities and experiences may focus on only one or two dimensions at a time.

> Objectives should promote learning in all three dimensions.

Figure 8:4. The Three Dimensions of Balanced Learning

The first dimension, *understanding*, often can be demonstrated by explaining or describing a truth. *Ministry skills* can usually be demonstrated by doing a particular activity, such as preaching, witnessing, building, or planning. It may be helpful to remember, however, that the third dimension, *being*, often is not best measured by behavior or action. Inner *character qualities* are more subtle, intangible, and therefore more difficult to quantify or measure. *Values* and *feelings* also are more difficult to demonstrate and measure. That doesn't mean we can't evaluate progress in the area of character formation, but it does mean that we must exercise care and discernment in writing objectives that are appropriate for that dimension of ministry growth.

A balanced view of learning prevents curriculum planners and trainers from placing too much emphasis on mere information and knowledge gained in an academic setting, apart from the being and doing dimensions. Growth and development biblically understood keep knowing and obedience inseparably linked. Truth is "known" only when it is obeyed.

The Place of Objectives in Teaching and Learning

Setting objectives is a necessary step in developing a ministry training curriculum. "If you aim at nothing, you will be sure to hit it" is a self-evident truth. Unfortunately, setting objectives is a step often omitted by trainers. As you look at the primary learning needs of your trainees, you should begin to develop specific objectives to meet those needs. Some needs or learning tasks may require more than one objective in order to have that need adequately met. In other cases, perhaps one objective will meet several needs.

Writing objectives can be understood as defining the specific learning steps to bridge the "gap" between what is and what is not yet. The statement of an objective answers the question, *What does the trainee need to be able to* **understand** *(know), to be (character qualifications), or to* **do** *(behavior or ministry skill)? How can the trainee demonstrate that he or she has achieved the learning goals?* Objectives describe a desired state in the trainee.

A meaningfully stated objective is one that succeeds in communicating the trainer's intent to the trainee. That implies that the trainee shares responsibility with the trainer for the learning process. It is not enough for the trainer to state clearly his or her purposes for a course or lesson, then proceed as if successful learning depends only on the skill of the trainer. The trainee must respond to the trainer's stated intent and must actively participate in the activities in order for an objective to be realized.

Before we proceed to specific instructions for writing objectives, a word of caution is in order. Some efforts at writing objectives may be unsatisfactory because the goals which are sought cannot be reduced to behavioral terms. It is dangerous to assume (as some educators teach) that only observable behaviors or qualities evidenced through behaviors are real. In Scripture we see a number of commands that are not stated in behavioral terms. For example, the Great Commandment in Matthew 22:37, "Love the Lord your God with all your heart and with all your soul and with all your mind," is not behavioral. While Jesus' words to his disciples, "If you love me, you will obey what I command" (Jn 14:15), seems to be behavioral, yet we know that commandment-keeping does not always indicate genuine love (note the Pharisees!).

Another mistake is to assume that stating a desirable outcome in behavioral terms makes it a helpful objective. Sometimes a "means-end" shift occurs that is totally counter-productive. Suppose a trainer, in a course on "The Missionary's Prayer Life," set a goal to enlarge the role of prayer in the life of her trainees. That certainly is a worthy goal. Yet notice what happens if we announce the behavioral objective, "By the fourth week of the course, the trainee will pray sixty minutes each day." Praying sixty minutes a day, which was intended to deepen communication with God, easily can shift to become an *end* in itself. The number of minutes trainees "pray" can become the goal! For those who believe God is more concerned with the heart than with outward behavior, this is a fatal shift.

- Objectives define specific learning steps.
- Objectives answer the questions of what the trainee needs to understand, be or do.
- Objectives communicate the trainer's intent to the trainee.

Caution: Observable behaviors (i.e., praying 60 minutes per day) do not constitute an objective.

Ted Ward suggests that instructional objectives are most helpful for the lower levels of cognitive learning (e.g., recognition, recall, and comprehension), but they are not as helpful, even useless, for the higher levels of thinking (e.g., evaluation, application, and synthesis).[6] You will discover that you cannot write specific objectives for every value, behavior, or character trait that you want people to develop.[7]

To the extent that writing learning objectives helps you identify the understanding, skill, or quality that you wish trainees to develop, use learning objectives to guide your lesson planning. Remember, though, that there are understandings that are difficult to quantify, skills which cannot be measured or observed easily, and character qualities that defy definition in behavioral form. When you encounter these issues, state "faith goals"[8] rather than behavioral objectives.

Finally, writing objectives is a dynamic and developmental activity. It requires changes, additions, and refinements as the trainer interacts with trainees—their uniqueness and growth—and with change in the training or ministry context. I often have regarded objectives I have written with great pride, only to realize two weeks into my course that my objectives were incomplete, that the verbs I selected no longer seem accurate, or that the students actually need to spend time on different qualities or skills than I had anticipated. This situation forces me to rewrite some objectives and to draft entirely new ones I had missed.

Writing Objectives That Communicate

The most helpful teaching-learning objectives adhere to specific standards:[9]

✓ There is no doubt on the part of the trainee about what is required.

✓ Action is the trainee's, not the trainer's or anyone else's.

✓ Performance is unambiguous. After an attempt is made, it is possible for the trainee or the trainer to tell clearly whether the objective has been achieved. (This is easiest when the performance can be measured in some meaningful way.)

✓ Clear, precise, action words are used (whenever possible and when appropriate).

There are three essential ingredients to writing clear objectives. The first is the *performance* or *behavior*—what you want the trainee to be able to do. The second is the *condition* under which the performance is to be obtained. The third is the *standard of performance*. Let's take these steps one at a time.

---

6   Ted Ward, Personal conversation with S. Hoke, July 18, 1994.

7   Jarrold E. Kemp (*Instructional Design: A Plan for Unit and Course Development*, (Belmont, CA: David S. Lake Publishers, 1977), pp. 34-38), highlights the difficulty in specifying objectives in the affective area—attitudes, values, and appreciations—in clearly observable and measurable terms. Realistically, there are many important training goals that cannot be reduced to measurable objectives. Elliot Eisner ("Instruction to the Teaching Ministry of the Church," Course syllabus, (San Clemente, CA: Chrysalis Ministries, 1969), pp. 13-18), a critic of behavioral objectives, suggests the term "expressive objectives" for those specific outcomes which cannot be stated readily in behavioral terms.

8   James E. Plueddemann, "Behavioral Objectives, No! Faith Goals, Yes!" *Intercom*, no. 144 (August-October, 1994), p. 8.

9   Tom W. Goad, *Delivering Effective Training*, (San Diego: University Associates, 1982), p. 65; cf. Warren S. Benson, "Setting and Achieving Objectives for Adult Learning," in *The Christian Educator's Handbook on Adult Education*, ed. K.O. Gangel and J.C. Wilhoit, (Wheaton, IL: Victor Books/SP Publications, 1993), pp. 192-175.

Step 1: Identifying Desired Behavior

First, *identify the final performance or behavior with a specific action word.* Unfortunately, there are many common verbs which are open to a wide range of interpretations, which mean different things to different people. Consider the following verbs in this light:[10]

Words Open to Many Interpretations	Words Open to Fewer Interpretations
To know	To write
To understand	To recite
To *really* understand	To Identify
To appreciate	To differentiate
To *fully* appreciate	To solve
To enjoy	To list
To believe	To compare
To have faith in	To contrast

Step 1:

- Identify performance or behavior (what you want the trainee to be able to do).
- Use specific action words that avoid requiring interpretation.
- State how you want the trainee to demonstrate the desired performance.

Why do the words on the left lead to discussions and debate regarding their meaning and application? It is because they require judgment, rather than simple observation. Whenever behavioral objectives are appropriate, it is helpful to ask, *Did I describe what the trainee will do (action word!) to show that he or she has acquired the knowledge, has mastered the skills, or evidences the character qualities which are needed?* Thus the statement that communicates best will be one that describes at least clearly enough to avoid misinterpretation – a *behavior* which indicates the intended learning.

Evaluate the following example objectives. Which is more helpful in determining whether a candidate actually values the importance of language acquisition?

> **Objectives Regarding Language Acquisition**
>
> A. To develop an understanding of the importance of language acquisition.
>
> B. When the trainee completes the training module, he/she must be able to state three reasons language acquisition is vital to effective missionary work.

Figure 8:5. Example Objectives

Note that the word "understanding" is open to many different meanings, is difficult to measure, and doesn't indicate exactly what you want the trainee to be able to do after a course in language acquisition. The second objective (B) is accomplished only when the trainee can explain *why* language acquisition is vital to missionaries. The ability to *explain* a concept to others not only requires that a person comprehend the main ideas, but also assumes the ability to state the reasons that language acquisition is important. Thus, "to state" is a more helpful verb because it identifies more precisely what you want the trainee to be able to do.

---

10   Robert F. Mager, *Preparing Instructional Objectives*, 2nd ed., (Belmont, CA: Pearon Publishers, 1975), p. 20.

There is no doubt about what is expected when objectives are complete and precise. The key is to use *action* words, denoting something that can be measured and/or observed. It is easy to see that "understanding" is extremely difficult to measure. The words "state," "show," and "solve," on the other hand, are precise and measurable.

Which of the following objectives has identified the *end result* most specifically?

Objectives Identifying the End Result

A. The trainee will learn the Bible verse presented in this lesson

B. The trainee will memorize the Bible verses presented in this lesson.

C. The trainee will love the Bible verses presented in this lesson.

Figure 8:6. Example Objectives

Step 2:

- Describe the conditions under which the behavior will be expected to occur.

- Ensure the conditions do not indicate outcomes which are unintended.

Note that the word "learn" is somewhat ambiguous—does it mean "memorize" (as in B)? or "state the meaning of"? or "obey"? "Loving" God's Word certainly is the highest goal, and it is not ambiguous, but it is manifested in many different ways, and recognizing love does demand judgment. The most specific objective, therefore, is "to memorize."

Try your hand at writing a few objectives. How would you want a candidate to demonstrate the following?

Character Quality	Possible Objective
Acceptance	
Endurance	
Forgiveness	
Joy	
Peace	

Step 2: Describing Conditions for Behavior

The second element of a learning objective is a statement of the conditions for behavior. After identifying the desired behavior, try to define that behavior further by *describing the important conditions* under which the behavior will be expected to occur. Be detailed enough to assure that the behavior will be recognized by another competent person and that it will not be mistaken as indicating understandings, skills, or character qualities other than those intended. Conditions may specify time, place, participants, or other aspects of the expected situation. Note how the condition is illustrated in Figure 8:5, Objective B, above:

Condition: When the trainee completes the training module...

Performance: ...state three reasons language learning is vital

Now evaluate the following objectives. Which is more helpful in describing the conditions under which the behavior will be expected to occur?

> **Objectives Regarding Interpersonal Conflict**
>
> A. The trainee will be able to resolve interpersonal conflicts on the mission field.
>
> B. Given a typical interpersonal conflict situation occurring on the mission field, the trainee will be able to describe at least two different but culturally appropriate ways to resolve the conflict.

Figure 8:7. Example Objectives

By providing a specific case in which the trainee is to resolve an interpersonal conflict, the second objective narrows the broad area of interpersonal conflict resolution to a manageable task.

> *Performance*:   ...the trainee will be able to describe at least two different but culturally appropriate ways to resolve the conflict.
>
> *Condition*:   Given a typical interpersonal conflict situation occurring on the mission field...

See if you can detect which of the following three objectives describes the important *conditions* most specifically:

> **Objectives Describing Conditions of Behavior**
>
> A. Given an encounter with a non-Christian Pokot woman in northwest Kenya, the trainee will pray powerfully.
>
> B. When anxious, the trainee will pray powerfully.
>
> C. When under direct spiritual attack, the trainee will pray powerfully.

Figure 8:8. Example Objectives

Step 3:

- Specify the standard of acceptable performance.
- Standards should be identifiable to the trainer and the trainee.

Step 3: Specifying the Standard

The third step in writing clear learning objectives is to specify the standard of acceptable performance. This is done by describing how well the trainee must perform to be acceptable. Examples of how standards may be stated include the following:

✓ an accuracy of 80%

✓ according to the plans provided

✓ [listing] at least five characteristics for each

✓ in a culturally appropriate way

✓ in keeping with biblical principles

Which of the following objectives is more helpful in describing the conditions under which the behavior will be expected to occur?

> **Objectives Regarding Language Acquisition**
>
> A. The trainee will speak Japanese fluently.
>
> B. After nine months of language study, the trainee will be able to converse at an intermediate level with a native Japanese speaker on topics of home and community life.

Figure 8:9. Example Objectives

This example helps us see that it sometimes is necessary to specify several conditions for demonstrating learning, but we also see the usefulness of clearly stated standards. Consider this analysis of Figure 8:9, Objective B:

Performance: the trainee will be able to converse

Conditions: After nine months of language study,...

                [converse] with a native Japanese speaker

                [converse] on topics of home and community life

Standard: [converse] at an intermediate level

Stating the standard in each learning objective you write is not absolutely necessary. Whenever it makes sense to do so, however, and whenever it helps you specify the kind of performance you want, try to indicate a meaningful standard.

See if you can detect which objective specifies the *standard* or *criterion* most clearly:

> **Objectives Specifying the Standard of Performance**
>
> A. Upon completion of this course, the trainee will effectively experience a deepened prayer life.
>
> B. Upon completion of this course, the trainee will experience a deepened prayer life, as assessed by the trainer.
>
> C. Upon completion of this course, the trainee will experience a deepened prayer life, evidenced in a growing love for God, an expanding desire to pray, and increasing power in intercession.

Figure 8:10. Example Objectives

Did you observe that all three of the objectives stated in this box include standards of performance? In A, however, "effectively" affords little guidance for either trainer or trainee to assess the learning that was achieved. Objective B affirms the right and responsibility of the trainer to judge the trainee's development. At times this may be appropriate—even necessary—but it is of little help to the trainee. The specific standards included in Objective C, on the other hand, may be the most helpful to trainers and trainees alike.

In Conclusion...

The paragraphs above describe all but one of the necessary ingredients for a clearly written objective. The missing ingredient is assumed yet primary: the Holy Spirit directs and shapes your thinking in the process. To ensure the proper mix of this ingredient, bathe your assessing, thinking, and planning in prayer. Ask the Lord for discernment and direction in your writing and decision making. As he leads your thinking, you will sense that your objectives are truly Spirit-led.

Three further words of caution: First, build into your objectives some sort of accountability. *Who* will check to see if an objective has been achieved, and *how*? Who is responsible to verify that the objective has been accomplished? Is verbal evidence (oral or written) appropriate? Is simulated ministry (a role play or case study) a reliable context for assessment? Should the trainee be observed in ministry?

Second, involve as many people as possible in developing and approving the objectives. A highly participatory process could involve several trainers, former students, and even some current or future students, not just one trainer.

Third, continuing discussion of learning objectives with your trainees is vital. It will keep your trainees focused on the target. Start each instructional unit by listing the learning objectives, refer to them as you proceed through the exercises, and review the objectives as you conclude a particular module. Without continual discussion of objectives, it is easy for trainees to lose track of what you are doing or why you are doing it.

Chapter 8: Exercises

Writing Learning Objectives

On your own:

1. Practice writing your own learning objectives:

    Under each general area outcome copied below from the Training PROFILE of a Cross-Cultural Church Planter (pages 91-92), write two different learning objectives for three of the listed outcomes of your choosing.

    Example:

General Area:

1. **Spiritual Maturity**

    Outcome 1: *Knows & loves God & exhibits fruit of Spirit*

    Objective A: *By the end of the community residential phase of the program, the trainee will exhibit love for the Lord by demonstrating the regular use of Christian spiritual disciplines and, by means of a 1-2 page reflection paper, will list the fruit of the Spirit chosen for prayerful and intentional improvement giving specific examples of how this growth occurred.*

General Areas:

1. **Spiritually Mature**

    Outcome 1:

    Objective A:

    Objective B:

    Outcome 2:

    Objective A:

    Objective B:

    Outcome 3:

    Objective A:

    Objective B:

2. **Family Wholeness**

    Outcome 1:

    Objective A:

    Objective B:

    Outcome 2:

    Objective A:

    Objective B:

    Outcome 3:

    Objective A:

    Objective B:

3. **Cultural Adaptation and Contextualization**

    Outcome 1:

    Objective A:

    Objective B:

    Outcome 2:

    Objective A:

    Objective B:

    Outcome 3:

    Objective A:

    Objective B:

2.   Evaluate your learning objectives:

Do your learning objectives clearly express the intended dimensions of:
- knowing (understanding),

- doing (skills),

- and being (character qualities).

Are your learning objectives specific enough?
- Does the verb express the right action?

- Does the condition express a clear time frame and setting?

- Is the objective measurable providing a clear standard?

Make the needed improvements to ensure your learning objectives are clear and specific, balanced and complete.

3.   With a group of your fellow students or ministry partners, evaluate a curriculum you know in light of Ralph Tyler's "Principles of Curricular Planning" (on the following page).

Principles of Curriculum Planning

Three basic principles—continuity, sequence, and integration – will help you in the process of planning your curriculum and organizing learning experiences.

Continuity

Continuity refers to the repetition or recurring emphasis of major curriculum elements. The trainer seeks to achieve a flow or connection between different units of learning so that there is an unbroken unity and cohesion to what is being learned.

- A young convert may receive teaching on communion and later receive further Bible institute or seminary instruction on the same subject.

- Principles for culture learning that are acquired pre-field should be reinforced by on-field internship and mentoring by experienced missionaries.

Trainers must recognize the necessity of providing recurring and continuing opportunities for these skills to be practiced.

Sequence

Sequence stresses organizing instruction over time (i.e., longitudinally) in a way that encourages meaningful learning. Each successive experience should build on the preceding one, with increasing breadth and depth.

- Succeeding exercises in preparing a sermon should stretch trainees into broader issues and push them deeper into disciplined biblical study. Merely repeating an assignment at the same level leads to little or no positive development in attitude, understanding, or skill.

- Development of observation and culture learning skills should focus on more complex social situations, broader hypothesis formation regarding behavior, and greater depth of analysis.

In this way, a second-year missionary would not simply repeat the learning experiences of the first year, but would explore the surrounding culture more broadly and with more depth of insight.

Integration

Integration refers to organizing concurrent instruction so that topics and principles in various subject areas "fit together." The organization of learning experiences should help trainees gain a holistic perspective by discovering ways in which all the separate pieces fit together into a cohesive whole.

Integration of learning activities involves pointing out patterns and relationships (e.g., between church history and missions strategy, between culture and evangelistic methods). Integration is the process of drawing linkages between evangelism and discipleship, between "pastoring" and "teaching" skills, between one's personal character (being) and ministry effectiveness (doing).

Source: Ralph Tyler, *Basic Principles of Curriculum and Instruction*,
(Chicago: University of Chicago Press, 1949), pp. 84-86

Chapter 9

Designing Learning Experiences

Stephen Hoke

Kweku was both excited and a little apprehensive. The first group of missionary candidates was scheduled to attend the three-week pre-field orientation session at the West Africa Training Centre, and Kweku was planning the sessions he would lead.

This would be his first opportunity to train young candidates, and he was eager to plan interactive sessions that would actively engage all participants and significantly improve their self-awareness and skills. He wanted to translate into the daily schedule of experiences the objectives he had written with the training team. He wondered if he would be as effective as he hoped in combining reading, writing, discussion, exploration, prayer and worship, group work, and learning projects into a meaningful course of instruction. Kweku wanted to build on the Centre's existing curriculum, but he also intended to add some spice with new learning experiences. As he sat down in the Centre library, he bowed his head to ask the Master Teacher for wisdom and insight.

Like Kweku, many ministry trainers are faced with a task that is at once awesome and exciting. Around the world the opportunity exists for ministry training to become highly responsive to the needs of emerging missionaries, flexible to local needs and resources, and contextualized within the cultural setting in which the training is conducted. There is a need to look back and borrow from what has been done in the past, as well as to look forward and design new training models and learning experiences for the next generation of cross-cultural missionaries and church workers.

This chapter is written for two groups of people at two levels of experience. The first group consists of those persons with little or no previous teaching or training experience, for whom the task of creating a ministry training program is a totally new and challenging experience. The step-by-step approach presented in this chapter is designed to make the design process as clear and simple as possible. Try using this approach, because it works. Learn the basic dynamics of designing an instructional program, so that you will be equipped to branch out on your own the next time you engage in this activity.

The second group consists of those persons with some or a great deal of previous training experience. You may want to skim this chapter in search of new ideas to improve what you are already doing and for training tips on how to go beyond where you are now.

Chapter Objectives:

This chapter is designed to help you:

- Understand and apply key principles of learning and development to course design.

- Be able to use a sequential process in designing effective instruction.

- Apply the most appropriate learning contexts, methods and experiences for generating specific outcomes.

Overview

All the planning you have done to this point has prepared you to select your methods and design the teaching-learning activities for your instructional plan. Only after you have clarified your training commitments, set training goals, assessed the needs of your trainees, and identified clear learning objectives can you effectively design appropriate training strategies and choose the right methods. Now you must decide how to achieve your objectives in order to meet your trainees' needs.

Principles of Learning and Development

The term "learning experiences" refers to a variety of interactions between the trainees and the external conditions in the environment to which the trainees can respond. A learning experience might take place in a classroom or in a sanctuary, on a campus or on a field trip, alone or in a small group with other trainees.

Instructional Planning Is a Creative Process

If (as suggested in Chapter 8) the role of the educator-trainer is a mix of science, art, and gift, then developing one's repertoire of teaching-learning strategies is critical to the success of both the scientist and the artist in us. Clearly, this process includes relationship building and community building strategies, not merely plans for transferring ideas into heads or onto paper in an efficient manner.

Designing and preparing for instruction, then, is a creative process that follows certain patterns, while constantly surprising both the trainer and the trainee with the unexpected. Using the image of learners and disciples as *pilgrims*, Jim and Carol Plueddemann warn against being too rigid or predetermined in this learning process:

> Precise goals are alien for pilgrims who are facing unpredictable dangers on the road. There are too many precarious experiences along the path. Pilgrims must have a strong sense of direction and destination, but they are not specifically sure where the path will lead in the near future. Leaders (and trainers) who get bogged down with measurable, short-term objectives often miss unfolding opportunities that arise around them... We are headed to a heavenly city. We are concerned with the inner character development of pilgrims. We are fighting for the souls of people. The most important things in life and in eternity are not easily measurable: "So we fix our eyes not on what is seen, but on what is unseen. For what is seen is temporary, but what is unseen is eternal" (2 Cor 4:18).[1]

The Plueddemanns' concluding caution provides a helpful balance:

> Pilgrim educators who are deeply committed to promoting the development of people for the glory of God are not afraid to stumble about. But the stumbling is not random or irrational—but purposeful. We need to plan with much common sense and clearly focus on a vision. But for some reason, God intended for

---

1   James E. Plueddemann and Carol Plueddemann, *Pilgrims in Progress: Growing Through Groups*, (Wheaton, IL: Harold Shaw Publishers, 1990), pp. 73-74.

life to be unpredictable—at least from our perspective. Educational administrators and management experts long to be in control of results. But while God gives us a significant task, he does not allow us to be in control of our own lives or want us to control the lives of other people. And yet our stumbling is not aimless or purposeless. We stumble about led by the unseen hand of a loving Father who delights in giving us joyful surprises.[2]

Learning Proceeds Best in Community

Learning is not primarily an individual endeavor. It is a small group experience. Living and learning together provides a setting where sustained, personal interaction can take place. This is not a "hit and run" approach. Rather, it is life-on-life exposure in familiar, non-threatening settings. The more closely ministry training centers can reproduce a family environment—a learning community—the more powerful will be the teaching-learning impact on trainees. A learning community provides for loving acceptance and trust of each member, nurtures the growth and development process, and creates frequent natural settings in which people can share needs, reflect on their experience, talk about what they are discovering, and be vulnerable in admitting what is difficult to apply to themselves and change about themselves.

Action Is Essential to Learning

Currently, training practitioners advocate using strategies related to experiential, active, or discovery learning. This means that trainees participate in activities—such as role play, discussion, hands-on practice—that help them discover how to be effective in ministry. In contrast, didactic strategies involve telling or showing trainees what to do. Learning takes place through the active participation of trainees—not essentially or necessarily through activities of the trainer. (Note the comparative retention rates in Figure 9:1.) That is not to say the trainer's role is unimportant. The trainer's most fundamental influence, however, is in designing an environment to stimulate and encourage learning.

Instructional Method	Recall 3 Hours Later	Recall 3 Days Later
Listening along ("telling")	70%	10%
Looking alone ("showing")	72%	20%
Listening and looking ("show and tell")	85%	65%

Figure 9:1. Recall Rates of Three Instructional Methods
(Source: John Detonni, "Introduction to the Teaching Ministry of the Church," (San Clemente, CA: Chrysalis Ministries,1993), p. 110.

> The key to effective instruction is active participation of trainees.

The key to effective instruction is active participation of trainees. Participatory strategies in which students take an active role in listening, looking, and doing instructional activities contribute to a more "holistic" learning experience, in which various senses are employed and both the logical/analytic and sensory/artistic sides of the brain are used.

Reflection Enables Learning to Be Developmental

Effective ministry training will best be done in learning communities characterized by love, acceptance, and trust. It will feature dialogue and reflection on present realities and

---

2   James E. Plueddemann, "Purposeful Stumbling About in Search of Surprises," *Bridge: Wheaton Graduate School Alumni Newsletter*, (Fall, 1991), p. 3.

ministry methods in light of biblical truth and the Great Commission.[3] This critical reflection, which is so vital to adult learning, draws upon three skills: 1) critical reason to evaluate the present (observe the obvious and probe beneath the surface to causes and meanings); 2) critical memory to uncover patterns and principles from the past so as to break open new understanding in the present; and 3) critical imagination to envision what God desires for all peoples in the future.[4] Thus, adult, nonformal, professional training should emphasize principled instruction and reflection, modeling and reflection, case studies and reflection, field trips and reflection, simulated ministry experiences and reflection, immersion experiences and reflection, journaling and dialogue reflection, etc.

An Instructional Planning Sequence[5]

Planning instruction comes easily to some trainers and much more slowly and laboriously to others. We have observed that teaching is a science, an art, and a gift. To some, planning instruction is the natural outflow of the "art" of teaching; to others, it is the disciplined labor of teaching as a "science." Designing learning experiences, as discussed in this chapter, really has much more to do with the art of relationships and community building than with the mere science of connecting pieces into a whole. The science is there, but often art is dominant.

Although not everyone will plan instruction in a sequential manner, it is useful to lay out a simple sequence of activities that flows logically from start to finish. In Figure 9:2, the main steps are connected with heavy arrows, indicating sequence; the light arrows indicate the interaction between the different steps while the creative process is under way.

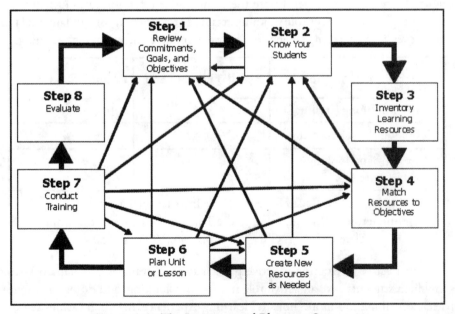

Figure 9:2. The Instructional Planning Sequence

---

3   Thomas Groom, *Christian Religious Education*, (New York: Harper and Row, 1980), pp. 184-195.

4   Groom, pp. 185-187.

5   The planning sequence which follows focuses on planning individual lessons or training sessions. Planning a training curriculum or a unit must precede planning learning experiences. Curriculum planning should be guided by principles of continuity, sequence, and integration. For an explanation of these principles, see "Principles of Curriculum Planning" on page 109.

Step 1: Review Commitments, Goals, and Objectives

It is wise to begin by reviewing your commitments and goals and by placing them foremost in your planning efforts. A review of the missionary or ministry profile is equally important to maintain a "big picture" perspective. In instructional design, it is too easy to "lose track of the forest for the trees."

While the big picture is important, we will not make significant headway toward designing learning experiences unless we also have our lesson objectives clearly in view. Reviewing these objectives is the last step in preparing ourselves to engage in lesson planning. Consider the following practical ways to review your objectives:

- *Review and focus.* Read over your commitments and training goals, and spend time in prayer, alone and as a training team. Ask questions like these:

  - How do our training commitments inform our understanding of this objective?

  - How do our training goals inform our understanding of this objective?

  - What learning environment is most conducive to achieving this objective?

  - What specific learning activities will enable us to achieve this objective, understood in terms of our broader commitments and training goals?

- *Review and discuss.* Conducting this review with colleagues in a small group setting will allow members of the group to question and sharpen each other's thinking. In such a friendly setting, we can ask questions like these:

  - Are we clear and in agreement on what the *focus* of this unit or lesson should be?

  - Do we agree that the activities planned are appropriate to our objectives, goals, and commitments?

  - Are there other, more appropriate ways to accomplish our objectives than those we have planned?

Step 2: Know Your Trainees

Transformational training focuses on the needs of trainees entering our programs and attempts to customize the training to their level of education, skills, and maturity. This assessment can be done at application and entrance to our programs through review of their experience, transcripts, and testimony. Assessment by trainers also continues throughout the training in order to see how the trainees are progressing. It is easy and natural to know one another when trainers and trainees are a part of "communities of learning."

There are two closely related reasons that knowing our trainees is essential. First, every learner is unique. Second, learning, especially formation, is relationally grounded. My wife, who teaches thirty fifth graders in our local public school, is constantly telling me stories of how important she finds it to draw on the divergent backgrounds, interests, and expertise of her elementary children. They represent eight ethnic groups, their parents range from poor to wealthy, some have traveled the world, and all bring a range of life experience that is fascinating. How much more important it is for ministry trainers to perceive their trainees as resources, as well as recipients.

Step 1: Review Commitments, Goals and Objectives

- Maintain a "big picture" perspective.
- Have lesson objectives clearly in view—review, focus and discuss.
- Pray together and as a training team.

Step 2: Know Your Trainees

- Assess students at training entrance and throughout training.
- Trainees are resources as well as recipients.

Step 3: Inventory Your Resources

- Individuals
- Events
- Places

Step 3: Inventory Your Resources

Both scientists and artists are limited in their activities by the media available. Trainers can "broaden their vision" of what is available by recognizing the resources that are readily available in their community—individuals, events, and places (historic, cultural, and religious). Be sure to include the resources of local congregations and affiliated mission agencies.

Jesus' model is instructive at this point. Review how his encounters with people—women, children, scribes, Pharisees, prophets, beggars, and lepers—were incorporated into his teaching. List the natural events of life—weddings, funerals, dinner parties, farming, eating, shopping, Sabbath observance, praying, tithing, and marketplace meetings—which he turned into training environments. Count the different places in which he taught—temple courtyards, private homes, markets, open fields, fishing boats, shaded hillsides, synagogues, and mountaintops. In the same way, trainers who know what is locally available can provide a richer mix of training experiences.

Step 4: Match Resources to Objectives

- Move from all the resources available to the best one for the objective by listing resources, matching them to objectives and charting objectives and experiences.
- Use a check list to evaluate the activity.

Step 4: Match Resources to Objectives

You are now ready to determine what training activities best fit your learning objectives. You might adopt an existing activity, adapt a published learning experience, or combine several different activities into an integrated lesson. The key is to relate or link learning experiences and methods to the learning objectives you want to accomplish.

Each training activity should be designed to accomplish a specific training and development objective. The objectives you have written provide clues to appropriate methods and activities. To save time by focusing on the most powerful method to reach your objective is a matter of both stewardship and teaching effectiveness. What activities will achieve your objectives?

- *Start general; move to specifics.* Think in general terms initially to identify several alternative ways to achieve your objectives. Consider activities already going on in your area as identified in your inventory of local learning resources (see Step 3, above). Look at each activity to determine how well it will fit into your situation.

  For example, if an objective says trainees will analyze the host culture, appropriate methods might include observation reports, field trips to ethnic neighborhoods, case studies of people groups or cultures, and research and reports describing the designated culture.

- *Divide and match.* After looking over your broad goals and objectives for the entire unit, divide the learning into smaller, bite-sized parts for daily or hourly instruction.

- *Chart your objectives and experiences.* A chart is a useful display of objectives and possible learning experiences that can help you visually link or match different learning experiences to particular objectives. To use the worksheet in Figure 9:3, list your unit or lesson objectives in the left column. In column two, jot down any specific needs or characteristics of your trainees which may influence what you teach or how you teach it. In column three, list as many different and creative ways (i.e., methods and strategies) to accomplish each objective as you can, including what is available and what may need to be designed. In the fourth column, write only the learning experiences you will use to achieve each objective.

Learning Objectives	Trainee's Needs	Possible Learning Resources	Learning Experiences Selected
1.			
2.			
3.			

Figure 9:3. Worksheet for Matching Resources and Strategies
to Objectives and Trainees

Once you have charted the information in this way, draw lines from the learning resources and activities on the right to the particular objective on the left that you think is the best "fit." This visual exercise will help you see which learning experiences you are using most often and which activities are not used at all.

In matching learning activities to training objectives, there are four tests which can be applied to guide the planning process. A simple checklist, like the one illustrated in Figure 9:4, can help you in applying these tests.

Checklist for Selecting Learning Activities

1. Is it appropriate:
   - to the training objective?
   - to the trainees' stage of development?
   - to the trainer's skills?
   - to the group size?
   - to the setting?

2. Is it learning focused?

3. Is it fresh?

4. Does it support all training commitments and goals?

Figure 9:4. Checklist for Selecting Learning Activities

1. Is it appropriate?
The nature of the training objectives, the knowledge, skill, character, and language level of the trainees, the abilities of the trainer, the size of the group, the size of the room or location of the setting, and the arrangement of the learning environment all influence the choice of methods and activities.

- Jesus led the twelve disciples on frequent field trips, interspersed with mini-lectures, demonstrations, and debriefing discussions. At other times, he lectured to thousands in the natural amphitheaters provided by hillsides. He waited until meal times for more intimate dialogues behind closed doors. His teaching method always matched his learning objective, taking into creative account the natural setting and the group size and composition.

Learning experiences must be appropriate to the trainees—neither too difficult nor too easy. The trainer should begin where the trainees are, not where he or she thinks they should be. Trainees cannot be stretched beyond their capabilities nor forced to go beyond their present abilities. The trainer must judge trainee readiness for the tasks to be performed.

- In the LAMP (Learning Acquisition Made Practical[6]) approach to language acquisition, students are urged to "Learn a little; use it a lot." This moves beginning language trainees into a variety of cross-cultural learning experiences appropriate to their present stage of development.

2. Is it learning focused?

In designing learning experiences which aid learning, focus on the learner learning rather than on the teacher teaching. A simple method to ensure focus on the trainees is to use a present participle (i.e., an "-ing" word) when specifying a method. Your description of the learning experience might read:

Tell me and I'll forget; Show me and I may remember; Involve me and I'll understand.
- Chinese proverb

- In this unit, trainees are analyzing case studies, observing village life, interviewing community members, journaling, facilitating discussions, preaching sermons, teaching lessons, writing reports, and designing community development projects.

Focusing on the trainee also means he or she must gain satisfaction from completing the behavior implied by the objective. If the experiences selected are not enjoyable or if they are distasteful and unsatisfying, learning is less likely to occur.

- New missionary candidates can see the relevance of learning a new language, for example, when it helps them make new friends and do evangelism among their friends.

It usually is best to begin ministry training from the experiences of life. This is how Jesus most often began his teaching. When he didn't know people, he started right where they were. He began with people's questions and used those questions to stimulate growth. Jesus didn't immediately tell Nicodemus how to enter God's kingdom, but he aroused Nicodemus' curiosity and stimulated him to ask leading questions. Neither did Jesus tell the woman at the well that he was the Messiah until he actively involved her in thinking about physical water, living water, and true worship.[7]

3. Is it fresh?

In ministry training for cross-cultural ministry, trainers often use certain methods in frequent combination—observation and discussion, case study analysis and discussion, discovery and discussion, mini-lecture and application discussion, etc. Discussion may be the most common learning activity, but it should be used in different ways and in combination with various other "input" or discovery activities.

Traditionally, lecturing has been the most common method of presenting new information in a short amount of time. Lectured material is not always the most memorable, however, and lecturing can easily be supplemented by activities such as films, videos, role-plays, and case studies which present new information in more "user friendly" ways.

---

6   Tom Brewster and Elizabeth S. Brewster, *Language Acquisition Made Practical (LAMP): Field methods for language learners.* (Colorado Springs: Lingua House, 1976) p. 383.

7   James E. Plueddemann, "Behavioral Objectives, No! Faith Goals, Yes!" *Intercom*, no. 144 (August-October, 1994), p. 56-57.

4. Does it support all training commitments and goals?

Whenever we design learning experiences, we must be concerned about balancing all three dimensions at once—knowledge, skills, and character development. Although certain activities and experiences may focus on only one or two dimensions at a time, don't forget to include activities which integrate all of these dimensions.

Trainers facilitate true attitudinal and character change when they sensitively blend learning about God with genuine first-hand learning from God. This is done when trainers recognize the way in which truth must be felt and obeyed, as well as understood.

- Bob Pierce, the compassionate evangelist and founder of World Vision, moved by the needs of children orphaned by the Korean War, once prayed, "Let my heart be broken with the things that break the heart of God."

Every learning activity also must be consistent with the commitments which guide the training program and with the program's goals. A strategy which violates principles taught elsewhere in the training program is always the wrong choice, irrespective of its efficiency in achieving a specific training objective.

Step 5: Create New Resources as Needed

A range of training strategies exists. Ferris has pointed out, "The poverty of our individual repertoires is testimony to the effectiveness with which we allow our own experiences to limit our imagination and practice."[8] For ministry training to become more effective, the emerging generation of trainers and facilitators must develop more creative and diverse teaching methods than their predecessors.

It would be nice to be able to outline an easy-to-follow, step-by-step process for creating learning experiences that achieve our training objectives. Unfortunately, creativity cannot be reduced to a formula. Perhaps the most helpful stimulus to creativity is an appreciation of the range of training options available to the trainer and program developer.

Ministry training strategies may be classed in two categories:[9]

> ### Step 5: Create New Resources as Needed
>
> - Employ creativity and diversity.
> - Consider classroom-based and field-based training or a combination of both.

Classroom-Based Strategies	Field-Based Strategies
Lecture	Field observation and reflection
Dialogue	Trainer modeling and reflection
Case studies	Directed field assignments and reflection
Role play	
Structured Simulations	Field ministry and reflection
Research and reflection	

Figure 9:5. Categories of Missionary Training Strategies

Traditionally, classroom-based training has relied on lecturing, answering questions, writing on the chalkboard, demonstrating, and showing audio-visual materials. Trainees worked individually by reading the text, solving problems, writing reports, using the library and other print resources, and sometimes by viewing films or videos or listening to tape recordings. Interaction between trainers and students and among students often

---

8   Robert W. Ferris, *Renewal in Theological Education: Strategies for Change*, (Wheaton, IL: Billy Graham Center, 1990), p. 6.

9   Ferris, 1990, p. 6.

took place by means of discussions and small group activities, student projects, and reports.[10]

Classroom-based learning experiences for adults also can include role plays, case studies, dramas, worksheets, games, simulations, projects, quizzes, presentations, small group work, stories, interviews, and skits. The list is almost endless. This process of creating and selecting learning experiences requires both artistry and careful evaluation. The critical concern for trainers is to select experiences which "fit" the learning objective.

For candidate and in-service training in spiritual maturity, classroom-based strategies could help in knowing *about* holiness without experiencing it. A *discipling* method and a *modeling-with-reflection* strategy that is situated in life and ministry, in the field or around the training center, would be preferred.

In a field-based strategy, such as discipling, each candidate is mentored by a mature believer. Discipling will include Bible study, prayerful reflection, and discussion of character development goals as each quality is modeled by the discipler. This strategy necessitates life exposure between discipler and candidate. Two programs which incorporate such discipling for developing spiritual maturity are the JIFU program at China Graduate School of Theology (Hong Kong) and All Nations Christian College (Ware, Hertfordshire, UK). Without doubt, many other examples exist on each continent.[11]

Classroom-based instruction is a beneficial supplement to discipling, however. Classes on Missionary Life and Work, Missionary Biography, The Life of Christ, and Missionary Ministry in Acts are among many which afford opportunities to reflect on principles for Christian living and on historical models of holiness and spiritual power. To achieve character development goals, however, learning activities and reflection must focus on the character qualities to be developed.

For developing cross-cultural communication skills, *both* classroom-based *and* field-based strategies could be employed effectively. Classroom strategies may include case studies, role plays, and cultural simulations in addition to mini-lectures and discussions about the skills to be developed. Trainers must have extensive cross-cultural experience for effective personal illustration of the principles and skillful demonstration of the skills taught. Field-based strategies might include language learning forays into the surrounding community, venturing into the neighborhood as "cultural detectives" to observe and reflect on what was seen, observing effective national communicators, and practicing non-verbal skills such as bowing, gesturing, and listening.

Field observation and field ministry opportunities might be jointly debriefed with reference to principles discussed in classroom studies. Frequent field trips to village and urban communities, as well as one or more extended immersions in field environments, will be beneficial to several areas of the curriculum, provided they are effectively debriefed.

Step 6: Plan the Unit or Lesson

You are now ready to lay out your training plans. Planning learning activities for each session can be aided by using a "Lesson Planning Sheet" (see Appendix G). If you are just beginning to teach, this may seem like an unnecessary discipline. Over time, however, you will see yourself developing greater skill in shaping lessons which meet the needs of the trainees and which fulfill your training objectives.

---

10   J.C. Galvin and D.R. Veerman, "Curriculum for Adult Education," in *The Christian Educator's Handbook on Adult Education*, ed. K.O. Gangel and J.C. Wilhoit, pp. 178-189, (Wheaton, IL: Victor Books/ SP Publications, 1993), p. 184.

11   cf. Ferris, 1990.

A simple three-phase model is helpful for sequencing activities in a way which leads naturally from one phase to the next.[12]

Reflect

Start any learning experience (i.e., class, trip, or discussion) with a short time for reflection. Use simple exercises and activities which help trainees think about the topic, recall what they already know, and review their past experience related to the topic or issue. You can do these things by using one of the following activities:

- *Questions* - Have trainees write their response to a provocative opening question.

- *Quotes* - Have trainees think about the meaning of a striking quote.

- *Statistics* - Ask trainees to write for two minutes on their response to statistics.

- *One-page reflection sheets - Use one-page handouts with questions, cases, or Bible passages for discussion.*

- *Values clarifying exercises* - Have trainees rank the top ten values of their culture in contrast to the top values of the kingdom of God.

- *3" x 5" card reflection questions* - Have trainees write out on a 3" x 5" card their thoughts on an issue, topic, or dilemma.

- *Journal exercises* - Give trainees five minutes to record a recent lesson from God.

These and other activities can serve as "warm up" exercises for the mind, make trainees aware of how much they already know, and focus the trainees' concentration on the subject to be addressed.

Detect

During the second phase of the learning experience, trainers help the trainees discover new information, theories, and meanings for themselves, in addition to developing new skills and character traits. This phase focuses on helping the trainees learn new information or put information together in new and more meaningful ways.

A variety of different types of activities can be used to stimulate individual and group learning. "Input" methods range from the traditional lecture to discussions, games, simulations, forums, panels, question and answer periods, media starters, field trips, interviews, observation exercises, self-study modules, etc.

Project

In the third phase, trainees are helped to make specific application to their lives from the general kinds of learning gained. Trainees may be asked to think ahead, i.e., to project how the learning will apply, what changes they will need to make, what activity they will need to adjust or adapt, and to write guidelines or personal applications of theoretical principles.

"Project" activities include those which encourage and facilitate trainees' sharing with each other, such as buzz groups, brainstorming, question and answer, open-ended discussion, writing action plans, etc.

The goal of effective curriculum design encompasses much more than achieving individual training objectives. The greater goal is to equip whole people from the whole church to take the whole gospel to the whole world. In order for this goal to be accomplished

---

Step 6: Plan the Unit or Lesson

- Start any learning experience with time for reflection.

- Help trainees discover new information, meanings, skills, and character traits.

- Help trainees make specific application to their lives from the learning gained.

> The greater goal is to equip whole people from the whole church to take the whole gospel to the whole world.

---

12   Ted Ward, Unpublished notes, College of Education Doctoral Seminary (East Lansing, MI: Michigan State University, 1975).

Step 7: Conduct the Training

- Planned lessons help the trainer focus on what is important.
- Be ready to modify lessons based on:
  - "Reading" the student
  - Unexpected opportunities
  - Student questions

Step 8: Evaluate the Training

- Asses the effectiveness of achieving your training objectives.
- Plan in advance how and when evaluation will be done.

effectively, missionary candidates need help integrating their learning into a cohesive fabric of biblical thinking and living. Trainers need to help trainees "re-connect" the pieces of their training experiences, synthesizing the parts into a whole.

Step 7: Conduct the Training

You will be eager to lead your training after having invested so much energy in planning your instruction. You soon will recognize how critical is the linkage between planning and instruction. Step-by-step planning can make the teaching-learning process seem simple and straight-forward. In reality, good teaching and effective learning can be extremely complex and messy. The complexity of learning (due to its relational nature) and our frailty in anticipating future interactions inevitably cause even the best instructional designs to fail if they are implemented woodenly.

Teaching is an active vocation, and professional teacher-trainers approach it interactively and reflectively. When we teach, we constantly "read" the class. We look for those who may not understand our instruction, who may be emotionally absent, who need to say something we didn't anticipate. We have learned to expect surprises. We must be willing to modify or abandon planned activities and objectives to pursue unanticipated learning opportunities. We often stop lecturing to follow up on a trainee's question. We allow a trainee's sharing of a recent experience to introduce a more immediate or relevant path toward our training goals. We talk, we listen, we weep, we laugh, we pray, we worship, and often none of these things were in our lesson plans. This approach is what Plueddemann [13] calls "purposeful stumbling about."

The plan is a helpful starting place, nonetheless. Gifted trainers, after years of experience, may walk into a class with only a Bible and their life as the textbook. For most of us, however, lesson plans help us focus on what is important: on the principles to be learned in that session, and on how we will approach the topic at hand. Lesson planning is a tremendously helpful discipline for trainers to focus on instruction and to ensure that trainees' learning experiences match our training objectives.

Step 8: Evaluate the Training

How will you assess the effectiveness of each learning experience and assure that learning is successful? On-going evaluation and adaptation can improve the effectiveness of any training plan and its component training experiences. Consider in advance how you will evaluate the effectiveness of each learning experience:

- What specific outcomes will you look for to determine success?
- Who will be responsible for assessment?
- When (by what date) will assessment be done?
- To whom does the observer or evaluator report?

View this final step of evaluation as a means of discovering how to improve. Don't get caught in the trap of thinking of evaluation as *assessing trainees*, as on a report card or as a pass/fail grade. You want to find out *how to be effective* in achieving *your training objectives*. Through trial and error experience, you will be able to determine which learning experiences are best suited to achieving your learning objectives and which experiences do not bring your trainees to your desired learning outcomes. Chapter 10 will provide more specific guidance for evaluating your lessons and your training.

---

13   Plueddemann, 1991, p. 3.

Conclusion: Expanding the Range of Trainers' Roles and Abilities

Professional competence in teaching is an increased ability to fulfill a variety of roles effectively—including counselor, facilitator, instructional manager, curriculum designer, academic instructor, evaluator, and mentor. A large part of teaching effectiveness consists in mastering the repertoire of approaches to teaching that are appropriate to those roles[14]. Joyce suggests that one's training "competence is expanded in two ways: first, by increasing the range of teaching strategies that we are able to employ; second, by becoming increasingly skillful in the use of these strategies."[15]

Unfortunately, there is no formula for matching learning activities to objectives. What may work for one trainer in one class or with one group of students can be unsatisfactory in another situation. You need to know the strengths and weaknesses of alternative methods and of various materials and curriculum. You will develop this familiarity through experimentation and practice. Then you can make your selection in terms of the student characteristics and needs that will *best* serve the objectives you have established.

---

14   Marlene D. LeFever, *Creative Teaching Methods: Be an Effective Trainer*, (Elgin, IL: David C. Cook Publishing, 1990); Detoni, 1993, pp. 113-119.

15   Bruce R. Joyce, *Selecting Learning Experiences: Linking Theory and Practice*, (Washington DC: Association for Supervision and Curriculum Development, 1978), p. 3.

Exercise 9:1
Identifying and Designing Learning Experiences

1. Inventory: List the types of learning experiences that are currently used in your training center or program.

2. Select *four* learning experiences that are used most often and evaluate the effectiveness of each in terms of your program's purpose, goals, and/or objectives.

    Learning Experience   **Effectiveness**

    a.

    b.

    c.

    d.

3. Identify at least three *additional* learning experiences which might teach the competencies for which you wrote learning objectives in Exercise 8:1.

    a.

    b.

    c.

4. From the learning experiences listed in #2 and #3 above, identify *five* experiences which promise to have the fewest negative consequences and the most positive outcomes in your cultural setting. Be prepared to explain your list to a colleague.

    a.

    b.

    c.

    d.

    e.

5. Use the following "Lesson Planning Sheet" to design learning activities for a lesson you plan to teach soon.

Lesson Planning Sheet

UNIT TITLE: _____

UNIT GOAL: _____

Lesson Title: _____

Focal Passage: _____

Background Passage: _____

Lesson Goal: _____

Lesson Objectives: *To achieve this goal the learner will...*

1.   _____
   _____
   _____

2.   _____
   _____
   _____

3.   _____
   _____
   _____

Materials Needed:

-
-
-

Lesson Outline:

Notes:

Chapter 10

Evaluating Ministry Training Programs

Robert Ferris

It is common for non-educators to view program development as a start-up activity, something which must be tackled once, at the outset of a new training program. Anyone involved in training, on the other hand, understands that program development is an on-going process. To remain vital, relevant, and effective, training programs must continue to develop.

Evaluation is the step which closes the loop on program development. As set forth in this manual, program development begins with clarifying training commitments, then employs a profiling process to identify training goals. The program of training becomes real when training goals are distilled into specific objectives and are implemented through planned and structured experiences. We can't stop there, though. We need to observe the effect of our training and ask how the training can be improved. This is the task of evaluation. By assessing training outcomes and identifying implications for future instruction, evaluation closes the program development loop. A disciplined review of training experiences and outcomes can assist in the reconsideration of commitments, training goals, training objectives, and training strategies.

Three Aspects of Evaluation

Any evaluation should attend to three distinct aspects of the training program: training processes, training outcomes, and stewardship of resources.

Training processes include all the intentional activities and relationships by which the training program seeks to shape the understanding, skills, and character of the trainee. This may include trainee selection, in-class instruction, on-campus training (e.g., survival, sanitation, health, gardening, construction, home-making, mechanical skills), in-field training (e.g., community orientation, evangelism, church planting), trainer demonstration or modeling, discipling or mentoring, cultural immersion, internships, group worship and prayer, recreation, community life, personal counseling, and ministry or career guidance. Please note that this list is intended to be suggestive, rather than exhaustive; the training processes evaluated for any program should be those employed by the program.

When training processes have been identified, each should be examined for consistency with the program's training commitments and goals and for stewardship of the program's resources. A simple table (see Figure 10:1) which provides ample space for recording observations and findings can simplify this task.

To use this table, list training processes in the first column, comment on the appropriateness of each process factor in the second column, and record conclusions and recommendations in the third column.

Chapter Objectives:

This chapter is designed to help you:

- Value outcomes-based evaluation and its importance to program improvement.
- Understand three different aspects of evaluation and their relevance to a program.
- Be able to use a specific procedure for program evaluation.

Take time to identify the training processes in your program.

Training Process	Commentary on Consistency with Commitments, Goals, and Stewardship	Satisfaction Level and Recommended Steps to Improvement
Trainee selection		
In-class instruction		
(Etc.)		

Figure 10:1. Sample Table for Recording Process Evaluation Findings

There are two kinds of *training outcomes*, each of which requires a different method of evaluation. *Intended outcomes* should be assessed in terms of training goals and objectives. If commitments have been agreed to and recorded (Chapter 6), and training goals have been specified (Chapter 7), and if lesson objectives have been defined (Chapter 8), this is a straightforward exercise. As with training processes evaluation, tables can simplify the task.

List the "intended" outcomes of your program.

Training Commitments (See p. 77)	Evidence of Attainment (Pro and Con)	Satisfaction Level and Recommended Steps to Improvement
Objectives determined by standards of performance		
Training is church-related and community based		
(Etc.)		

Figure 10:2. Sample Table for Recording Commitments Evaluation Findings

Use this table like the previous one. List training goals (or lesson objectives) in column one, then enter evidence of goal or objective attainment in column two. Since it is rare for all goals to be attained with equal effectiveness, the third column should record observations and recommendations to improve the training program.

Training Goals and Objectives	Evidence of Attainment (Pro and Con)	Satisfaction Level and Recommended Steps to Improvement
Knows how to inform the church about the missionary task		
Is eager to practice language learning at every opportunity		
(Etc.)		

Figure 10:3. Sample Table for Recording Outcome Evaluation Findings

Unintended outcomes are quite different from intended outcomes. Although any individual or group activity—especially an activity as complex as teaching and learning—has unanticipated effects, these often are overlooked by inexperienced evaluators. In fact, however, unintended outcomes can delightfully enhance or tragically mitigate the effects of a program which, in systems terms, attains all (or most) of its stated objectives.

> A "slum living" experience was designed to teach missionary trainees skills needed for survival in urban ministry situations. Annually, however, the training staff observed that the weeks spent in the slums produced strong friendship bonding among trainees which persisted throughout the balance of the training program and into their missionary careers.

One danger of identifying specific objectives for training is a tendency to produce a kind of "tunnel vision." Like individuals without peripheral vision, we see only what we are looking at. Like them, also, our greatest jeopardy or blessing may lie just outside this narrow field of vision. To resolve that problem, we need deliberately to broaden our area of focus. Instead of looking only at goal attainment, we need to ask, "What *other* positive or negative effects is our training producing?"

> We need to ask, "What other positive or negative effects is our training producing?"

Just asking that question is the first step in the evaluation of unintended outcomes. The question itself is also crucial. Only as we recognize the unintended outcomes of our training can we adjust our training plans to capitalize on and enhance positive outcomes or to diminish or eliminate negative outcomes.

The procedure for evaluating unintended outcomes is like that for evaluating program processes. First a list of unintended outcomes, both positive and negative, must be developed. This may involve brainstorming by the training staff, polling current trainees and alumni, and interviewing constituent church and mission leaders. When a responsible list has been assembled, the outcomes identified should be examined against the program's commitments and training goals. (A table similar to Figure 10:1 is very useful, but instead of listing training processes in column one, list the unintended outcomes that have been identified.) Often the evaluation of unanticipated outcomes leads to the most significant insights toward immediate program improvement.

Finally, evaluators must consider the program's *stewardship of resources*. As Christians, we own nothing; everything we have is held in trust for God. We are stewards; we are held accountable for the way we use the resources entrusted to us. Again, we need to think broadly. Resources include financial resources and physical resources (land, buildings, and equipment), but also personnel resources and environmental resources. A few minutes' reflection usually will yield a respectable list of individuals, organizations, and points of cultural or religious interest existing in the environs of the training center which can be used to strengthen missionary training.

Evaluation Procedures

Any procedure which enables us to reflect knowledgeably on training in terms of our commitments, training goals, and stewardship of resources qualifies as "program evaluation." Although the time and energy invested in evaluation will vary, it is useful to consider the variety of strategies available to program evaluators, whether the evaluators are program staff or an external individual or team.

Tests of trainees' knowledge or skills are the most commonly employed means of evaluating effectiveness and the attainment of training goals and objectives. Whenever tests are employed, evaluators should assure that the information or skills tested are consistent with stated learning objectives. It also is important for trainers and evaluators to recognize, however, that tests administered at the training center afford only an indirect and intermediate measure of trainees' readiness for ministry. The ultimate goal of information and skill training is the formation of Christian character and life-long, growing effectiveness in ministry.

Exhibits, such as trainer or trainee portfolios or products demonstrating trainee skills, afford a second evidence of training program effectiveness. A garden can provide convincing evidence of trainees' mastery of cultivation principles. A garment sewn by a trainee can demonstrate the effectiveness of preparation for "self-supporting" ministries. A tape recording of a sermon preached by a trainee, or a Bible study taught, can effectively document mastery of preaching and teaching skills. Likewise, a doctrinal statement developed by a trainee can evidence his or her grasp of basic Christian truths. When several similar exhibits, produced by different trainees, are examined, evaluators can observe the effectiveness of the training program.

> Often direct inquiry methods are the most useful way to obtain information about persons and their opinions.

Direct inquiry methods include interviews and questionnaires. Generally interviews are preferred, except when the persons to be questioned are widely distributed geographically or when the number of individuals is relatively large. Often direct inquiry methods are the most useful way to obtain information about persons and their opinions. Direct inquiry may be used to collect self-reports, peer reports (i.e., reports by one or more friends), trainer or supervisor reports, and congregational or ministry team reports (i.e., collective judgments in ministry contexts). Since character qualities are not accessible to testing or exhibition, direct inquiry is almost the only means for assessing attainment of character development goals. Congregational or ministry team reports, along with trainer or supervisor reports, also provide a useful index of ministry skill development. We sometimes have felt that we could learn more about a training program by interviewing four alumni in their ministry setting than by spending four days at the training center!

Finally, some aspects of a training program can be assessed only by ***direct observation***. Especially when evaluating program processes and stewardship of resources, evaluators may need to observe training procedures, interpersonal relations, institutional records,[1] physical facilities (i.e., buildings and equipment), and environmental resources.

Two Types of Evaluation

There are two ways we can evaluate training: through on-going evaluation and periodic evaluation. On-going evaluation provides a stream of information, sometimes imprecise and often informal, on training effectiveness. Periodic evaluation, on the other hand, affords a larger and more systematic assessment of training program effectiveness. For most training programs, it probably is not useful to schedule periodic evaluations more often than once in five to seven years. If your program is seven years old and you have not conducted a periodic evaluation, however, we believe you would find this a valuable discipline. This chapter will provide guidance for conducting on-going and periodic evaluations of missionary training.

On-going Evaluations

Evaluation may occur at any point in a training program, and it probably should. Most commonly, however, we evaluate our training daily, at the end of each training unit, and at the conclusion of each program cycle. To be sure, the formality of these evaluations may differ, but the means employed are similar and the criteria applied are the same.

> Most commonly... we evaluate our training daily, at the end of each training unit, and at the conclusion of each program cycle.

Daily, following each training session, a wise trainer will ask himself or herself, "How did it go today?" This is the time to make notes on parts of the lesson which were particularly effective or ineffective, including especially positive experiences or insightful discussions, problems encountered by trainees, illustrations which did not illustrate, demonstrations or explanations which require more clarity, etc. Daily evaluation typically depends on the trainer's subjective assessment of the training experience in light of the commitments which guide training and the objectives set for the day. Trainers who take time to make such notes, however, will find them invaluable aids to future preparation.

Assessment ***at the end of each training unit*** (lectureship, internship, course, or term) often is more formal. Usually some measure of trainee achievement (e.g., a grade, fluency level, etc.) is part of unit completion. While we typically view these measures as assessments of the trainees, it is helpful to view them as assessments of training effectiveness as well. Assuming that admission standards are appropriate, effective training should result in high levels of trainee achievement. When trainees fail to learn, it is safe to conclude the trainer has failed also. It is useful, furthermore, to supplement records of trainee achievement with the trainer's assessment of the unit's success vis-à-vis training commitments and unit objectives.

It is also helpful to request trainees to evaluate each unit of the training program as the unit is completed. We recommend an evaluation form that lists training commitments and asks trainees to rate (from high to low on a 5-point scale) how effectively each commitment was demonstrated in this unit. A second section of the evaluation form lists unit objectives and asks trainees to rate the extent to which the training achieved each objective. A third section may list specific topics or activities included in the unit,

---

1   Institutional records examined may include any or all of the following: official documents and minutes, policy statements, staff personnel records, trainee admission records, trainee assessment reports, alumni records, financial records and statements, income and development plans, and property development and maintenance plans.

requesting assessment of their effectiveness in promoting unit objectives. We also have found it useful to include a fourth section, in which trainees are invited to provide any additional comments or suggestions. Often trainees have nothing to add, but at other times this fourth section will yield the most encouraging or most insightful feedback.[2]

Usually student evaluations confirm the trainer's subjective assessment, but occasionally students will identify weak areas of which the trainer is unaware. Trainers who are unaccustomed to trainee evaluations may find this practice unsettling. Nevertheless, by submitting ourselves to trainee evaluations, we demonstrate a willingness to humble ourselves to learn from our trainees. Besides the insights gained for strengthening our training programs, trainee evaluations provide a strong positive example for our trainees.

At the conclusion of each program cycle,[3] usually annually, it is worthwhile for the training staff to review the cycle as a whole, assessing the staff's faithfulness to training commitments and their achievement of program goals. The conclusion of a program cycle provides a particularly appropriate occasion for a global review of the training program. Reflection on the ministry preparedness of the recent graduates affords the training staff an opportunity to assess the outcome of their training in very specific ways. By discussing the effectiveness of each unit of the program and the interaction of those units, training staff can gain insight for improving the program units or for refining the training program as a whole.

Every healthy training program has a systematic plan of on-going evaluation. This is the staff's only means of assuring that areas of weakness are identified and addressed and that program improvement is continuous. Methods may vary, but on-going evaluation always is oriented to three considerations: (1) faithfulness to program commitments, (2) achievement of program objectives, and (3) stewardship of program resources. On-going evaluation provides the shortest and surest route to program improvement.

> The (evaluation approach) which best fits the commitments and values of ministry trainers has been termed "responsive evaluation."

Periodic Evaluation

Occasionally it is useful to step back from our training programs, to look at them holistically in a fresh light, to attempt to see them as others do. Formal program evaluation is a science. Although various approaches exist, the one which best fits the commitments and values of ministry trainers has been termed "responsive evaluation."[4] This approach is responsive in that evaluation is concerned with the responses of various groups of people affected by the training program.

Responsive evaluation proceeds from a set of assumptions which ministry trainers can endorse. Its view of reality is holistic, its stance is participative, its goal is program improvement, its interest is to learn from human responses and assessments, and its assumptions are sensitive to moral and educational values.[5]

---

2   For a sample evaluation tool, see the Module Evaluation Form on p. 209 of this manual under "Evaluation Tools" in Section 3: Additional Resources.

3   Cyclical evaluations may also be referred to as *formative*. Periodic evaluations may also be referred to as *summative*.

4   This term was coined by R.E. Stake, "Program Evaluation, Particularly Responsive Evaluation," in *Evaluation Models: Viewpoints on Educational and Human Services Evaluation,* ed. G.F. Madaus, M Scriven, and D.L. Stufflebeam, (Boston: Kluwer-Nijhoff Publishing, 1993), pp. 311-333. The same model is sometimes identified as "naturalistic evaluation" because of its attention to interactions in natural contexts (E.G. Guba and Y.S. Lincoln, "Epistemological and Methodologial Bases of Naturalistic Inquiry," in *Evaluation Models: Viewpoints on Educational and Human Services Evaluation,* ed. G.F. Madaus, M Scriven, and D.L. Stufflebeam, (Boston: Kluwer-Nijhoff Publishing, 1993), pp. 311-333.

5   Guba and Lincoln, 1993, pp. 313-323.

Definition of Terms

Before proceeding to a description of this approach to periodic evaluation, three terms must be defined and five groups distinguished. Although periodic evaluation need not be complex, it will be helpful to clarify our use of terms at the outset.[6]

"Merit" is the presence of values affirmed broadly among educators of a particular type —in our case, missionary trainers. Where shared values have been codified, as in lists of accreditation standards, assessment of "merit" is quite straight-forward. Missionary trainers rarely have reflected collectively on the values and commitments which direct their training programs. In the absence of a more broadly based statement of values, the training program's own commitments, clarified and owned through the process described in Chapter 6 of this manual, can be used.

"Worth" is the presence of values specific to one program and its context. These values are the factors which make one missionary training program distinct. "Worth" includes, but goes beyond, the stated goals of a training program. "Worth" is a function of the needs and expectations of a training program's constituency—the churches, mission agencies, and individuals it serves. The "worth" of a training program also relates to the program's appropriateness to the cultural contexts from which trainees come and into which they will be sent.

"Integrity" relates to the way the periodic evaluation is conducted. It is the appropriateness of the procedures employed and the seriousness with which the evaluation is pursued.

In addition to these terms, we also need to identify five groups who are significant to the periodic evaluation process.

The *training center staff* is the community of trainers who staff the missionary training center. In some cases the center staff may be known as the center's "faculty." Generally both full-time and part-time trainers are considered center staff. It usually is not helpful to consider as staff non-residential trainers who participate only occasionally in the center's training programs.

The *center administrator* bears responsibility for directing the daily operation of the training center. Sometimes the center administrator is known as the center's "director," "principal," "dean," or "president." Although she or he may function as "first among equals," the center staff are responsible to the center administrator.

The *center's board of directors or trustees* are a small group of mature Christian individuals, external to the training center but committed to its mission, to whom the center administrator is responsible. If the training center is operated by a church, a denomination, or a mission agency, the center's board may be a committee charged with oversight of the training center. Even when the training center is organized as an independent ministry, it is generally accepted that the center administrator needs a clearly identified group to whom she or he can look for accountability and advice. If the training center is an independent ministry, the center's board may be a legally constituted body.

When legally constituted, the board may hold title to any property belonging to the training center and may be responsible for appointing the center administrator and the

> Create a list of persons that should be involved in a periodic evaluation process concerning your training program.

---

6   The concepts and language described are drawn from the sources cited in the paragraph above, with one exception. "Integrity" is a factor recognized by a team of educators appointed to develop a scheme for accrediting TEE in Asia (Ferris and others 1986). Robert Ferris ("Accreditation and TEE," in *Excellence and Renewal: Goals for the Accreditation of Theological Education*, ed. R.L. Youngbood, pp. 59-79, (Exeter, Uk: Paternoster Press, 1989)), has provided a full description of that project.

staff. Usually it is not advisable for members of the administrator's extended family or for training center staff to serve on the center's board of directors or trustees.

The *evaluation team* consists of two or three persons, including one from the training center staff, who are charged with conducting the periodic evaluation. At least one member of the evaluation team should be familiar with the procedures of social research. To avoid conflicts of interest, the center administrator should not be appointed to the evaluation team.

The *evaluation guidance committee* is a group representative of the training center's stakeholders.[7] It is convenient for the evaluation guidance committee to be no larger than necessary. Usually one carefully selected representative of each stakeholding group is satisfactory. The center staff is a stakeholding group and should be represented on the evaluation guidance committee.

The Evaluation Procedure

A periodic evaluation of the training center's program can be pursued as a ten-step process.

1. The decision to conduct a periodic evaluation should be taken by the center's board of directors or trustees. It may be necessary, however, for the center administrator to recommend that a periodic evaluation is needed. When the board authorizes evaluation of the training center's programs, it also should appoint the evaluation team.

2. The first task of the evaluation team is to identify the training program's stakeholder groups. The center's board, administrator, and staff should be consulted regarding the list of stakeholders, since the credibility of the evaluation will be diminished if any significant stakeholder group is overlooked. At the same time, it is advisable to identify an individual, as well as an alternate, who can represent the interests of each stake holding group. (The alternate will be needed only in the event that the original individual is unable to serve.) These stakeholder representatives, when recruited, will constitute the evaluation guidance committee.

3. The evaluation team should call a meeting of the evaluation guidance committee. The agenda of this meeting is to identify factors relevant to the "worth" of the training program. After the stated training goals of the center are reviewed, each member of the committee should address (a) the perceived purpose of the training center; (b) issues or concerns related to the design, operation, or impact of the training programs; and (c) sources of evidence perceived to relate to the effectiveness of the training center in meeting the needs and expectations of the representative's stakeholding group. With various perceptions on the table, it then is the task of the evaluation guidance committee to negotiate any differences in order to produce a coherent statement of factors relevant to the "worth" of the training program. This is essential to the continuing work of the evaluation team.

4. The evaluation team next must develop a strategy for assessing the training program's stated objectives, its "merit," and its "worth." The evaluation team should be assured full and uninhibited access to all records maintained by the training center. Survey or interview data collected from the training administrator and staff, current trainees, alumni of the training center, and selected stakeholder groups will be critical to the evaluation. Special attention also should be given to sources of evidence identified by members of the evaluation guidance committee in their first meeting.

---

7   The concept of "stakeholder" was is discussed in detail in Chapter 6. Readers who are not familiar with this term may find it useful to review that section before proceeding.

5. A second meeting of the evaluation guidance committee should be called to review the evaluation strategy developed by the evaluation team. Following presentation of the proposed strategy, discussion should focus on the adequacy of the strategy and any adjustments which may be required. At the close of this meeting, the evaluation guidance committee should assure the evaluation team that the amended strategy is an acceptable approach to assessment of the training program. If this is impossible, steps 4 and 5 must be repeated.

6. The evaluation team should proceed with the evaluation, according to the strategy approved by the evaluation guidance committee. Findings should be analyzed, and a report should be prepared addressing the training center's achievement of its stated objectives, and the "worth" and "merit" of the training program. The evaluation team also should identify any adjustments in personnel, facilities, or program design which are indicated by their findings.

7. A third meeting of the evaluation guidance committee should be called to review the evaluation team's report. The evaluation team should present its report section by section, allowing opportunity for members of the evaluation guidance committee to question the team's findings, interpretations, or recommendations. Objections raised by any member of the evaluation guidance committee must be addressed by the evaluation team and by the committee as a whole. If added perspective permits reinterpretation of the evidence collected, and if this new interpretation is acceptable to all members of the evaluation guidance committee, the report may be amended in that meeting. If any member objects to the way evidence was collected or interpreted or to the sources from which evidence was drawn, the evaluation team either must defend its procedure to the satisfaction of the committee or must collect additional evidence which addresses the stated concerns. When the evaluation guidance committee is satisfied that the report of the evaluation team accurately reflects the "merit" and "worth" of the training program, the committee's work is done.

8. The evaluation team should review its report, as approved by the evaluation guidance committee, with the training center administrator and the training center staff. Unlike the evaluation guidance committee, the training center administrator and staff do not have the prerogative to require amendment of the evaluation report, although any overlooked information should be noted. This review is provided as a courtesy to the administrator and staff, inasmuch as they will be responsible for implementing any recommendations included in the report which are mandated by the training center board.

9. The evaluation team should draft a statement on the "integrity" of the evaluation project, describing the procedures and strategies employed and specifically noting and justifying any deviations from the approach outlined here.

10. The evaluation team should present its full report, addressing the "merit" and "worth" of the training program and the "integrity" of the evaluation project, to the training center's board of directors or trustees.

When the evaluation team's report has been received by the training center's board, the team's work is completed. The board, then, is responsible to determine which of the recommendations included in the report should be implemented and to provide for their implementation.

Although this process may appear complex, in practice it can function very smoothly. The most difficult problems are encountered when various stakeholding groups hold

> The most difficult problems are encountered when various stakeholding groups hold deeply divergent understandings of the center's purpose. In such a case, *achieving a common understanding of the training center's mission may be the most significant product of the evaluation.*

deeply divergent understandings of the center's purpose. Despite the complexity of negotiating these differences, the training center cannot be successful in the midst of such division. In such a case, *achieving a common understanding of the training center's mission may be the most significant product of the evaluation*. When differences exist, it is critical to the work of the evaluation team that they avoid taking sides; they may facilitate the negotiation, but they must not "get caught in the middle." The stakeholders themselves must resolve any differences; then the evaluation team may proceed on the basis of the negotiated understandings.

Much will depend on appointing the right persons to the evaluation team and on providing them the time and resources needed to do their work. It is not realistic to expect members of the evaluation team to fulfill their responsibilities while maintaining a full workload. The budget required to underwrite the evaluation project will depend on the geographic distribution of the members of the evaluation guidance committee and on the evaluation strategies employed. If travel expenses of the evaluation guidance committee members can be minimized, and if the evaluation team can collect its data without extensive travel (e.g., by sampling alumni opinion via postal survey, rather than personal interviews), periodic evaluation need not be expensive. It is unrealistic, however, to assume that evaluation can be cost free.

The costs of periodic evaluation must be weighed against the benefits it affords. Periodic evaluation is the most effective way to assure that the training center is fulfilling its mission and is serving well its various stakeholders. Periodic evaluation also is the most effective way to identify areas in which the training center's programs can and should be improved. Another way to say this is, the periodic evaluation provides information which is essential to the on-going development of the missionary training program. We have never encountered a training program board which regretted the time and resources invested in a periodic evaluation, but we know of several which have made significant adjustments in training programs on the basis of information obtained through a periodic evaluation using the process described here.

> We have never encountered a training program board which regretted the time and resources invested in a periodic evaluation.

Conclusion

When training is not evaluated, training center administrators and staff have no informed basis on which to improve their programs. Program evaluation, however, "closes the loop" on program development. In this chapter we have described procedures for both on-going and periodic evaluations. In both types of evaluation, training outcomes are compared with training goals, and training methods are compared with training commitments. Periodic evaluation broadens the scope of inquiry to assure that the training center's stakeholders are well served. The findings of program evaluation afford perspective for reassessing training commitments and program goals. Thus, the program development "loop" is closed, and the way is opened for continuing, significant improvement of missionary training.

Chapter 10: Exercises

Evaluate Your Evaluation Process

1. If you are a part of a training program or ministry, how often and in what ways do you deploy evaluation tools and techniques? In light of this and other chapters in this manual, in what ways can you reinforce this activity?

2. If you are doing this course with a group of students, evaluate the delivery of this course. Use the following criteria:

   a. How consistent has this course been in employing the principles it promotes in relation to a biblical philosophy of education and adult learning?

   b. In what ways has this course been valuable to you as a person or to your institution? What could make it more valuable?

Section 3

Additional Resources

Program Descriptions

In 2005, we asked ministry training programs around the world to submit case studies that described innovative, strategic, and best practices from our global missionary movement. Several are represented in this chapter. Responders were asked to provide the following information:

- **Part 1:** Demographic details in chart form, student and staff description, history and objectives.

- **Part 2:** Provide a detailed account of methodology used in the training program that addresses the following question. Fill this out with specifics of circumstances or situations addressed by this methodology. This is primarily a description of what is done.

  Question: There is an established correlation between non-formal (experiential), practical cross-cultural ministry involvement and the development of needed skills and attitudes. There is also a correlation between the intentional use of "community" (living situations, activities or relationships) in attitude formation and character growth. How does this training program use non-formal practice and experiential learning to develop skills, and/or how does it intentionally use community to generate growth in character?

- **Part 3:** Use your expertise to interpret what has been described in Part 2 in terms of the process that was used to implement the above described learning practices.

  Question: The ongoing evaluation and assessment of a training program leads to the introduction of improvements. Through trial and error, the effectiveness of changes can be affirmed. How has this training program progressively improved learning activities addressing the development of essential ministry and/or cross-cultural skills, or the formation of attitudes leading to character growth?

Share the journey with the following organizations....

«1»

Program: Asian Cross-Cultural Training Institute (ACTI)

Country: Singapore

Sponsor: Mission agency partnership

Contributor: Henry Armstrong

Part 1: Demographics

Name	Asian Cross-Cultural Training Institute (ACTI)
Address	11 Pasir Ris, Drive 2, Singapore, 518458
Contact information	Email address: admin@acti-singapore.org Web-site: www.acti-singapore.org Phone/Fax: (65) 6583-0085/ (65) 6583-0084
Other contact	Henry Armstrong, Dean Henry@acti-singapore.org
Language of instruction	English
Affiliations and sponsors	The ACTI Board consists of representatives from OMF Singapore, SIM East Asia, OC International, Interserve, The Navigators, Wycliffe Bible Translators, Bethesda Pasir Ris Mission Church, CNEC (Partners Int'l). Also affiliated but less involved are the Singapore Centre for Evangelism and Missions (SCEM), WEC International, and CB International (WorldVenture). Residential trainers for the last 10 years have been from World Team.
Length of program	ACTI offers a 3-month pre-field training course in very basic English, with 1 month extra if intensive English language training is needed. For the majority of our trainees, English is a second language.
Number of students	We normally run 2 courses per year with an average of 7 students per course. Our maximum would be 15 per course; optimum would be 10 to 12.

Students:

Trainees of the Asian Cross-Cultural Training institute (ACTI) come mainly from East and Southeast Asian countries, Korea, Hong Kong, Japan, Singapore, the Philippines, Malaysia, Thailand, India, Myanmar, Indonesia, and Nepal. The admission requirements are a Bible school or seminary degree, but applicants are weighed on a case-by-case basis. They must also be approved and sponsored by a sending church or mission agency. Upon completing their training most become involved in church planting and evangelism ministries. Some serve as tentmakers. Graduates from ACTI are serving in various countries in Asia and around the world.

Staff:

One residential training couple, Westerners who have lived more than half their lives in Southeast Asia, undertakes approximately one third of the classroom teaching. Other training resources are gathered from the missionary community in Singapore. These volunteers come and provide lectures for a morning or two. Alumni and visiting missionaries are called upon to share their experiences. Lecturers are chosen, not only because of their cross-cultural experience, but also because of an evident heart for the Lord, and a love for people. Frequently, they will have experienced 10 to 20 years of cross-cultural living, and are usually active or retired missionaries or area leaders of mission agencies. The ethnic diversity of lecturers is as follows: 40% North American missionaries who have served in Asia, 40% Singaporean, 10% other Asian countries, 10% from New Zealand, Australia, and the U.K.

History and Objectives:

The original aim of ACTI was to provide pre-field cross-cultural training for missionary candidates, tentmakers and bi-vocational workers intending to serve in a cross-cultural environment in an Asian country. The course was structured to provide trainees with: 1) experience in cross-cultural community living in preparation for working with a cross-cultural team; 2) skill for cross-cultural evangelism and church work; 3) knowledge of Asian cultures and religions, and perspective on missions strategies; 4) reflection on one's own and family identity in the context of cross-cultural living and working. These objectives have remained constant since the inception of ACTI.

ACTI began in 1984 as the Asian Mission Training Centre, a ministry of Overseas Missionary Fellowship. The founders saw the need for missionaries to be better prepared to handle the challenges of cross-cultural life and ministry. A few years later ACTI opened the doors to include other agencies and served primarily to train Asians going to other Asian nations. Over the years Joshua Ogawa, Titus Loong, Paul Han, Kim Gi Mun, Melville Szto, Kim Chong Pae, and Henry Armstrong have each held the position of dean.

Due to the shift in missionary sending patterns, ACTI shortened the course of study from 10 months to between 3 and 4 months. Some of the Singaporean agencies and churches believe this is still too long. Over the years, ACTI has become less visible in Singapore. It appears many do not see the need for this kind of training, especially those churches that send missionaries directly to the field.

The initial years of training were marred by instability due to the lack of a permanent facility. Ten years ago ACTI found a more permanent home by moving to the new Bethesda Pasir Ris Mission Church building, where it enjoys a combination of good facilities and a good working relationship with the church. A large percentage of the trainees come from developing countries, and ACTI continues to seek financial sponsorship from Singaporean churches to enable them to receive this training. This produces a serious challenge to the school to determine the real motivation that brings trainees into the program. After years of experience, ACTI now requires that the trainees be sent through a church or missionary agency.

Part 2: Non-formal and Community-Based Learning

How does this training program use non-formal practice and experiential learning to develop skills, and/or how does it intentionally use community to generate growth in character?

As far as formal learning is concerned, not too much has changed over the years in the way things are done, although the content of many classes has changed. Monday to Friday mornings are scheduled for classroom learning from 8:30 to 10.00, with a tea break till 10:20, chapel till 10:55 and class again from 11:00 to 12:30. Lunch is at 12:45, and afternoons will vary with different activities: study time, meeting people in the larger community around us (pre-evangelism), cleaning duty, volleyball at another school.

Once a week is "Family Night" where each person or family has an opportunity to host the others to an evening of information on their country, games and ethnic foods. Other evenings are usually taken up with studies. With trainees from different cultural backgrounds, and going to different cultures for ministry, ACTI by default must remain a bit generic in the curriculum. We cannot focus specifically on any one culture or religion.

Core Emphases: ACTI's curriculum and residential living arrangement are designed to prepare cross-cultural workers with growth in character and competence in order to be effective in working in another culture. With this in mind our core courses are based on six keys to effective cross-cultural ministry:

- Spiritual Formation
- Team Building
- Phonetics and Linguistics
- Contextualization in Asian Religions
- Cultural Adaptations
- Practical Case Studies

Besides the six core emphases listed above, ACTI also teaches the following individual courses: Principles of Church Planting, Spiritual Warfare and Intercessory Prayer, Modes of Tentmaking/Creative Access Options, Stewardship in Missions, Understanding Spiritual Gifts, Trends in Mission Today, Church/Mission/Missionary Relationships, Communication Skills. Trainees must also read various parts of the Perspectives course material, as well as parts of several other books, and write short reports about what they have read.

Part 3: Program Improvements and Development

How has this training program progressively improved learning activities addressing the development of essential ministry and/or cross-cultural skills, or the formation of attitudes leading to character growth?

ACTI has intentionally created its own sub-culture to accommodate learning servant leadership among the trainees. Everyone agrees to address each other on a first name basis, in order to illustrate that all are on the same level, and trainees learn that even the leaders of the institute are still learning to be servant leaders. English is the required language for public speech. This is an attempt to model the importance of respecting the language of the host culture, and to be respectful to each other by not speaking a language that is not understood by everyone.

The community living situation helps trainees to see the importance of building good relationships with the people they will be working among. ACTI, as a residential cross-cultural program, benefits from having trainees and trainers from various cultural backgrounds living together in a fairly close-knit community. Everyone experiences some degree of culture shock, even the trainers, and we work as a local body of Christ (community) to help each other adapt to the situation and to each other.

Besides eating meals together, the trainees together with the trainers are responsible to set tables, serve the meal, wash dishes, and do general cleaning of the premises. For some trainees this is a quite a shock! ("The Dean also washes dishes?") In his home culture, a man may never even enter the kitchen, but in his future host culture it may be completely different. Servant leadership must be modeled. A key phrase here is, "You teach what you know; you reproduce who you are." Some other key emphases are: the importance of community, flexibility, life-long learning, vulnerability, integrity, servant leadership, and ministry that flows out of the "being" (as opposed to just "doing" ministry). Some of our staff members are gifted at finding "teachable moments" in the everyday activities.

Other activities include visits to culturally specific areas of Singapore such as Little India, Chinatown, and Malay village, and a one week cultural exposure trip to a nearby country for an additional opportunity to put into practice what is being learned in the classroom and ACTI community.

Once a week trainees go out to meet the public specifically with the aim of experiencing cross-cultural interaction with non-believers. Picnics and a weekly excursion to another school to play volleyball provide opportunities for more non-formal interaction. We have not always been as intentional as we should in some of these activities, mostly due to the fact that we are very short-staffed. A few of our lecturers use experiential learning techniques for their classes (e.g. team-building), but we need to work at developing or borrowing more of these types of activities.

Each trainee is assigned to attend an English-speaking church congregation on Sunday mornings. This is to give the trainees more exposure to English, as well as to enhance their Singapore experience. Many trainees are then also invited to attend a cell-group. This proves to be a highlight for most trainees, as the churches involved in this aspect of the training are always very caring. Some trainees want to attend a service in their own mother tongue. This is only allowed if given permission by the Dean. The intention is not to prohibit fellowship with one's own people, but these contacts can become an additional burden. The desire is for trainees to keep a Sabbath day rather than wear themselves out by going to too many services, especially if they are called upon to participate.

It is this contributor's belief that small schools become a reflection of the attitudes and beliefs of the dean. A recent curriculum review initiated by the Chairman of the Board helped to define and refine the key emphases, and to sharpen the teaching focus in the classroom. It is the prayerful expectation of the staff that the Lord will help others recognize the valuable learning experiences waiting at ACTI.

«2»

Program: Global Missionary Training Center (GMTC)

Country: Korea

Sponsor: Mission agency partnership

Contributor: David Tai Woong Lee

Part 1: Demographics

Name	Global Missionary Training Center (GMTC)
Address	231 - 188 Mok Dong, Yang Chun Ku, 158-052, Seoul, Korea
Contact information	Phone: 82-2-2649-3197 Fax: 82-2-2647-7675 Email: gmtc@chol.com Web-site: gmtc.or.kr
Other contact	Director: David Tai Woong Lee dtwlee@hanafos.com
Language of instruction	Korean
Affiliations and sponsors	Primary affiliation: Global Missionary Fellowship Inc. The GMTC ministry is extended to different denominations and missionary organizations, and as such is an interdenominational, inter-organizational missionary training center.
Length of program	We have two tracks in our training center. One is from January to June of a given year, while the other is from August to December. The former is approximately six months and the latter is three months.
Number of students	We normally take 30 adults plus their children for each session. For the last several years we have had from 30 to 38 adults. For the January to June 2006 sessions there will be 37 adults plus 24 children. Annually we train 60 to 75 adults plus 50 to 60 children.

Students:

The trainees come from missionary organizations such as: Global Missions as Pioneers (GMP), Global Bible Translators (GBT), Helping Overseas Professionals Employment (HOPE), OMF Korea, Interserve Korea, WEC Korea, Korea Baptist Mission, Hapdong Presbyterian Denomination, Hapsin Presbyterian Denomination, etc. GMTC requires the trainees to have at least an undergraduate degree from a university, for the principal member of the family. As for the spouse, in a few cases graduation from high school has also been accepted. The majority, however, have graduate degrees, either from seminaries or universities. All must have been called to a missionary ministry, and preferably recommended by a missionary organization. They are planning to enter ministries such as: Bible translation, ministry to missionary children (MK's), community development through farming, computer related work, and church planting and discipleship ministry. Most trainees plan to work in church planting as well as discipleship ministries. The other ministries altogether make up about the half of the trainees. Our graduates are scattered all over the world, although the greater number serve in Asian countries, particularly China and the Central Asian region.

Staff:

There are currently 17 people on staff at GMTC. Among them are 8 tutors, 5 supportive office staff, and 4 children's workers. Currently one tutor is on study leave for higher education. By mid 2006 the school expects to gain two (husband and wife) teams and another two tutors by 2008. In order for the whole staff to function as a "high impact team," each member of the staff must be a team person. The tutors especially must be able to work as a team. The staff must have adequate experience both in practical training as well as a balance in understanding theory, such as missiology and counseling. While cross-cultural experience is important, it does not exempt one from understanding something about training. Currently all of our tutors have some sort of experience living in different cultures. Out of eight tutors, two have been ministering on the mission field.

History and Objectives:

GMTC was founded in 1986 by a group of Korean pastors who had a missionary vision for training Korean cross-cultural missionaries. From the beginning it was an interdenominational organization, ministering in cooperation with various denominations and mission organizations, with the support of the Korean church. It was designed to maintain balance between academics and practical aspects of training. Internalization and reflection upon their learning were required from the students.

It was felt that GMTC could best serve the Korean church by training its potential leaders and pioneers so that they would not only pioneer new fields, but also build infrastructure for the new missionaries. Eventually some would become leaders in the home office as well. In the beginning, the school lacked facilities, staff, trainers and experience. For the past 20 years GMTC has continually built up its staff. Now the school enjoys a "high impact team," and the facilities have been expanded beyond what was originally imagined. The school can now host up to 38 adults, plus around 25 children. In contrast, during the first year, all the training was done in a rented house, and limited to just one full day a week, without communal living. Now each of the trainees must live in community. This gives the trainer adequate time and opportunity to observe and help trainees in all areas of their lives.

The present objectives include a greater emphasis on servant leadership. The desire of the school is to see mid-level leaders emerge as a result of the training so that they serve their own entities better. Another important objective is to see better personal and family relationships.

Looking to the future, two of the biggest challenges will be: 1) to find suitable and well experienced trainers who understand both traditional people from seminaries, as well as modernists coming from secular Korean society, and 2) how to become contemporary without losing the cutting edge in producing well-trained people. All of this boils down to a question of leadership. Who would be able to actually help make this transition?

Part 2: Non-formal and Community-Based Learning

How does this training program use non-formal practice and experiential learning to develop skills, and/or how does it intentionally use community to generate growth in character?

Focus on the whole family as an integral team:

GMTC training requires all trainees to bring their whole family to the center and live communally for the duration of the training. Trainees experience leading the entire community for a short period through the Haba (house father) and Hama (house mother) system. Each trainee unit will take his/her turn serving a team of 3 or 4 members for several weeks. This provides an excellent opportunity for exercising team leadership in the community, similar to a set of parents in an extended family.

A marriage workshop, offered at the beginning of the training, gives the families (singles have their own single's seminar) opportunity to work on improving their marriage relationship. Lectures on raising children (parenting) both at home and abroad, allow each family to put theory into practice while living at the center. These are samples of some of the training elements that are offered as non-formal educational components in a community setting. All of these are done with a view toward each family living in a cross-cultural setting for a life-long period. The "life cycle" of a missionary family is emphasized, as most Korean missionaries still opt to stay on the field for the rest of their lives.

Group/Teamwork in learning and in life situations:

Almost all of the important assignments are done in groups. This gives each group opportunity to interact so that they will know what it is like to be a part of a team and how to do things through teamwork. Studies in missiology are done in the classroom setting. But even these classes are conducted in informal and nonformal manners. There are discussions, question and answer periods, and workshops. It is hoped that through these exercises and learning experiences that the trainee's worldview will be challenged, changed and strengthened.

Trainees are divided into groups after the orientation. A tutor is assigned to these tutorial groups consisting of 6-7 people per group. As part of a Life Formation course that runs throughout the period of training, every week trainees will spend time together as a group to discuss different themes that will help form their lives. Tutors then share about the life of each trainee in tutorial meetings conducted each week. Each trainee is prayed for in this meeting. Trainees are expected to grow in their character as well as in competence through these sessions.

Planned and scheduled "socialization" as an important learning activity:

As the training begins, the first step in the process is for everyone in the community to share their life journey. They are expected to share something about their past, their present, and their extended family—particularly the relationships with their parents and brothers and sisters in their formative years. This is to provide an opportunity to understand first oneself, then others, so that the process of socialization can begin. It is expected that much learning will be done by this informal way of teaching and encouraging one another.

Emphasis on spiritual formation through devotional life together:

Some of the learning activities that bring spiritual and personal growth are: family nights (usually fun and recreational activities to break the ice), Friday late night prayer meetings conducted approximately every other week from 9 p.m. to 11:30 p.m., and early morning quiet time workshops from 6 a.m. to 7 a.m. twice a week (other mornings are for individual quiet times). Almost all of these activities are done in anticipation of living in a cross-cultural environment where little or no help is available for personal and spiritual growth.

Counseling sessions geared towards the whole person:

Each trainee receives counseling at least three times from his/her tutor. If there are character issues or other personal problems, extended periods of moral or spiritual counseling are offered. A number of tools are used in these sessions. The Taylor-Johnson Temperament Analysis (T-JTA) determines the type of character a person has, using nine dipoles such as: nervous vs. composed, depressive vs. light-hearted, hostile vs. tolerant and self-disciplined vs. impulsive, etc. This is just one of the tools that is used to help trainees better assess themselves, and thus be better equipped for the cross-cultural living involved in some kinds of team ministries.

Life formation:

The Life Formation sessions are like a training thread woven throughout the whole training program. Teachings are done on life formation each Friday prior to tutorial group meetings and are geared toward helping trainees learn about practical life issues such as emotional healing, personal management, understanding spiritual gifts, etc.

Community worship services: the backbone of the whole curriculum

A team is assigned by turn for a period of one to two months to plan a meaningful worship service on each Wednesday evening. The whole community will participate in the worship in one way or the other. Through expository biblical preaching on such themes as the "Crucified Life," "Spirit-filled Living," "Discipleship," "Power of God," "Dedication," etc., the community is fed as well as challenged to experience further growth. This is a vital part of the curriculum, usually well-planned to cover most of the important themes for mature Christians and a biblical worldview.

Noon prayer time and communal noon meals:

Every day at noon the whole community stops and gathers together for one hour to pray for the world, identifying particular issues. They also pray for country and local issues, as well as requests that come in throughout the month. Lastly, there is prayer for each of the graduates since the founding of the center, close to 900 people plus their children. This is usually an intense time of prayer, covering many needs and addressing problems that arise. Trainees learn firsthand how prayers are answered. It is hoped that they too will pray for various problems and needs while on the field.

Prayer is followed by the noon communal meal for the entire community. On any given day there will be around 100 people who will share this meal together. It is a prime time for families to mix and fellowship as they eat together.

Living in a "normal environment", the best setting for training:

GMTC is situated on a corner in a normal town. The majority of missionaries will probably reside in this kind of environment when they are on the field, particularly those who will be ministering in urban areas. Trainees are encouraged to live a normal life, and in the process, the tutors as well as the trainees themselves identify areas of weakness and strength. Tutors continue to keep their eyes and ears open for clues to issues that concern the trainees. This can help them with their "real needs" in addition to their "felt needs." For the past 20 years this informal way of identifying and helping resolve problems has proven to be one of the most effective, and one of the strengths of training in community.

Day of prayer and retreat:

One day per month is set aside for the trainees, tutors and part of the administrative staff to spend in prayer. Mornings are for communal prayer, followed by fasting at the noontime meal. The afternoon is spent alone with God. Those who have children are encouraged to take them for a walk or do activities together.

There is one retreat on the prayer mountain or conference center during each training session. This usually occurs during the middle of the training. The whole family goes to the center together, spending two to three days in the countryside. It provides an excellent time for prayer, worship, fun and sharing deeply what is in their hearts.

Final summary time and final exam:

At the end of the training, the trainees are given three to four days (depending on the length of the program) to summarize all that they have learned throughout the entire training period. This is a difficult and intense period, as they recall what they have read and notes they have taken, as well as review handouts they have received during the entire period of training. This gives each trainee time to process the learning experience and integrate the material, and reflect on what they have learned. Following this time, they are given a half-day exam period. They are usually allowed to use their own written summary. The exam is graded and kept as a record in the event that they need credit for further studies. Permission to graduate usually does not depend on how well they do on the exam. It is only one of many factors that are considered. Rather, the whole of the training—informal, nonformal and formal—is taken into consideration in the final evaluation.

Part 3: Program Improvements and Development

How has this training program progressively improved learning activities addressing the development of essential ministry and/or cross-cultural skills, or the formation of attitudes leading to character growth?

The following description includes two levels of evaluation—the tools used to evaluate the program and the way that information is used for feedback in order to improve the training system. The tools used for evaluation are as follows:

Weekly tutorial meetings:

The tutorial meetings are primarily designed to evaluate trainees by the tutors in a private setting. Each tutor gives a report concerning their group members on family life, finance, health, spiritual life, children, progress, problems of any kind, and relationships both within the community, as well as outside the community, such as in the church and with other organizations. After the report by tutors concerning the status of their trainees, there is an extended period of prayer for each of the trainees and their children. Although this tool is primarily for evaluating the trainees, it is also an excellent tool for evaluating the team and the training program. Whatever changes, improvements and reinforcements that need to be made will be implemented as quickly as possible after a thorough review made by the tutors themselves.

Bi-weekly survey sheet filed by each trainee:

Every two weeks each trainee is asked to fill out a survey of important information. This form may include, for example, how they are doing spiritually, what is happening in their daily devotions, new things that they have learned, difficulties they are facing, relationship problems, logistical inconveniences, etc. Each tutor will read and take appropriate steps to work things out. If major changes are involved, tutors will be called together to discuss and make necessary changes.

Noon prayer time:

The noontime community prayer meeting includes a time slot to share personal prayer needs. This is a good opportunity to get to know the needs of the trainees. Tutors are very sensitive to do whatever possible to help meet needs. It also provides an opportunity to recognize areas that should be improved for the good of the community, and for the effectiveness of the training.

Longevity of trainees on the field as a means of evaluation:

As of January 2006, GMTC has trained 907 people. Thirteen of them received training the second time, after serving some time on the field, making 894 people who have been through our training for the first time. In 20 years, there has been approximately 3% attrition among the entire group of graduates. This means that average attrition rate for a given year has been somewhere around 0.16%.

GMTC monitors the graduates every day through the noon prayer time. In a sense, this serves as a barometer for the training center. The prayer letters and notes of the graduates posted on the website provide clues as to areas of strength and weakness.

Feedback from the heads of the sending arms of the wider mission community, both within Global Missionary Fellowship (GMF) as well as outside GMF:

As of January 2006, 38% of GMTC graduates are involved in missionary activities among the GMF community, of which the school is a part. The remaining 62% of the graduates are scattered among a number of other Korean missionary organizations. Within the GMF community, there are three sending arms, and the heads of these sending bodies periodically give evaluations of their members who have completed training at GMTC. On one hand, it is an awesome thing to be evaluated long term for the quality of the graduates' lives, and on the other, it is a privilege to be continually evaluated, so that necessary changes can produce better results. This feedback is related to both the personnel, as well as the content of training. Recent responses after an evaluation indicated that it is felt that GMTC graduates lack an "adventurous spirit" or "Ya-Song" as we say. They feel graduates seem too tame for rigorous life on the field, such as the Indian village lifestyle.

Tutors have been trying to implement changes, first by incorporating this need in the philosophy of training. Then, changes are made in the curriculum. A few examples of these changes are: giving greater attention to discipline, living a simpler lifestyle without harming the health, perseverance in completing assignments even when time and energy are limited, etc.

Detailed evaluation made by the graduates on the integral part of the training:

By far the most effective tool has been the evaluation by the graduating trainees themselves. Evaluation is made on almost all aspects of the training program and can be done anonymously if desired. Evaluation ranges from the quality of tutors, methods of training, the staff, and the children's program, to training facilities, living situations, acoustics, costs, and the way of handling training. Trainees are also asked to rate how much they feel they have learned on a scale of 1-10 on the most important learning elements upon which the training program is built. They are also asked to list in order of priority what they feel the training center is trying to accomplish, from the following kinds of values: the combination of theory and practice, non-formal and informal education, changes in worldview, holistic thinking, integral mission, etc.

Bi-weekly expanded staff meetings also serve as an evaluative tool and an opportunity to make needed improvements in each part of the training program such as: the office, children's school, facilities, and networking and webpage work.

Final evaluation:

Following the graduation of each group of trainees, the whole community usually goes on a retreat to do further evaluation of the completed training and incorporate the results of the evaluation made by the trainees, as well as the staff, before a new training session begins.

In conclusion, all the results of the evaluations are ultimately fed back into the training system.

GMTC is now looking toward the next six months to bring in new tutors from among the graduates who have served several terms on the mission field, as well as having completed studies in missiology. This is to prepare for the new generation of missionary candidates who have grown up in the post-modern era. The program may have to change radically to accommodate younger and more secularized Korean young people of the future. This will be the challenge of training the next generation. To meet these ever-increasing changes, one must grow accustomed to a lifestyle of continuous evaluation.

«3»
Program: Nigeria Evangelical Missionary Institute (NEMI)
Country: Nigeria
Sponsor: National missions movement
Contributor: Peter Boma

Part 1: Demographics

Name	Nigeria Evangelical Missionary Institute (NEMI)
Address	NEMI Campus, Mista Ali Village, PO Box 5878, Jos, Plateau State, Nigeria
Contact information	Phone/ Fax: 08037984008 Email: nemitoday@yahoo.com Web-site: www.NigeriaMissions.org
Other contact	Rev. Peter Boma piboma@hotmail.com or nemitoday@yahoo.com
Language of instruction	English
Affiliations and sponsors	Interdenominational, sponsored by Nigeria Evangelical Missions Association (NEMA)
Length of program	One year
Number of students	This varies from year to year, but an average of 15

Students:

Most of the students at NEMI are sent from mission agencies. After the training they return to the agencies that deploy them. Other private self-sponsored students come into the program. Before their graduation, they are linked up with agencies of their choice. The candidate must be a mature Christian, called to missions, sent by an agency, able to read and write, and pass the prescribed interview. They are involved in church planting, discipleship, training, administrative work, and serve within and outside Nigeria.

Staff:

NEMI is staffed from three sources: those seconded by their mission agencies, those on voluntary service and those employed. The expectations regarding staff eligibility are: relevant qualifications, experience, maturity and personal testimony. The present list of staff includes those who have served as missionaries in local and foreign fields, trainers of missionaries in a foreign setting and those who have over 20 years experience serving as mission executives.

History and Objectives:

NEMI was founded by the Nigeria Evangelical Missions Association (NEMA), which is a coalition and fellowship forum for more than 95 mission agencies and churches. The school is interdenominational and has 20 years of operating history (1986 to date) training for cross-cultural missions. NEMI exists to provide practical training in cross-cultural ministry and skills to those called of God, and to facilitate the empowerment of NEMA member institutions in leadership and manpower development for a qualitative missionary thrust within and from Nigeria. Our basic philosophy of training is based on an integrated approach with emphasis on character, competence and skill development. Some of the changes experienced over the past years include change of leadership, relocation from a rented apartment to a permanent site with buildings, administrative structure, and introduction of the advanced Training of Trainers program. The current objectives are to provide: 1) Pre-field practical cross-cultural one year training program to qualified candidates, 2) Training of Trainers (TOT) Program, 3) Refresher courses for in-service missionaries, 4) Seminars for church leaders, mission executives, and directors of Christian organizations, (5) Short intensive courses for administrators, secretaries, researchers and skill acquisition for female missionaries. One of the challenges faced by NEMI includes finding resources to develop and position NEMI in order to effectively train missionaries and service the training movement in Nigeria.

Part 2: Non-formal and Community-Based Learning

How does this training program use non-formal practice and experiential learning to develop skills, and/or how does it intentionally use community to generate growth in character?

Through the NEMI community life, people desire to set good examples for others and thereby refrain from ungodly behavior. Once ungodly behavior is noticed, effort will be made to put it under check. In so doing, there is intentional growth in character as everybody desires to do what is acceptable in the community.

The training methodology includes the following:

- Class work: Classes are organized on a modular basis which affords the opportunity to bring in experts to teach the courses.

- Fieldtrip: A week-long fieldtrip is planned in which staff and students go to a chosen field, stay, work, interact, learn, eat, pray and fellowship together.

- Fieldwork: The fieldwork is four months long. Previously, students chose their field, but after recently reviewing this approach, it was determined that agencies should choose and place their students. Now, NEMA member agencies need to request a student for the fieldwork. This commits the agencies to care for and supervise the student, and also identify with NEMI in his/her training process. NEMI receives three fieldwork reports: one from the agency's supervisor, another from a NEMI staff person who visits, and a third from the student. The student report is an ethnographic research project, based on the people group he/she served. When all the students return, they do a debriefing.

- Sports: There are two days in the week that the staff and students come out for various games.

- Manual work: Students are required to carry out manual work as part of their training. A duty roster is drawn up for each semester.

- Meals: NEMI does not operate central cooking but encourages students in the same room to cook together. Those who have food are to share with those who do not.

- Family nights: Family nights are held every Sunday evening. We organize a variety of programs such as quizzes, testimonies, singing of special numbers, film shows, etc. There is usually a "Hot Seat" where someone sits and participants can ask the person any question.

- Outreach: Every Saturday the students and resident staff go to the nearby communities for evangelism.

- Community life: There is freedom for the students to visit the homes of staff and share in discussions, work and food whenever available.

- Care and share: This program occurs once a semester. At the beginning of the semester, everybody picks the name of a person written on a sheet of paper. No one knows who picked what name. Each person is expected to pray for the name he/she picked till the end of the semester and buy a present for the person.

- Chapel: We hold chapel services every day except Saturday. The roster is drawn in such a way that everybody has opportunity to lead prayer and to preach.

- Worship/Fasting and All-Night Prayer Meetings: Every Wednesday is a day of fasting and prayer. In the morning between 5:00 a.m. and 6:00 a.m., the resident staff and students meet just to worship. The fasting continues till evening. People are placed into small prayer groups. Later, all the groups come together for corporate intercession. The last Friday of every month is the All–Night Prayer Meeting.

- Week of spiritual emphasis: This program is held once a semester. A minister is invited to speak on a chosen theme for the week. The guest minister also makes time available to listen to and counsel students.

- Evaluation of staff and students: This is an age-old practice in the school. We ensure that the staff and resource persons evaluate the students, and also that the students do the same for them.

Part 3: Program Improvements and Development

How has this training program progressively improved learning activities addressing the development of essential ministry and/or cross-cultural skills, or the formation of attitudes leading to character growth?

The above description incorporated the formal, informal and non-formal methods of the training process. The classes are formal. The lecturer comes to deliver his lectures, gives reading assignments, expects lecture reflections, sets the exam, marks the scripts and submits the grade.

The Fieldtrip and Fieldwork are elements of the informal learning process. They provide opportunity for the staff to discover certain behavioral traits among the students, and ensure proper modelling and accountability.

The Fieldwork enables the student to stay in a new cross-cultural field, discover the people, establish relationships and put into practice the principles he/she was taught in class such as language learning techniques, interpersonal relationships, cross-cultural church planting, etc.

Using a non-formal process, the trainer and other staff who are residents on the campus visit and interact with the students. Sometimes they engage in discussing what had taken place in class, and share in the joys, difficulties and struggles.

In NEMI, evaluation and assessment have been an integral part of our training process. The regular evaluation process has helped both the staff and students and school leadership to improve on methodology, choice of resource persons, courses, self-development, program schedule, etc. It has promoted growth and dynamism in our institute. The most recent evaluation was held in December of 2005.

This recent evaluation included both staff and students. The names of each staff member and student were typed on sheets of paper and given to everybody to evaluate, including both the positive and negative aspects of the person. The intention was to allow each person to know how others felt about him or her. The leadership then compiled the completed sheets and gave the comments made by everyone to the person concerned. It was like a revelation. We saw ourselves through the eyes of others. This resulted in praises to God for the positive elements and determination to improve in the negative areas.

≪4≫

Program: Ghana Evangelical Missionary Institute (GEMI)
Country: Ghana
Sponsor: National missions movement
Contributor: Patrick Nuwode

Part 1: Demographics:

Name	Ghana Evangelical Missionary Institute (GEMI)
Address	PO Box 2632, Accra, Ghana, Africa (GEMI is located in Amedzofe, Ho District of Volta Region)
Contact information	Phone: 233-021-405212/233-0931-22015/020-8495491 Email: gemisint@yahoo.com
Language of instruction	English
Affiliations and sponsors	GEMI is a non-denominational missionary focused training institution
Length of program	Initially, GEMI offered only a two-year Certificate in Missions and a three-year Diploma in Missions. During the past two years, offerings at GEMI include: a two-year Bachelor of Arts program for diploma students; a three-year Diploma in Ministry, with concentrations in Christian education and pastoral ministry; a three-year Diploma in Theology, in addition to the certificate and diploma in missions.
Number of students	GEMI trains an average of 20 students annually.

Students:

Students are primarily from Bible believing churches from different regions of Ghana. Some come from the West African coast, namely: Liberia, Gambia, Nigeria, and Togo. The admission requirements for the certificate, diploma and degree programs are the following: evidence of conversion and clear commitment to Christ, evidence of ability to pursue an academic program with a general education standard that enables students to participate meaningfully in all courses (Senior Secondary School certificate or General Certificate of Education 'O level'). Those who seek to study missions must have previous Bible school education. Some of the methods of assessment include: producing a 10 page write-up, spelling out significant experiences that have contributed to their personal and ministerial development, independent testimonials, and the assessor's own evaluation.

Most of our students are Christian workers in their own churches. They occupy positions such as Sunday school teachers, lay evangelists, deacons, and elders. Undergraduate students have often served as pastors and evangelists after their diploma course before coming to GEMI. After their courses, most of them serve as pastors in their local congregations and some as home missionaries sent to different tribes within Ghana for church planting. A few of them were able to cross national borders to other African countries such as Togo, Liberia, and Nigeria. It is worth noting that on rare occasions students were able to travel as far as East Africa, the United Kingdom, and the United States of America.

Staff:

The institution employs staff with a B.A. degree to teach the certificate and diploma students. The staff with master's and doctor's degrees, as well as visiting lecturers, teach the B.A. courses. The selection of staff depends on the following essential areas: he or she must be a committed born-again Christian, he or she must be a graduate from a credible institution, he or she must hold a B.A. to teach at certificate and diploma levels and an M.A to teach at the undergraduate level, he or she must have served as a missionary, pastor, church planter or mission administrator and possess the relevant field experience. The staff has a wide range of experience. They are from different cultural backgrounds and have served in different milieus and ministries, and are therefore able to offer the students a culturally contextualized and balanced training diet. We believe this dimension is often missing in mission work today and is the only way Scripture can go deeper than the usual surface level.

History and Objectives:

Ghana Evangelical Missionary Institute (GEMI) is a non-denominational missionary training institution born in 1993, and the first missionary focused training institution in Ghana. GEMI is a ministry of Africa Christian Mission (ACM). The founding president is Dr. Seth Anyomi, a citizen of Ghana. In 1993, the school started with only a one-year certificate course. Then the following year, a two-year diploma in missions was added to the training program. With the assistance of two Western mission agencies, human resource and finances were not problematic at this initial stage of our training institution.

The purpose of the training program is to assist the African church to evangelize and disciple African nations in this generation by offering a holistic biblical view of training that significantly accommodates to African cultures. In 1999, there was a need to revise the duration of both the certificate and diploma courses. The certificate course became a two-year program and the diploma course became a three-year program. The reason for the change in length was to enable students to be thoroughly familiar with a maximum of missions subjects prescribed for these levels. However, in 2003, the administration launched a general reform on the college's activities. To avoid refusing admission to mission students without previous biblical background, a one-year course in Biblical Studies was introduced as a foundational course and inserted into the certificate and diploma in missions programs.

The current objective is to maintain and vigorously pursue this reform, which has enabled the school to extend our programs to other areas of ministry. Currently, courses offered include: diploma programs in pastoral ministry, Christian education, theology, and missions, as well as a B.A. in missions program for diploma holders.

Looking to the future, the greatest challenges that the school faces are: How do graduates relate to their churches after their graduation from GEMI, as most have had only minor support from their churches during their studies? What are the difficulties encountered by the graduates on the mission field? How successful are they in applying the knowledge acquired at school? Is the training methodology effective enough to help them make an impact?

Part 2: Non-formal and Community Based Learning

How does this training program use non-formal practice and experiential learning to develop skills, and/or how does it intentionally use community to generate growth in character?

GEMI combines classroom work with field work at certificate, diploma, and degree levels. The school seeks to use the principles of adult learning, combining both enculturation and acculturation to enable students to function as missionaries to their own people as well as to people from other cultures.

Classroom Work:

No doubt most of the textbooks used in teaching missions subjects are authored by Westerners. Fortunately, most of these authors speak significantly to the African context. GEMI places much emphasis on the practicality of lectures, and urges local lecturers to use practical illustrations as much as possible to help students deepen their understanding of the course being taught. Likewise, foreign visiting lecturers are urged to open up dialogue during lectures, and encourage students to participate by making local examples in the course of their interaction. An operating assumption is that vivid interaction between two different contexts (that of the student and foreign lecturer) provides a clearer picture of the study in question.

Classroom lectures are presented in such a way that students see the urgent need for application, rather than learning theories for informative purposes only. The class assignments and examinations require answers with practical illustrations from students rather than merely reproducing what is written in the textbooks. Students are encouraged to go beyond informative scholarship to transformative scholarship. By so doing, the field work is not seen as tourism, but rather where God proves Himself as dependable, reliable, and faithful.

Field Experience:

Learning through field work implies demonstration of acquired theories. There is undoubtedly a mutual relationship between practical cross-cultural ministry involvement and the development of skills and attitudes that students need in their missions work. Even though the development of skills and attitudes is strengthened in part by the accumulation of essential classroom theories, these areas are sharpened by practical cross-cultural ministry involvement. It is much like believing the Word of God by faith after hearing a sermon or teaching. Until we experience a situation and see God in action fulfilling his promises, that Word in us is not fully alive and part of us.

To this end, field work at GEMI is one of the top priorities and is given serious consideration during the course of training. The school often identifies a mission field in a foreign culture and develops a relationship with churches in that locality. For example, the Republic of Togo has frequently been used for the students' field work. Small groups of students are assigned to each church to carry out evangelism, counsel troubled people, and preach and teach to an audience of a different cultural background. This cross-cultural experience helps students put into practice the acquired cross-cultural communication theories and measures their impact on the audience. Cultural values and beliefs are learned from their host churches and people outside the church. In fact, lively significant interactions do take place and enrich students' cross-cultural experience.

Nevertheless, during field work students face many difficulties. The problem of limited financial resources is not uncommon. They learn how God visits such situations in a very special way, beyond their expectation, and how to trust Him. They often face strong opposition from traditional authorities who find it difficult to understand that Christ could have anything to do with their local tradition. The few Christians in their community have often proven to them that Christ is entirely against their culture. Encountering these complex situations and many more, the students are able to apply their cross-cultural communication knowledge to seek appropriate solutions. Students have seen power encounters displayed many times. They have come across both surmountable and insurmountable cultural shocks. They have seen the need to go beyond the classroom prescribed theories to resolve complicated situations. However, these varied living situations play a vital role in the students' attitude formation and generate growth in character.

At the end of the course students are required to write a project or senior paper, based on a topic that reflects acquired theoretical and practical knowledge. The development of needed skills and attitudes to enhance mission work depends on the degree of serious commitment to practical cross-cultural ministry. The attitude formation and character growth of students is correlated to intentional living situations, activities or relationships.

Consequently, the above training methods consider practical cross-cultural ministry through field work a means of developing necessary skills and attitudes for successful ministry. The field work is a confirmation of the reality of what is taught in the classroom. Classroom work helps lay the foundation for the field work. It is the policy of the college not only to train the head, but also the heart and hands for service. The emphasis is not only on academics but also on spiritual and practical aspects of ministry.

In fact, teaching and learning at GEMI have taken on a new dimension. The college is no longer satisfied with academics only, which accorded little importance to the transformational aspect of ministry. While the school continues to use the services of foreign visiting lecturers, they are now required to receive a short orientation on our training methodology. This is simply because lectures were previously presented from the perspective and methods of the visitor. The administration has also resolved to progressively train local faculty staff. To this end, three lecturers have been raised up to teach at certificate and diploma levels.

Part 3: Program Improvements and Development

How has this training program progressively improved learning activities addressing the development of essential ministry and/or cross-cultural skills, or the formation of attitudes leading to character growth?

Evaluation: The process of evaluation at GEMI can be improved by carefully considering past mistakes and aiming towards more innovative training methods. Contributions to the process of teaching and learning at GEMI come from three major sources:

1. *Admission Requirements:*

The admission requirements, as described above, play an important role in the promotion of healthy training because they prescribe the qualifications of people to be trained. Past difficulties with admissions included making exceptions to increase the student body, failing to filter out uncommitted Christians, and allowing people into the program who lacked a call to missions or were improperly motivated (seeking scholarships, easy admission or those pursuing a vocation). Consequently, the development of skills and the formation of attitudes that lead to character growth were less effective. However, it is worth noting that those who truly met the admission requirements did develop in those areas. After thorough consideration, only qualified candidates are now accepted into the program – those with a commitment to Christ, and a sound call to missions. Scholarships, if available, go only to the proven needy students. Students with no previous Bible knowledge must pass through the foundational course in biblical studies during their first year. The enforcement of the admission requirements has been very helpful, even though it decreases the student population.

2. *Staff Contribution to the Process of Teaching and Learning:*

The idea of a teacher being simply a sign post has been eliminated at GEMI. Students want to see the same qualities in the teachers or other administrative staff that are demanded of them. By the grace of God, the college seeks to carefully comply with the above-mentioned criteria (see staff) in recruiting staff. Their diverse cultural backgrounds enable students to learn from a variety of contexts. The staff are a living testimony of the skills, attitudes and character needed in ministry, making it easier for students to take the steps of faith that bring about transformation. Plans for more innovative teaching methods are under exploration. The college also intends to seek and apply local traditional training methods that will help students develop skills and form attitudes leading to genuine character growth based on the students' worldview.

Although the contribution of foreign visiting lecturers has been very helpful, the need was seen to revise their collaboration. It appeared that visiting lecturers trained in the West used only those same methods in training others. The college believes that local lecturers who were trained in the West would inevitably have the same problem of using Western methodology. While some say that this issue is not of great importance, the school believes the opposite. GEMI is in the planning and development phase of an orientation short course for foreign visiting lecturers. The hope is that the course would help them to acculturate appropriately with traditional methods before giving their valued assistance. Local lecturers trained in the West would take the same orientation course.

3. *Training Methodology:*

As indicated above, training methods are based mainly based on classroom and field work. The goals set for both methods are to help the student develop cross-cultural skills and form attitudes leading to character growth. As the classroom training methods indicate, learning of abstract or propositional truth is not totally excluded but is combined with as many practical illustrations as possible. The aim is to develop improved training methods which effectively combine both formal and informal methods, bringing them to an experiential level through contextual practical illustrations. GEMI students view knowledge not just as information, but also as a means for transformation to take place in themselves, in their relationship to God and with others in their community. Students are eager to live this reality. This concept of learning also helps students to bring Scripture into fulfilment and focus, in spite of the contrary daily events that surround them. Time spent in the classroom has always been lively under the direction of the Holy Spirit and the instrumentality of the lecturer. There is no doubt that the theoretical aspects of learning in the classroom lay the foundation for the development of the student's skills, attitudes and character.

GEMI students, after acquiring needed knowledge in the classroom, test the quality of what has been entrusted to them on the field. The theoretical is made practical as they seek to impact the lives of others. In the field, students encounter many difficulties, and are encouraged and counseled by the field supervisor who provides guidance during the field assignments.

«5»

Program: Center for Cross-Cultural Missionary Training (CCMT)

Country: Argentina

Sponsor: National mission movement

Contributor: Jonathan Lewis

Part 1: Demographics

Name	Center for Cross-Cultural Missionary Training (CCMT)
Address	Villa Retiro, Cordoba, Argentina
Contact information	Phone: (54) (0351) 499-0505 Email address: ccmt@ertach.com.ar Web site: www.ccmt-online.org
Other contact	Fabian Chinnati (advanced program): fryta@ciudad.com.ar Omar Gava (master's program): ogava@ciudad.com.ar
Language of instruction	Spanish
Affiliations and sponsors	The CCMT is governed by the Asociación Campos Blancos. This is a non-denominational organization based in Cordoba. As a center, it has strong ties with the Argentine Evangelical Alliance and COMIBAM International.
Length of program	The CCMT offers an advanced program for missionary candidates that lasts approximately 10 months. It also offers an introductory 12 week course by extension and on-line, as well as two-year master's level course for missionary trainers, offered by extension in modules.
Number of students	There are typically 8-12 persons that take the advanced course.

Students:

For the advanced course, students come from all over Latin America and occasionally from Europe. They are mostly sent by their churches for the training and are serious missionary candidates. They must be 21 years old and have met the biblical training standards set by their church or sending agency. While not large in numbers, this program has seen the majority of its trainees placed in long-term cross-cultural ministries on several continents. The internet course has been taken by Spanish speakers in 30 countries. The master's level course primarily serves participants from the Southern Cone region (Argentina, Bolivia, Chile, Paraguay, and Uruguay) of Latin America, but has drawn students from as far away as Mexico. These students are generally involved in administrating missionary training programs.

Staff:

The CCMT over the years has been staffed by full-time missionaries and part-time staff. Missionary staff bring their own support. Currently, there are two full-time couples and two full-time singles in major roles of responsibility. They come from Uruguay, Chile and Argentina. Instructors are recruited for modular courses from the Southern Cone region and North America.

History and Objectives:

Argentina's first National Missions Congress was conducted in June 1986. The Argentine Evangelical Alliance's Missions Commission (Misiones Mundiales) also sponsored a series of regional consultations leading up to the continent-wide Missions Congress, COMIBAM '87, in Sao Paulo, Brazil (November, 1987). Consultations on missionary training followed and Argentine seminaries and Bible institutes began offering courses in cross-cultural missions during the next few years.

In July 1991, the Argentine Missions Commission along with COMIBAM, and the WEA Missions Commission sponsored the First Consultation on Missionary Training for the Southern Cone of Latin America. Over 60 delegates from missions and training institutions from Paraguay, Uruguay, Bolivia, Chile and Argentina were present. A descriptive profile of the entry-level missionary was developed that demonstrated the need for dedicated missionary candidate training. During an evaluation session, two-thirds of the participants identified the establishment of a regional missionary training center as the highest priority coming out of the consultation. Planning for the proposed center began shortly after this historic consultation.

In January of 1995, four families joined together to establish the new Center for Cross-Cultural Missionary Training (CCMT). In July of 1995, a large house was acquired near the center of the city that provided administrative and teaching space as well as living quarters for the residential program. The first group of candidates arrived in August. Since its inception, over 100 missionary candidates have gone through the training and many hundreds have been served through extension and internet programs. In 1998, the program was moved to a 5 hectare property on the outskirts of the city. This has enhanced the community aspect of the training as well as allowing for infrastructure growth.

Right from the start, it was apparent from the Argentine missionary training profile that candidates needed much more than lectures to equip them for the field. A whole person training approach was needed—something that would address the very character of the candidates and help them develop much needed skills. Another lesson learned early on was that field internship could not be offered simply as an option. Both the residential program and a guided internship were found to be essential to form necessary attitudes and equip candidates with the skills they needed to succeed after the training was finished.

Part 2: Non-formal and Community-Based Learning

How does this training program use non-formal practice and experiential learning to develop skills, and/or how does it intentionally use community to generate growth in character?

The curriculum was developed based on the characteristics described in the missionary training profile. As with any program, improvements have been made both to the design of the training and methods utilized. The ten month training currently includes a five-month residential program and a five-month internship among a northern Argentine tribal group. A week-long debriefing session is always held after the internship period.

The residential program is organized around modules that cover the basic areas described in the training profile. These vary in length from one-day workshops to a six-week English immersion program. Besides the coursework, informal learning is emphasized through the community experience. Facilities are limited and often cramped, providing ample opportunity to refine interpersonal skills. Students prepare meals and participate in maintenance activities. Full-time staff members live with the students and act as mentors. During this time, trainees are also involved on weekends in church-planting efforts nearby.

The period of cross-cultural immersion has historically been done as a group in the north of Argentina in native villages. This has facilitated periodic visits by staff members. Recently, students have gone to different groups and locations, including one couple who carried out their internship in Spain among Arab immigrants. This has limited staff visits. The immersion experience is the heart of the program and where the teaching of the previous five months has an opportunity to become "learning." Students follow a prescribed course of language learning, ethnographic study, and identification with the people they are living with. These are testing grounds that have allowed most of the trainees to mature their skills, understanding and commitment to cross-cultural ministry. The occasional candidate also comes away with the understanding that they are not cut out for this kind of experience or that they really need further training before heading to the field.

The debriefing session is critical. Trainees are given assignments that help them sort through their issues and find a way to communicate what they've experienced to their churches and supporters. Trainees work on the final version of a paper they have been working on during their cross-cultural internship. Staff members meet at length with candidates and they are given ample opportunity to talk about their experiences with empathic listeners. This time helps candidates sharpen their plans for their next steps. The staff also prepares a personal report for the sponsoring church or agency.

Part 3: Program Improvements and Development

How has this training program progressively improved learning activities addressing the development of essential ministry and/or cross-cultural skills, or the formation of attitudes leading to character growth?

The challenges of integral ministry training are many. Staffing is a critical element. Staff must be qualified as missionaries as well as have the desire to open their lives to students. It is nearly impossible to be intentional about speaking into trainees' lives if the staff members are not living in community with trainees. This is how we really get to know each other. Living with students means that staff members' lives are continually exposed to the students, and the dynamics of community living never seem to be dull. This dynamic produces nearly constant stress, and burn-out seems to be inevitable, if staff members aren't able to find adequate means to cope with it. We need to assure that our staff can get away periodically and that they are given a minimal amount of privacy.

Living in community also means having a facility that allows for this, and that creates challenges in the area of infrastructure. In the case of the CCMT, the original building was adequate to house a dozen students, but not to house staff members. We found out that this was a real flaw in the program. The current site is more ample and several buildings have been constructed to meet infrastructure needs. But the location is also a bit isolated from the city, and difficult to reach by public roads and transportation. The addition of broad-band internet service has been the most recent enhancement to arrive at the site.

Holding to the ideal of being "intentional" in everything we do in the program has also been very challenging. It calls for constant alertness and accountability. While guest lecturers are given outlines and oriented to the philosophy of training, they may ignore or be unable to fulfill these requests, and both their methods and content can fall short of the CCMT's goals. Training or culling these trainers is a challenge.

The nature of the training and a lack of resources encourage a tendency to add "filler" courses when adequate instructors aren't available for those courses which would most directly address specified learning objectives. There is a continuous drift towards routine lecture approaches and filling modules with "good" teaching but not that which is "essential" to meet the training profile objectives. There is a great temptation to use "free" resource persons with a "have-course-will-travel" ministry, even though the courses they offer don't meet specific training criteria. Annual reviews of the courses in light of the original training profile, as well as a review of the trainers, allow the CCMT to fight "drift" and keep up the quality of what it does.

The internships have been excellent for encouraging learning. This is proportional, however, to the trainees' engagement in the assignments that they are given. It is not easy to provide careful supervision on the field. When the whole group of trainees do their internship in the same place, it is much easier. But there is an increasing demand to be able to have a wider range of internships and this dilutes the resources that can be spent in supervision. There is no easy solution to this dilemma.

Perhaps the greatest challenge faced by the CCMT, and many other programs that have adopted this highly "hands-on" and intensive integral training approach, is lack of buy-in by churches and agencies. We have found that the minimum size of group to achieve some level of community interaction is six. It is assumed that this kind of program could handle about twenty trainees in each course, but there has not been an opportunity to prove this. Every session struggles to meet minimum group requirements to run the session. This puts pressure on entry qualifications with the result that candidates are sometimes accepted that don't meet initial screening standards. This has a negative impact on the program and begins a downward spiral.

The CCMT has built a fairly strong reputation over time, and that is helping to assure an adequate group will form for each session. The internet and extension courses as well as the web site have helped in marketing and recruitment. But the main challenge remains in convincing churches and agencies that they must provide integral cross-cultural training to their candidates if they hope to have them succeed on the field.

«6»

Center: Focus Team Leadership Training (FTLT)
Country: South Africa
Sponsor: National mission movement
Contributor: Adriaan Adams

Part 1: Demographics

Name	Focus Team Leadership Training
Address	669 Church Street, Arcadia, Pretoria, South Africa 0082 PO Box 36147, Menlopark, Pretoria, South Africa 0102
Contact information	Phone: +27 (0) 12 343 5206 Fax: +27 (0) 12 343 1167 Email: info@ftlt.org Website: www.ftlt.org
Language of instruction	English
Affiliations and sponsors	FTLT functions and serves interdenominationally and receives funding and support from various sources that believe in the vision and calling of the program. The school started under the covering of the World Mission Centre (WMC) but has recently registered as its own organization.
Length of program	11 months
Number of students	Between 8 and 20 students per session

Students:

Focus Team Leadership Training (FTLT) trainees are drawn from our interaction with churches, secondary schools, youth groups, universities and various other learning institutions. Although there is no age bracket, our target group is between 18 and 35 years of age. Any person interested in doing their missionary training at FTLT needs to be, first of all, a believer in Christ that has gone through a basic discipleship process. Secondly, the minimum educational requirement is a grade 12 school certificate or equivalent.

Nearly every person that has gone through FTLT is serving in some ministry capacity. Some are mobilizing their congregations to missions, while others are at university mobilizing their friends. Others have gone into the business world, supporting missions financially. On a more full-time basis there are graduates currently serving the FTLT in a leadership capacity, some at the World Mission Centre in the office, and also in Malawi, reaching out to the people along the southern part of the lake. Another has started a mission school with the help of WMC in Zanzibar, training locals to reach out to their own people.

Staff:

No person can become a staff member unless they have done the year of training and served for two years as a student leader. Student leader recruitment is done according to the tasks at hand, cross-cultural experience and individual potential as observed while in training. Key values attached to our staff are a personal relationship and commitment to Jesus Christ as Lord and Savior, plus devotion to the task of world evangelization in obedience to God. They must not only be willing to see change, but be committed to act for change to occur. We purposely go out of our way to have an international staff. This is essential to give the students a practical, first hand, cross-cultural experience.

History and Objectives:

Early in 2003 a group of young people in South Africa came together and shared their frustrations in ministry with one another. Through these discussions and previous research they came to the following conclusion. *"...we can wait until we are in leadership to change the way things are done or start now to influence our generation and the upcoming generation so that when we are in leadership things are already moving in a different direction..."* Through this dynamic process Focus Team Leadership Training was birthed.

At FTLT we make use of the *Live School* curriculum. The *Live School* is a video curriculum developed by the World Mission Centre, available on DVD. An International coalition was assembled to design the curriculum by Pastor Willie Crew, founder and International Director of World Mission Centre. Some of the important issues addressed are:

- Character development.
- The high rate of attrition.
- The difficulty of adjusting to cultural and ethnic customs.
- The skills needed for a successful missions outreach.

The school has a policy of continual change. Our objective is to train young people who will impact their sphere of influence through a focused lifestyle, working with others in a team, expressing godly character and continuing to develop themselves and those around them into better leaders.

Part 2: Non-formal and Community-Based Learning

How does this training program use non-formal practice and experiential learning to develop skills, and/or how does it intentionally use community to generate growth in character?

The length of our training program is 11 months. For the first month, the major focus is on character development and dealing with personal issues of the past. Thereafter the students are introduced to the biblical fundamental issues regarding missions; why missions, who we are in Christ, perseverance in ministry, etc. In the fourth month they are taken on a one month "Bush Phase" training where they are exposed to some of the realities they might face in pioneering a field; sleeping in tents, limited water, food preparation on an open fire, hiking, training in radio communication, navigation and even evacuation. After the bush phase there is a greater focus on the practical issues important to missions; Cross-Cultural Communication, Cultural Anthropology, Ethnographic Process, Chronological Approach, etc. For the last three months students are sent on outreach to one of the least reached people groups of the world. After their outreach they go through a re-entry phase lasting one week, after which comes graduation.

Because of our understanding of the importance of personal development for both life and ministry, FTLT includes the following non-formal practices in their training:

Dance and Drama: There are designated days where the trainees are exposed to different forms of art as a tool for communicating the Gospel and in developing their skills and creativity.

Street Evangelism: The trainees' ability to communicate the Gospel is shaped by weekly exposure in the streets where they are expected to share their faith. This is specifically and purposely done to ensure that all grow in their ability to interact and effectively communicate to people with whom no prior contact had been made.

Weekend Ministries/Mobilization: Students visit and spend time with various churches and ministries on weekends and learn the different dynamics involved in practical ministry such as planning, coordination and teamwork, as well as public speaking/preaching and leadership skills.

Fundays: To ensure the trainees' wholesome growth and development, days are set aside for everyone to go out and have fun as a team or with family and friends.

Fundraising: The ideas and participation in organized fundraising activities enables us to validate the students' commitment to what they believe God has called them into, as well as to check their individual attitudes.

Physical Training: Physical training is designed to build the student's stamina for physical challenges in the mission field and for general health and fitness as we target some of the geographically remote areas where the physical wellbeing of a missionary is as important as their spiritual wellbeing.

Bush Phase/Survival Training: This is specifically designed to prepare the trainee for the harsh realities they are likely to face in the field. Trainees are purposely put under maximum pressure with very minimal provisions and accessories, a reality in most mission fields. Key values taught in this period are attitude, excellence, determination, perseverance and commitment.

Communal Housing: All the trainees stay in a hostel setup. Everyone rotates as a house leader and is given various responsibilities over others.

Menial Tasks: These tasks are intended to build and cultivate in the trainees the principle of diligence, faithfulness and general attitude to work and leadership.

Time of Encouragement: This is a time during which trainees and leadership mould and shape one another as they lay their lives before the group for correction, rebuke and teaching.

Coaching/Close Monitoring: Each FTLT staff member is charged with responsibility over a given number of trainees with whom he/she walks a closer road through the whole training period. His/her role is to train by walking side-by-side with his/her group in a Christ-centered relationship.

Three Month Outreach: This is the final phase of the training during which the trainees are sent on an outreach/internship where all the theory and informal learning becomes a reality.

Pastoral Oversight: During the three month outreach phase, an FTLT oversight team visits the trainees in the mission field to encourage, motivate, challenge and prepare the team further for effective ministry.

Basic Motor Mechanics: During this training time each student is taught how to look after the vehicles God has entrusted to them for use and to empower them to understand and address some of the common mechanical breakdowns they might face while on outreach.

Part 3: Program Improvements and Development

How has this training program progressively improved learning activities addressing the development of essential ministry and/or cross-cultural skills, or the formation of attitudes leading to character growth?

The lecture part of the program is more formal with pre-recorded sessions presented on DVD in the presence of a class facilitator who conducts a discussion session after every presentation. All classes run from 08:00 hours to 13:00 hours when the students break for lunch. Various activities occupy the afternoon session, from spring-cleaning and office duties to street ministry.

Four days per week, students meet for joint worship and devotions before the class presentation commences. Intercession takes place every Thursday and during this time each student is encouraged to share what he/she believes God has revealed to them. This creates the opportunity for everyone to grow in their walk with God.

FTLT has created a dynamic sub-culture in which both staff and trainees relate in a serving leadership empowerment process based on a Christ-centered relationship. House leaders stay with the trainee, sharing their lives with them.

You cannot expect of others what you cannot deliver. Based on this, upon arrival the students are treated to a special time in which the leadership literally does everything for the students as they seek to model a standard of excellence and clarify expectations. All the trainees will eventually be fully responsible for setting tables, preparing meals, doing dishes, and maintaining the best possible standard of hygiene, health and cleanliness.

Interpersonal relationships, dignity and respect for others are key ingredients in the process. Everyone must be at the table and pray together before anybody can start eating. Each person has a set place at the table. No room is allowed for gossip, name-calling or slander. If anyone has an issue with another person, the biblical principle is followed in facing that person, before talking to another brother or going the third step of approaching the leadership.

FTLT leadership is seeking to develop people who are part of the solution, as opposed to being part of the problem. As such, the FTLT leadership intentionally withdraws from certain active leadership roles to allow for the emergence and empowerment of natural leadership abilities in the trainees. The leaders live open lives, and where possible, take advantage of God's *kairos* moments in the students' lives to offer further guidance and instruction.

On a weekly basis the trainees are purposely sent out to share and learn what God is doing in their own lives and in the lives of those they meet. During the weekends they are exposed to actual ministry in various churches. At FTLT, teamwork is a key principle. The leadership therefore identifies a church ahead of time where all the trainees will attend the normal Sunday service. Due to the intensity and the ideals of the training phase the leadership tries to minimize outside influences that easily sway students from their focus.

Twice a week, the students have physical training. Team building becomes a key element and not just physical fitness. Although we believe in healthy competition, a team is only as strong as the weakest link or team member. Thus the trainees are brought to the point of taking responsibility for one another. This principle is further reiterated during the bush phase period when strategic thinking and planning, communication skills, submission and personal disciplines are put to the test.

FTLT firmly believes that true leaders are people of character, and that it is character that gives credibility with people. We therefore believe strongly in the "CAR" of leadership: Character, Accountability and Responsibility.

The leadership keeps a watchful eye on each trainee and has weekly meetings where observations are reported and discussed in detail. We also apply the use of a "Character Assessment Sheet" in which each student is assessed and areas needing attention are determined so that the leadership, together with the trainee, can work at improvement.

The three months of outreach are the climax of the training. The trainees are sent as a team to a pre-selected least reached people group where they'll spend time involved in cross-cultural ministry. During this time, feedback happens weekly between the teams in the field and the base office, either through radio or other channels of communication.

An oversight team extends pastoral care to the field as well as prepares the trainees for re-entry after the period of outreach. A special debriefing is arranged for the team when the students will reflect on and share those special things that shaped their lives or touched others while they were in the field. To facilitate this process, trainees are required to maintain a journal from which to share.

During this final time the trainees give a comprehensive evaluation of the entire training program as they experienced it throughout the year. This enables us to make necessary improvements to strengthen the program and make it as relevant as possible. While FTLT may be a young school, our aspiration is to see a generation that will rise up prepared to live a non-compromising lifestyle for God.

« 7 »

Program: Capacitación Misionera Transcultural (CMT)

Country: Mexico

Sponsor: Church-based

Contributor: Kerry Olson/Juan Carlos Gómez

Part 1: Demographics

Name	Capacitación Misionera Transcultural (CMT) del Instituto Cristo para las Naciones de México, (Cross-Cultural Missionary Training, Christ for the Nations Institute)
Address	San Felipe #138 Col. Xoco, C.P. 03330 México D.F, MEXICO
Contact information	Phone: (52-55) 5604-0449, 5604-0500 Fax: (52-55) 5604-9235 Email: secremisiones@hotmail.com Web-site: www.idportodoelmundo.com/cmt
Other contact	Kerry A. Olson kerry_olson@hotmail.com
Language of instruction	Spanish
Affiliations and sponsors	Open to all churches. The school is sponsored by the Amistad Cristiana church in Mexico City and is affiliated with Christ for the Nations in Dallas, Texas and Bethany College of Missions in Minneapolis, Minnesota.
Length of program	4 years – all students must have two years of Bible at our Bible institute or other. We offer one year of missions studies with a required one year cross-cultural internship.
Number of students	8 - 15

Students:

The admission requirements for Cross-Cultural Missionary Training of Christ for the Nations (CMT) is the following: 21 years old or more, high school diploma (though many have college degrees), a well-defined call to the mission field and commitment to cross-cultural missions, active concurrent service in a local church, the spiritual support from a local church, pastoral approval, and three acceptable references. Graduates tend to be involved in church planting, Bible translation, broadcasting ministry, evangelism amongst the unreached, mobilization and bi-occupational missions. Trainees serve the Lord primarily in Central and South America, Spain, North Africa, and China.

Staff:

CMT enjoys the advantage of being associated with the mega-church, Amistad Cristiana, one of the largest congregations in Mexico. The training staff are drawn from this pool, providing they have adequate experience, calling, passion and teaching ability. Most have been on the mission field and are experts in their field of study with master's degrees or the equivalent.

History and Objectives:

Christ for the Nations Mexico has operated as a Bible school since 1985 and began the specialization in missions in the year 2000. The school has been a tremendous asset for the advancement of the missions vision of the church, Amistad Cristiana. Students have served and are serving full time in Nicaragua, Panama, Paraguay, Ecuador, Spain, North Africa, Senegal, Kenya, India, the Philippines, Russia, China, England and with three indigenous groups in Mexico. One of the challenges this school faces is the retention of staff, since many end up on the field.

The immediate objectives are: to increase the number of students studying and going out on cross-cultural internships, to increase promotion of the school outside of Amistad Cristiana, to place workers in North Africa, India and China. The greatest challenge for the school is to promote the school outside of the church Amistad Cristiana.

Part 2: Non-formal and Community-Based Learning

How does this training program use non-formal practice and experiential learning to develop skills, and/or how does it intentionally use community to generate growth in character?

The experience of the staff and school has demonstrated that attitude is more essential than aptitude. As such, the school strives to get to know the students and to have a healthy balance between classes (20 hours per week), that is, what students must KNOW for effective ministry, and what the student must BE (in terms of spiritual dynamics, character qualities and interpersonal skills), and what the student must be CAPABLE OF DOING.

Most of the students come from the congregation Amistad Cristiana (around 10,000 in membership). The school is not residential, so students live at home. Although this can pose a challenge to getting to know the students, the school requires students to go through the Bible school for two years, as well as the mission school and a one year cross-cultural internship.

During the mission school, students go on monthly evangelistic outreaches to Mexico's indigenous peoples. They are mentored and have contact with teachers and the director of the school. They spend time in small groups in staff homes and other outings. They are also exposed to other Latin missionaries and sending agencies. Each mission candidate is required to serve in some capacity in their local church.

Part 3: Program Improvements and Development

How has this training program progressively improved learning activities addressing the development of essential ministry and/or cross-cultural skills, or the formation of attitudes leading to character growth?

Christ for the Nations Mexico instituted an interview session with the leadership from both the school and church in order to confirm a candidate's readiness to be sent out on the one-year cross-cultural internship. The internship requires the student to be under a mentor (a local pastor or experienced missionary) and to be learning language and culture as part of their field experience. Ministry is of secondary importance during the field experience. Internship evaluations are essential.

A significant need at this time is to strengthen the re-entry orientation for students returning from internship in order to better reflect on their experiences. The school is improving the methodology of field-based learning through increased communication; monthly reports and times of reflection and required reading.

«8»

Program: Logos Mission School
Country: South Africa
Sponsor: Church-based
Contributor: Pieter Vermeulen

Part 1: Demographics

Name	Logos Mission School
Address	3 Hebron Street Oakglenn, Bellville, Western Cape, South Africa
Contact information	Phone: +27 21 9193338 Fax: +27 21 9198871 Name: Pieter Vermeulen Email address: pieter@logos.org.za Web site: www.logos.org.za
Language of instruction	English
Affiliations and sponsors	Logos Christian Church
Length of program	1 year
Number of students	12

Students:

Students come to the school by invitation. We select only students who have a relationship with our church or with an organization we are partnering with – like the World Mission Centre. The main focus of our school is to train students from countries where little mission training is available. Our school will train them to start programs in their own countries. They must be involved in mission work and have a vision to start a mission training program, or be a key person who would be involved in reaching an unreached people group. Most students are mission trainers and have come from countries such as Uganda, Congo, Swaziland, Lesotho, Transkei, and Botswana.

Staff:

Because we are a church-based training center, we have volunteers from the church assisting with practical things like meals and student care, and the staff of the church providing for administrative services. Instructors are provided primarily through the *Live School* curriculum (www.liveschool.org), but we also use experienced missionaries and leaders from our church to teach. Those that teach all have at least ten years of field experience.

History and Objectives:

The Logos Mission School partners with the Live School in order to train trainers who will be involved in starting training centers in the Commonwealth of Independent States (CIS) and southern Africa. The school has been in operation for only two years.

Our greatest challenge is to maintain adequate contact with our students and assist them to be effective on the field. One of our objectives is to connect each student with a cell group in the church to ensure a lifelong relationship with them while they are in the field. The cell groups will visit them in the field and provide member care. The objective of the leadership of the school is to assist them in establishing an indigenous missionary training program.

In this program description, Parts 2 and 3 are combined.

Part 2: Non-formal and Community-Based Learning

How does this training program use non-formal practice and experiential learning to develop skills, and/or how does it intentionally use community to generate growth in character?

Part 3: Program Improvements and Development

How has this training program progressively improved learning activities addressing the development of essential ministry and/or cross-cultural skills, or the formation of attitudes leading to character growth?

The Logos Mission School course consists of four legs. The first leg focuses on character development and includes courses on discipleship, relationships, intercession, spiritual authority, and spiritual gifts. The main emphasis of all these courses is to put students in an environment that exposes them to the biblical standard of character. The lecturers we use in this leg will spend much time with the students in individual and group counseling. We also spend much time in prayer. One course is called *The Plumbline* and deals mainly with issues of rebellion and rejection. Our belief is that character is "caught not taught," so the lecturers' personal lives and interaction with the students are important. Also, during this first leg, an experienced mission counselor meets individually with each of the students. The duration of this portion is around two months. We have developed an evaluation process that defines all aspects of character/leadership. Students evaluate each other in a group context using this evaluation process, addressing each aspect. This first leg is the foundation to this evaluation process, but the evaluating does not occur until the last two months of the program, because prior to that time the students do not know each other well enough to conduct an accurate evaluation.

The second leg is a one-month cross-cultural boot camp, where students get to know the realities of the mission field. The boot camp follows the first leg that deals with character, because character is tested during the boot camp. The aim of the boot camp is to put the students through difficult circumstances, because this inevitably brings out "bad" attitudes, and negative aspects of character become evident. True character is revealed under stress. This process produces a self-awareness that serves as an opportunity for growth.

The boot camp is completed on a farm. When students arrive, they set up a base, dig latrines, build a kitchen and clear a parade ground where they will be drilled in military fashion. During the boot camp they are put under severe discipline. For example, they wake up at 5 a.m. and start making a fire for breakfast. One team will cook for the day, and another will clean. Then at 7 a.m. they will all be on the parade ground. The boot camp attempts to simulate the harsh realities of difficult field experiences. During the month in boot camp they will go on two hikes (treks) of about 150 km, each. They are also taught practical things like first aid, survival skills, map reading and trekking. During this second leg, students learn about team building and practice working on teams.

The third leg focuses on missiological theory, but with a strong emphasis on cross-cultural ministry. Through the Live School curriculum, students are given courses such as: Overview of Theology, The Books of the Bible (OT and NT), Church Planting, The Book of Acts, Perseverance in Ministry, Folk Religion, Islam, The Chronological Approach, How to study the Bible, Preaching, Cross-Cultural Communication, Finance, Cross-Cultural Anthropology, the Kingdom of God and Community Development.

The final leg of training is ministry experience. This involves being part of a cell group during their training and also reaching out to one of our communities on a weekly basis. This practical leg is done in an area where we have established a church, like Lesotho or an informal settlement close to the campus. The church has between 600-800 members (including children) and is an independent church, though part of a wider network. The cell groups are located all over Cape Town wherever our members live. We divide the students among the cell groups, based on a number of criteria – where the cell members are doing mission work, what relationships are already established, and the type of cell group (family, youth), etc. We will send the married students with families to participate in family cells. If the student is unmarried we will send him or her to the youth cell groups. If someone in the cell group has a heart for working in a specific area, when a student from that area attends the school, they will be put into that cell group.

During the training, students live in community and share a room with another person from a different culture and language (last year we had seven nationalities and this year we have eight nationalities). English is the official language. Every student is taken out of his or her culture and put into an entirely new culture during their training. This in itself is a training experience. Church life is experienced through the cell groups. The community outreach is done with an experienced leader who introduces them to the community. After a while the students are left on their own to minister in the community. Furthermore, every week the student leader changes, and after leading for one week, we evaluate them on the leadership skills exhibited. Student assessment is not only completed by staff, but every student takes part in evaluating each other. These assessments include the mission course and different aspects of the Christian life.

As a final assignment, all students must write a 20 page mini-thesis on their vision and future ministry. The purpose of this assignment is to help them formulate a clear vision, and since this is a church-based training program, it also gives the leadership time to pray with them and assist them in the formulation and understanding of their calling. In this way, they help each student prepare him/herself for ministry.

«9»

Program: Gateway Missionary Training Centre

Country: Canada

Sponsor: Mission agency

Contributor: Rob Brynjolfson

Part 1: Demographics:

Name	Gateway Missionary Training Centre and Gateway Training for Cross-Cultural Service
Address	21233 – 32nd Avenue, Langley, BC V2Z 2E7, Canada
Contact information	Ike Agawin (Director) c/o info@gatewaytraining.org
Other contact	Bev Lombard (Registrar) info@gatewaytraining.org Website: www.gatewaytraining.org
Language of instruction	English
Affiliations and sponsors	WEC International and other educational training partners Educational training partners: • Northwest Baptist Seminary: part of the ACTS consortium (Associated Canadian Theological Seminaries) • Christ for the Nations International, Surrey, BC • Pacific Life Bible College, Surrey BC

Length of program	Gateway has two programs of study:
	 • The Gateway program (TRAX):
	   o 7 months (non-certificate): 4 months of residential training followed by a 90 day cross-cultural internship, with a one week re-entry debriefing.
	   o Certificate in Bible and Mission with partner institutions: This 11 month program includes the 7 month Gateway program (already mentioned) plus a prior semester (4 months) of Bible and theology at one of the partner institutions. This is an accredited one-year certificate.
	 • English for Missionaries (E-TRAX): 7 months (May till December with August off). This program is designed to improve the English of missionary candidates seeking to serve in a context where spoken English is required.

Number of students	Between 6 and 15 students per session

Students:

Students come to Gateway from a number of sources. Some come through our educational partners who use the Gateway program as their missions program. Others are sent by WEC International. Frequently these students come from the international sending bases that want their candidates to learn English and experience training in a different context. Gateway believes it has a mandate to serve the broader mission community and often receives students channeled to Gateway through other missionary agencies. Gateway requires adequate English and Christian maturity. Other entry-level qualifications are set by the sending churches and agencies for their candidates. Gateway will only accept students into the program who are sent as missionaries by their local church or a missionary agency. Trainees come to the center with the intention of entering cross-cultural service, usually focused on one of two tracks: church planting or children in crisis. Our graduates are spread throughout the world with a strong representation in the difficult access countries.

Staff:

The center is staffed by volunteer personnel who have previously enjoyed a cross-cultural missionary experience. The majority are affiliated with WEC International. In the past, Gateway has had the participation of non-WEC staff, covering duties ranging from maintenance to executive director. Since Gateway is a residential community, with trainees and staff living together in the same building, the ability to relate well to others is critical. The staff are expected to model the values of a person committed to missionary life. This means that not only did they serve in effective cross-cultural ministry, but that they obviously enjoyed life overseas. Experience and passion for cross-cultural ministry are more important than academic credentials.

History and Objectives:

Gateway Missionary Training Centre operates as the North American missionary training center for WEC International (Worldwide Evangelization for Christ). Gateway serves WEC International and the broader missions community by training missionaries for overseas service, specializing in church planting and ministry to children in crisis. The present director of the center is Ike Agawin. Rob Brynjolfson is Program Director.

In 1991, WEC Canada decided that the changing educational context of North America, evident in the diminishing emphasis on overseas missionary training, justified their vision to start a training center entirely focused on preparing overseas workers. WEC envisioned a one-year hands-on missionary training program that did not compete with traditional Bible schools, colleges and seminaries in Canada. The vision became reality after five years and one unsuccessful attempt. The training center celebrated its tenth anniversary in 2006.

As in the past, the objective of Gateway is to continue to serve the missionary community of western Canada, the educational partners and WEC International. Gateway faces the challenge of increasing its student body. The staff has accepted the goal of establishing a second intake (or session), and by 2007, hopes to offer both fall and winter sessions. The ongoing challenges of running a training program like Gateway are to ensure adequate staffing and adequate student numbers. Since staff are unsalaried volunteers, the former is a challenge, but Gateway has never suffered from urgent financial pressures.

Part 2: Non-formal and Community-Based Learning

How does this training program use non-formal practice and experiential learning to develop skills, and/or how does it intentionally use community to generate growth in character?

Gateway was committed to an integral training approach from its inception. There was a clear mandate: a one-year hands-on missionary training program, but everyone had a different idea of what that meant. Some thought that Gateway should be a concentrated Bible program; others thought that the program should reflect a battery of missiological courses. Underlying these early concepts was the assumption that learning would primarily take place in the classroom. Gateway faced the problem of how to move from the familiar traditional schooling model to a truly integral approach to missionary training. The integral equation of "understanding, being and doing" was weighted in favor of the cognitive domain of understanding.

A commitment to growth in the affective domain was never an issue at Gateway. WEC International has always expressed a commitment to the value of community living and Gateway adopted this commitment from the very beginning. The program did not start until a facility was provided where staff and students could live together, with the intention of growing in desired character traits, spirituality and attitudes. However, the assumption was that this growth would simply happen as a result of "accidental" lessons arising from the context of community living.

The difficulty Gateway faced related to the expressed commitment to develop skills and attitudes, while maintaining a program that was significantly lopsided toward cognitive development. The next section tells the story of the process of evaluation and the improvements that led to the needed adjustments in this area. Suffice it to say that Gateway came to a determination that 50% of the learning would be directed at needed cross-cultural skills and abilities. This meant sacrificing classroom learning in favor of a structured and supervised cross-cultural internship, as well as practicums in church planting, urban ministry, and service to children in crisis.

The cross-cultural internships are an attractive program element for missionary candidates. Students usually bring their own internship ideas and come motivated to learn about missions under the agency they wish to serve. Gateway quickly learned the importance of coaching supervisors through the internship experience, clarifying expectations and setting up lines of communication. Most internships have been very successful, in spite of a broad diversity of missionary agencies, fields and teams. Gateway students arrive on the field with planned instructional activities that last the full 90 days. The culture and language instruction is pre-packaged, so students are kept occupied and do not present a burden to the field structure.

Part 3: Program Improvements and Development

How has this training program progressively improved learning activities addressing the development of essential ministry and/or cross-cultural skills, or the formation of attitudes leading to character growth?

Gateway undertakes annual cyclical reviews of the program and periodic full evaluations of the training programs. These serve to identify weaknesses and address concerns. Over the years, a number of improvements have been implemented. The following is the story of the initial development during the critical early years of operation.

Through research from various Mission Commission texts, Gateway began with a commitment to develop an outcomes-based training program. Initially, the staff simply used a profile inherited from WEC International and adapted it to the aims and goals of Gateway. Later, during the lull of the summer months, the staff took the time to develop their own missionary profile using the steps outlined in *Establishing Ministry Training*. Through this consensus process the staff determined to redevelop the program into an outcomes-based training program. This contributor believes Gateway faced the problem that frustrates many programs: the commitment in theory to an outcomes based approach, and perhaps even a lovely missionary training profile, but without following through with curricular adjustments which ensure that adequate methods are used in appropriate contexts to address all of the training needs expressed in the profile. For example, during the first two years, the hands-on elements that emerged were limited to evangelistic skirmishes by urban ministry in Vancouver, or aboard ships in the harbor in collaboration with the Lighthouse Seaman's Centre. These experiences certainly had value, and significant learning took place. However, the distribution of contact hours and learning activities was still overly biased to the classroom.

One of the first changes was a deeper commitment to integral ministry training. This meant training not only in knowledge, but also in desirable character qualities and skills. For example, attempts were made to make the residential program more intentional so that the need for growth in character and attitude could be addressed with more certainty.

A mentoring program was developed to deepen the intentional effort at character growth. Eventually a "Character and Attitude Training" program was developed using role-plays and simulations, which served to get people in touch with the emotions that can lead to changes in attitudes. Specific skills were identified (such as cross-cultural communication of the Gospel) and learning activities were designed to thrust students out of their comfort zones and give them opportunities to develop communication skills.

In the second year of operation, a visit by Jonathan Lewis turned into an *ad-hoc* consultation, which prompted Gateway staff and stakeholders to take the next step – to change the outcomes to specific learning objectives and activities. If one truly desires to develop students' critical cross-cultural skills, the learning activities must reflect this commitment. Thus, a significant number of classroom hours were replaced by a cross-cultural internship. The residential component was reduced to 15 weeks and the new internship was set at 90 days. The internship was strengthened by a debriefing experience, designed to produce further reflection and to synthesize the learning achieved by the residential component, classroom hours and the practical experience of the internship[1].

Partnerships:

Gateway found itself in the awkward position of being set up to serve the training needs of its parent organization, whose training requirements were more rigorous than Gateway's. WEC International required two years of Bible and theology, so Gateway alumni were forced to seek further schooling in order to join the mission agency. During Jonathan Lewis' time as director, the Lord provided the opportunity to meet Rob Buzza, the president of Pacific Life Bible College in nearby Surrey, BC. Gateway needed to develop Bible and theological training for its students, and Pacific Life Bible College wanted to expand their program to offer a degree in missions. A partnership was struck that suited the needs of both institutions. This model has worked so well that partnerships were developed with another college, Christ for the Nations, and also a denominational seminary affiliated with the Associated Canadian Theological Seminaries in Langley, BC.

Gateway possibly could have avoided some of its early growth pains, and the program could have filled more rapidly, if partnerships had been developed before actually launching the program. On the other hand, the important partnerships that are now enjoyed by Gateway would not have emerged if Gateway didn't already have a program to offer. It was the lean years that demonstrated the need to value others in the body of Christ. WEC International made significant investments in property, time and energy to make Gateway successful. Even so, the program is viable only with strong partnerships. No single agency has the wherewithal to produce the numbers of trainees needed to fill the programs. In the formation of a training program, it is wise to develop a coalition of stakeholders from the onset.

Conclusion:

If integral ministry training requires an appropriate balance of the three contexts of classroom, community and culture, then this will always be an ongoing developmental process. This case study ended by looking at partnerships because, in the long run, training programs, whether run by a school, church or agency, will recognize that they cannot effectively address every area of the triad. However, by valuing other members of the body of Christ and partnering with other entities, the weak elements of a training program can be bolstered and strengthened. Besides glorifying God, it produces excellent training results.

---

1   These internships may occur anywhere in the world as long as the conditions and requirements are met. Since most initial visitor's visas are granted for 90 days, it seemed expedient to maintain the internship for no longer than this period.

«10»

Program: Youth With A Mission (YWAM)—University of the Nations

Country: International

Sponsor: Mission agency

Contributor: Thomas A. Bloomer, International Provost

Part 1: Demographics:

Name	University of the Nations (Youth With A Mission)
Address	Office of the Provost Les Ormeaux 1268 Burtigny, Switzerland
Contact information	Phone: +41223663915 Email address: tom.bloomer@uofn.edu Web site: www.uofn.edu
Language of instruction	50 languages of instruction
Affiliations and sponsors	The University of the Nations is a network of the missionary training centers of Youth With A Mission. We have no formal ties to any denomination, but many working relationships with local churches from scores of denominations.

Length of program	Discipleship Training School (required): 12 weeks of lectures followed by 8-12 weeks of cross-cultural outreach.
	
	Students may continue taking other 12 week modular courses which lead to the following degrees:
	    Associate's degree – two and a half years
	    Bachelor's degree – four years
	    Master's degree – two and a half years
	
	These are offered in 7 colleges/faculties.

Number of students	Each year there are approximately 10,000 students enrolled in the DTS programs, and approximately 6,000 students enrolled in the post-DTS modules.

Students:

The students come from all over the world, as over 200 different passports are found in our database. Our biggest number of students comes from the USA, followed by Koreans, Brazilians, and Indians. There are no entry-level requirements other than being a Christian, although we do encourage completion of secondary school. Since we also want to include those who have not had access to secondary school, we have different remedial programs to help them come up to speed in their study capacity.

YWAMers serve currently in around 160 nations, and we have had at least short-term ministries in every country of the world. They enter all kinds of ministries, and often start new ones, such as Cowboys With A Mission. We train in diverse areas, such as Primary Health Care, Family Counseling, Education, Digital Communication, TESOL, etc. More examples may be found on www.ywam.org

Staff:

Staff are often recent graduates of our schools, educational theory and practice indicating that the best teachers are those closest in age and experience to the students. They are selected on the basis of teachability, hunger for God, and passion for the ministry that the school trains for. There are no academic requirements for staff or leaders. We make an effort to have as many cultures as possible represented both in the staff and in the student population.

Some staff stay on long-term, and many of us have 20-30 years experience in YWAM and in missionary training. Many of these more experienced missionaries travel and teach in different schools. We also rely heavily on visiting speakers, both from the nation where the training center is located, and international speakers. All who teach must be committed Christians who uphold the authority of the Bible.

History and Objectives:

YWAM began its first nonformal missionary training program in 1969, which then multiplied into 30-40 training centers in about 30 countries. In 1978 the University of the Nations was begun at our Kona, Hawaii campus, networking the existing YWAM schools and beginning many new ones. Presently about 900 different schools, seminars and for-credit outreaches are found in our catalog.

Ongoing efforts in quality control, staff training, and development of teaching resources have made our schools more effective. The use of interactive video conferencing has brought the teaching of international speakers to several locations at once, and is much appreciated especially by our people in remote areas of the world.

Our University's goal is to be a "multiplier for missions", and we have, in fact, trained 150,000 people who have done at least short-term missions. Many new ministries have begun out of our University of the Nations courses, especially the Leadership Training Schools, in which the course project is always the planning of new ministries by the students.

Our biggest ongoing challenge is staff training, since we constantly have new people coming on board. We are also endeavoring to prepare for the Matthean dimension of the Great Commission, discipling the nations and teaching them all that Jesus commanded. We do not just train missionaries, our University is a missions delivery system, and we want to learn better how to minister as a University.

Part 2: Non-formal and Community-Based Learning

How does this training program use non-formal practice and experiential learning to develop skills, and/or how does it intentionally use community to generate growth in character?

The University of the Nations network is composed of 300 missionary training centers located in 110 nations. Instruction takes place in 50 languages in around 110 nations. The required first course for all potential YWAM staff is the Discipleship Training School (DTS), which consists of 12 weeks of lecture phase followed by 8-12 weeks of cross-cultural outreach. The DTS is also the required first course for all those wishing to pursue further studies with us. Approximately 10,000 students take this course each year.

Many go straight into missions after the DTS, and then take further 12-week modules of instruction with us when they need further training as their ministries develop. These modules, which we call "schools", may be combined to make up the following degree programs: Associate's, (two and a half years of study), Bachelor's (four years), or Master's (two and a half years). Since every one of our schools in our seven college/faculties is focused on missions, any degree program or progress toward a degree consists of missionary preparation. The number of those taking post-DTS schools with us is about 6,000 per year.

As mentioned above, YWAM's first schools were nonformal. The formal dimension was added when we networked the schools into a University, beginning in 1978. At our first University of the Nations workshop, in 1989 in Lausanne, Switzerland, Dr. Ted Ward told us that holding formal and nonformal elements together in a University was impossible. Although we have managed to do so until now, we live in this constant tension.

Since our schools and training centers are cross-cultural, and since everyone begins with DTS with its cross-cultural outreach, a cross-cultural focus is part of our DNA. In addition, three short-term outreaches are required for graduation from the B.A. program, and also study in two different cultures (normally on two different continents).

As part of our monitoring of the formal-nonformal tension, each school leader is required to document for the University leadership not just the content and assignments of the course, but also the more nonformal elements. For example, we require three hours of intercession per week, and two hours of practical work serving the community every day. Worship is also required in each course, as well as a one-on-one meeting with a staff member once a week.

A part of each course grade is based on character growth, and for the DTS the pass-fail grade depends almost entirely on character assessment, the DTS being the least formal of all our programs.

Staff and students live together and eat meals together in the YWAM communities, and ongoing discipling is an emphasis for everybody. We encourage each training center to be a learning and worshipping community.

Part 3: Program Improvements and Development

How has this training program progressively improved learning activities addressing the development of essential ministry and/or cross-cultural skills, or the formation of attitudes leading to character growth?

Since the drift in Christian institutions of higher learning is always toward the formal, we have had to be more and more strict concerning the maintaining of the nonformal elements of our schools mentioned above. School leaders have to re-register their schools every three years, which gives us a chance to assess tendencies toward drift.

A less formal method of ongoing quality control is the traveling teaching ministry of many of our staff and leaders. As they teach a week in one school after another, they are also monitoring trends and giving input into the staff and leadership in each place.

Although staff training has been part of YWAM since the 1970's, a more focused effort in this area was begun just five years ago. An approved list of competencies has been drawn up for DTS staff and leaders, and is being developed for the staff of other schools. A best practices document for DTS outreaches provides guidelines for fruitful cross-cultural ministry.

Staff training workshops are multiplying, and staff training modules are in development. The Internet opens up new possibilities for staff to acquire competencies in different areas.

«11»

Organization: New Tribes Mission

Country: United States of America

Sponsor: Mission agency

Contributor: Robert Strauss[1]

Demographics:

Name	New Tribes Mission (NTM) Missionary Training Center (MTC), USA
Address	Camdenton, Missouri, USA
Contact information	www.ntm.org/train
Language of instruction	English
Affiliations and sponsors	The NTM is a non-denominational sending agency based in Sanford, Florida. It is a member of the Interdenominational Foreign Mission Association (IFMA).
Length of program	The NTM Missionary Training Center is a two-year residential program. For some missionary candidates an additional two-year New Tribes Bible Institute (NTBI) course is a prerequisite.
Number of students	The NTBI program averages 380 students. The Missionary Training Center has approximately 190 missionary candidates.

Students:

The missionary candidates in the two-year Missionary Training Center program are primarily from North America, although there are always a number of international students. All are committed to career missionary service with New Tribes Mission and are sent by sponsoring churches. Two tracks of training are available to candidates, the primary one is equipping for cross-cultural church planting in animistic tribal settings. A second track provides training for support personnel.

Staff:

Almost all the faculty and staff at the Missionary Training Center are members of the NTM agency. Occasionally adjunct faculty and guest lecturers facilitate modules. The staff, like all NTM missionaries, is faith-supported.

History and Objectives:

From its inception in 1942, the founders of New Tribes Mission required missionary preparation. Initially, missionary training was provided in Chicago at the former Hi-Hat Club purchased by NTM and converted also into its headquarters. In 1944 NTM moved its training program to Fouts Springs in northern California. Over many years additional training centers were added, some were closed, and by the 1990s NTM had two Bible Institutes, six Mission Institutes, and one Language and Linguistics Institute in the USA.

---

1   Robert Strauss is President and CEO of Worldview Resource Group (WRG), a nonprofit organization based in Colorado Springs, CO, providing training in cross-cultural church planting methodologies based on a worldview approach to ministry. Robert is also a Doctor of Missiology candidate at Biola University's School of Intercultural Studies. He lives with his wife, Carole, in Colorado Springs, CO, has two adult children, Carrie and Christopher, and three grandchildren, Seija, Ani and Rowan. This chapter is extracted from his dissertation research entitled "The Design and Delivery of Intentional and Integral Missionary Training: A Case Study of New Tribes Mission."

Beginning in 1994 the Executive Board of NTM approved an evaluation and redesign of all curricula aspects of the entire USA training program. Curriculum content was retooled with a tribal church planter profile or competency model as the basis. Training environments were changed. New trainers were recruited who qualified to facilitate the new curriculum. Rather than replicate the two-year training at multiple institutes, a process was initiated to consolidate locations and integrate all the course material.

In August 2006 a consolidated and integrated missionary training program was launched in Camdenton, MO. Like the program before it is residential, focusing on whole person training – character qualities, ministry capabilities, values, and relationships.

Case Study of New Tribes Integral Training Program:

New Tribes Mission started a process in February of 1996 to evaluate and revise its North American training program. The process, which began as a focus on training programs alone, ended up generating changes throughout the worldwide organization. These changes were not necessarily our intent, but became the outcome of powerful ideas that changed the way we thought about ourselves, and generated far-reaching symbols and rituals that decidedly impacted our agency culture.

Following the evaluation of the training programs, a report was presented to the New Tribes Mission[2] (NTM) Executive Committee. The Executive Committee determined to follow through on the findings, especially the criticisms of NTM members. The members, called for: (a) more field experienced trainers in the North America training centers and (b) training curricula that reflected the methodologies being implemented out in the tribal church planting contexts.[3] The Executive Committee therefore appointed me, having led the first evaluation team, to coordinate the next phase of evaluation by assembling a new team of experienced trainers and tribal church planters from within NTM.

> "To begin with the end in mind means to start with a clear understanding of your destination. It means to know where you're going so that you better understand where you are now so that the steps you take are always in the right direction."
> –Stephen R. Covey
> *The Seven Habits of Highly Effective People*

Discovering a Process

In July 1996, the newly formed Training Evaluation Committee spent several hours reviewing the first report to the Executive Committee. "What is our next step?" I asked. Dell Schultze, a church planter among the Ilongot people in the hills of Northern Luzon in the Philippines, suggested that we begin our discussions by looking at NTM's purpose statement, which reads:

> Motivated by the love of Christ, and empowered by the Holy Spirit, NTM exists to assist the ministry of the local church through the mobilizing, equipping, and coordinating of missionaries to evangelize unreached people groups, translate the Scriptures, and see indigenous New Testament churches established that truly glorify God.

Establishing indigenous churches that truly glorify God was the definitive end result of the agency's mission, and, consequently, the target at which our training arrow would be shot.

---

2   New Tribes Mission is an international, interdenominational mission agency of 3,200 missionaries.

3   In North America in the mid-1990s, NTM provided missionary training in three distinct phases at ten training centers: (a) Two Bible Institutes were located in Waukesha, WI and Jackson, MI; (b) There were seven Mission Institutes: Fredonia, WI, Durant, MS, Baker City, OR, Rochester, PA, Jersey Shore, PA, Cornettsville, KY, and Durham, Ontario; and (c) One Language and Linguistics Institute existed in Camdenton, MO. The Bible Institutes enrolled approximately 190 students each, the Mission Institutes about 25 students each, and the Language and Linguistic Institute typically had almost 100 students.

Intuitively, committee member George Walker reasoned, "If church planting is the ultimate purpose of NTM, then to evaluate and redesign training we must start at the end and work backward." We all understood what he meant. We must start with what church planters need to know, be, and do to be able to establish effective churches. Once we determined what church planters should look like, we could work backward in designing training to meet that goal. The idea sounded good, even novel. But how would we go about this process?[4] Providentially, Tom Steffen, from Biola University's School of Intercultural Studies, referred us to *Establishing Ministry Training: A Manual for Programme Developers*, edited by Robert Ferris.[5] This book described exactly what we had conceived in our planning meetings. The book confirmed our assessment that our approach was good (though not novel).[6]

Ferris' book was exactly what we needed. The evaluation committee read the book several times, and modified its process for conducting a profiling workshop to fit the NTM context. The concepts presented in the manual were clear and easily adaptable. After consulting Ferris in Columbia, SC, we included the important step of clarifying expectations at the beginning of the workshop.[7]

In early 1997, the evaluation committee conducted two profiling workshops, one in Michigan and a second near the Bena Bena village in the highlands of Papua New Guinea. Fifty-six stakeholders (trainers, agency leaders, tribal church planters, and support personnel) participated in the Michigan workshop. Several weeks later, 75 experienced field leaders and tribal church planters took part in the three-day profiling workshop conducted in Papua New Guinea. A clear consensus about the spiritual qualities and ministry capabilities a church planter needs to successfully plant a church in a remote tribal setting emerged from these two workshops. The consensus assumed that the church planters would be incarnational, i.e., living in the context of the host society, and acquiring culture and language to a predetermined level of proficiency.[8]

Applying an Innovative Approach

A helpful, profile-altering incident occurred in the Michigan workshop, the first to be conducted. The evaluation committee followed the modified process that fleshed out the qualities and capabilities of a tribal church planter.[9] However, participants were not comfortable talking about spiritual qualities as abstract subjects. We stopped the workshop process to discuss as a group the implications of this quandary. Finally, it was suggested by the participants that we discuss the abstract spiritual qualities in the context of relationships.[10] Thus, before identifying general areas of spiritual qualities, we named seven areas of relationships in which all spiritual qualities were rooted. These areas included relationship to: (a) God, (b) self, (c) family, (d) co-workers, (e) host society, (f) leaders, and (g) sending church. Training objectives, standards for evaluating candidates, curriculum content, training environments, and learning experiences were built upon these relational foundations. This strategy of embedding the abstract spiritual qualities into relationships demon-

---

4   The Training Evaluation Committee was familiar with Benjamin S. Bloom's learning taxonomies: cognitive, affective, and psychomotor skills [*Taxonomy of Education Objectives, Book 1 Cognitive Domain*, (New York: Longman, 1956)]. At the beginning of our work in the mid 1990s, we were not familiar with the three domains added by Malcolm Knowles [*The Modern Practice of Adult Education: From Pedagogy to Andragogy*, (New York: Cambridge, 1980)] and others: understanding, values, and relationships [Herbert L. Brussow and Dale W. Kietzman, *Essentials of Training for Effective Intercultural Service*, (Pasadena, CA: World Link Association of Missionary Training Centers, 1999), pp. 13-20]. These additional domains became key factors in the creation of competency models and all curricula components.

5   Robert W. Ferris, *Establishing Ministry Training: A Manual for Programme Developers*, (Pasadena, CA: William Carey Library, 1995).

6   Ralph W. Tyler [*Basic Principles of Curriculum and Instruction*, (Chicago: The University of Chicago Press, 1949)], a student of John Dewey, had written about the concept of backward mapping. Grant Wiggins and Jay McTighe argue the concept is hardly radical in that "Tyler described the logic of backward design clearly and succinctly about 50 years ago."(p, 8) and, "Indeed, more than anyone, Tyler laid out the basic principles of backward design" (p.154). Grant Wiggins and Jay McTighe, *Understanding by Design*, (Alexandria, VA: Association for Supervision and Curriculum Development, 1998).

7   See Chapter 6, *Integral Ministry Training Design and Evaluation*.

8   NTM requires that tribal church planters pass Check Four evaluation in culture and language proficiency levels before starting chronological Bible teaching and daily lesson translation. NTM's culture and language acquisition Check Four addresses, but is not limited to, the following: (a) complex grammar (imperative, contrary to fact conditions, passive versus active voice); (b) specific terminology that will be foundational to evangelism and discipleship; (c) worldview understandings (revealed in stories); (d) discourse understanding and storying ability; (e) motives and activities during times of crisis; (f) beliefs and rituals; and (g) themes that transcend cultural institutions.

9   See Chapter 7, *Integral Ministry Training Design and Evaluation*.

10   This relational emphasis is similar to the Indian Mission Association/World Evangelical Fellowship Indian DACUM Profile, September 21-23, 1992, Chennai (Madras), Tamil Nadu.

strates how relating, valuing, being, and understanding took precedence over mere knowledge acquisition. All agreed, and this adjustment was made before we continued. The adaptation was intuitive and easily accomplished

The emerging tribal church planter profile then identified 14 ministry capability categories. These categories included skills like culture and language acquisition, culture analysis, cross-cultural communication, chronological Bible teaching, Bible translation, curriculum development, church planting skills, management skills, and more.

Once the tribal church planter profile was created, the evaluation committee believed each category in the profile should be validated by a focus group of specialists. Almost twenty focus groups were assembled throughout the world to review and develop each relationship and each ministry capability category. For example, the Bible translation category included eight component items, describing the major subject areas within that category skill set. Over the course of several months, a focus group specializing in Bible translation reviewed this area, filled in gaps, arranged the component items into a sequential order of development, suggested what should be pre-selection, pre-field training, and on-field consultation, described standards for evaluation of students, clustered component items into meaningfully related subcategories (later to be reviewed as potential courses or modules within courses), and wrote suggested learning objective statements based on Robert Mager's behavioral model.[11]

The work of the focus groups was a foundational piece in the backward mapping design. Training objectives were not initiated arbitrarily based on intuition. They were grounded in data that emerged from consensus in the profiling workshops and focus groups. We started at the end and worked backward. In *Alice in Wonderland*, Cheshire Cat advised Alice that if you don't know where you are going, any road will get you there. NTM's purpose statement identified the right road for the agency, i.e., tribal church planting. Next, the tribal church planter profile identified the starting point on the right road of missionary training.

The Profile Informs All Aspects of Curricula

If you create a missionary profile using the techniques described in earlier chapters, you will see that the qualities and capabilities that emerge are far too many for all of them to be individual training objectives, but the profile will inform all aspects of the overall curricula. To begin with, NTM used the profile to inform its candidate selection criteria. Certain spiritual qualities were to be in place and functioning prior to acceptance into the formal NTM training program. Other components informed the pre-field and on-field training objectives. Finally, some components identified lifelong personal and professional development goals.

Using the backward mapping approach helps to organize and prioritize the critical training objectives. Wiggins and McTighe, leading the backward mapping movement in curriculum design, argue that the unique place of assessment is a key aspect in the curriculum development process.

> The backward design approach encourages us to think about a unit or course in terms of the collected assessment evidence needed to document and validate that the desired learning has been achieved, so that the course is not just content to be covered or a series of learning activities. This backward approach encourages teachers and curriculum planners to first think like an assessor before designing specific units and lessons, and thus to consider up front how they will determine whether students have attained the desired understandings.[12]

---

11 Robert Mager, *Preparing Instruction Objectives, Second Edition*, (Palo Alto, CA: Fearson, 1975), designed instructional objectives in a three-part system reflected in Table 1:

Parts	Central Questions	Examples
Student behavior	Do what?	Mark statements with an F for fact or an O for opinion
Conditions of performance	Under what conditions?	Given an article from a newspaper
Performance criteria	How well?	75% of the statements are correctly marked

Table 1: Mager's Instructional Objectives

12 Wiggins and McTighe, 1998, pp. 12.

The Training Evaluation Committee not only started at the end and worked backward, but they also clarified the expectations related to missionary candidates' growth and development in each domain: relationships, values, understandings, spiritual qualities, and ministry capabilities. Whereas the learning objective statements were written according to behavioral model,[13] the standards for evaluating candidates reflected broader domains of learning.[14] Once the standards for evaluating candidates were clear, curricula could then be created.

Implementing Change

From 1996-2001, the Training Evaluation Committee redesigned the entire North America training program, including the training philosophy. Rather than implementing wholesale changes at 10 training centers, with 210 trainers and over 650 missionary candidates, the evaluation committee started a one-year pilot program at one training center. At this center, the curricula was completely redesigned, including training objectives, curriculum content, training environments or contexts, trainer qualifications, learning experiences, and standards for evaluating candidates.15 Principles of Theory Y management, andragogy, and experiential learning were implemented throughout every aspect of the residential program. As the integrated curricula was being developed and implemented at the pilot program, trainers from other centers (including England and Australia) came to visit and participate in the process.

In 2001, the evaluation committee conducted a profiling workshop for NTM support personnel (pilots, teachers, administrators, IT, and general services). Stakeholders from all the support personnel sectors participated. The evaluation committee followed the same process as the tribal church planter profile to develop the support personnel profile. Using the profile and focus groups, the process ultimately led to the creation of specific training courses and modules for support personnel. A support personnel track of training was instituted in the fall of 2004, running parallel to the tribal church-planting track.

Organizational Change

The details related to taking the profile and turning it into specific training courses in a real context with qualified trainers is covered elsewhere in this manual. The complexity of this process cannot be minimized. My focus here is how the creation of competency models and the use of backward mapping design not only redesigned the NTM North America training program, but also impacted the whole international agency.

Many agency personnel participated in some way and in varying degrees in the process of redesigning the North America training. They were updated every two weeks on the progress of the evaluation and redesign through a Training Evaluation Committee email, which was distributed throughout the agency. Many members wrote letters of encouragement, support, and concern during the process. It has been said that whoever tells the stories shapes the culture. As the stories were told about what was happening in the training program through the evaluation committee updates—especially the why behind the what—the ideas embedded in the stories significantly impacted the agency. Today it is popular among missiologists to confront cultural structures of organizations in an effort to affect change. Does this approach always work? Is it really the best practice for long-term change? The changes that occurred in NTM took place at the worldview level first and from there impacted the structures.

---

13   Mager, 1975.

14   The NTM Training Evaluation Committee wrote the learning objective statements for each of its courses in all three phases of its four-year training program using Mager's behavioral model, but the standards for evaluating candidates were broader and integrated. Trainers and candidates measured attainment and achievement based on behavioral standards, defined understandings (analysis, synthesis, and evaluation), relationships, spiritual growth, and demonstrations of ministry skills in practical settings. The residential format (both candidates and trainers) of NTM's training program facilitated these kinds of assessment that are perceived as impossible in a formal classroom context.

15   David A. Kolb, [*Experiential Learning: Experience as the Source of Learning and Development*, (Upper Saddle River, NJ: Prentice Hall, 1984)] is the leading author on the subject of experiential learning. His model, built on the foundations of John Dewey [*Experience and Education*, (New York: Macmillan, 1938)], Kurt Lewin, and Jean Piaget, incorporates four components into one whole: concrete experience, reflective observation, abstract conceptualization, and active experimentation. See R. Michael Paige's *Education for the Intercultural Experience* (Yarmouth, ME: Intercultural, 1993) for selections from leading intercultural authors like Milton J. Bennett and James A. McCaffery on subjects related to experiential learning.

Lee Bolman and Terrence Deal[16] describe organizations in terms of frames. They have identified four primary frames in every organization: (a) symbolic, (b) human resource, (c) political, and (d) structural. Table 2 identifies each frame and describes its function in the overall organizational development:

Symbolic	Human Resource	Political	Structural
The symbolic frame is first in organizational development. It has to do with organizational culture, stories, rituals, and meaning. Other frames will emerge from these worldview assumptions.	Although people and organizations need each other, organizations exist to serve human needs. When individuals find meaningful and satisfying work, organizations get the energy and talents they need.	Coalitions always form within organizations, each developing agendas and establishing power bases. The degree to which the symbolic frame is undeveloped will be the degree to which coalition differences will struggle for power.	Often addressed first in organizational development, the structural frame is really the final frame of consideration. A workable structure within an organization provides clarity about what to do and who is to do it.
Included in this frame are ideology, vision and mission statements, value statements, logos, tag lines, slogans, and images.	Included in this frame are human relationships, selection, allocation, training, and empowerment.	Included in this frame are resources, conflict, power, and negotiation.	Included in this frame are goals, guidelines, maps, roles, systems, and informal networks.

Table 2: Bolman and Deal's Four Frames of Organizational Development

The symbolic frame, including stories and leading to worldview assumptions, is the beginning point of change. In the early stages of design, Ferris had stressed the importance of the profiling workshop expectations (shared assumptions). It would be these shared assumptions, often made explicit, that impacted so many facets of the overall agency. For example, the competency models for the training program bespoke of competency standards overall in every role at every level. "If the ax is dull and its edge unsharpened, more strength is needed but skill will bring success" (Essles. 10:10). "Like an archer who wounds at random is he who hires a fool or any passer-by" (Prov. 26:10, New International Version). Increasingly, the process of choosing new leaders and allocating personnel was done through the evaluation grid of competencies, both spiritual qualities and ministry capabilities.

Another example of how shared assumptions in the redesign of training influenced the agency, was applying adult learning principles. The redesigned training program emphasized the important role of the learner. One of the new training program assumptions stated, "The missionary candidate must take personal responsibility for her or his own development and ministry effectiveness." Working under this assumption was no small change in the training program. Adult learning theory affirms the principles of participative management, which view people in a fundamentally different way that we were used to. A broader agency movement of participative management followed, not always understood clearly and sometimes implemented inappropriately, but nevertheless unfettered.

Conclusion

The influences of changes at the training level led to expansive changes throughout NTM. Training became more focused, based on targeted competencies. Through shared story, broader expectations were clarified and new standards were raised. The process of gathering together, focusing around our shared mission and clarifying the expectations of who we needed to become to achieve the mission, changed our organization from the ground up.

---

16   Lee G. Bolman and Terrence E. Deal, *Reframing Organizations*, (San Francisco, CA: Jossey-Bass, 1997).

«12»

Program: Redcliffe College, Centre for Mission Training
Country: United Kingdom
Sponsor: Academic institution
Contributor: Colin Bulley

Part 1: Demographics

Name	Redcliffe College, Centre for Mission Training
Address	Redcliffe College, Wotton House, Horton Road, Gloucester, GL1 3PT, U.K.
Contact information	Phone: +44 (0) 1452 308 097 Fax: +44 (0) 1452 503 949 Email address: admin@redcliffe.org Web site: www.redcliffe.org
Other contact	Principal, Rev. Dr. Simon Steer ssteer@redcliffe.org
Language of instruction	English
Affiliations and sponsors	Redcliffe College is not affiliated to any denomination but it has adopted the Statement of Faith of the Evangelical Alliance in the UK and is a member of Global Connections.
Length of program	Redcliffe offers the following courses of study: • One-year Certificates of Higher Education in Applied Theology and in Applied Theology in Cross-Cultural Contexts, the latter also being known as Professionals in Mission • Two-year Diploma of Higher Education in Applied Theology. • Three-year Bachelor's (B.A.) Honours degree in Applied Theology. • One-year full-time Master's (M.A.) in Global Issues in Contemporary Mission, also offered in a three-year Blended Mode involving two short periods of intensive study at the college and supervised study at a distance. All these are validated by the University of Gloucestershire. The college also offers the non-validated, three-month Across the Cultures course and "Pick 'n' Mix" courses of various lengths in which students choose from what is on offer in the timetables for each term.
Number of students	There are usually around 70 full time students.

Students:

Requisites for admittance to the M.A. course are: a good first degree in a cognate discipline and, normally, completion of some theological and/or mission studies. For the other university-validated courses, two 'A' levels and five GCSEs or their equivalent are necessary. For non-validated courses, proof of motivation and ability to benefit from the studies chosen are needed. For non-native-English speakers the college requires an overall grade of 5.5 for undergraduate and 7 for M.A. students on the International English Language Testing System.

Over the past nine years the college has seen an average of 40 full-time equivalent students join its training programs and an average total student body of 70. About half have come from the UK and half from overseas. Of those from overseas the largest contingents come from the Netherlands country-wise and from Africa and Asia (after Europe) continent-wise. The great majority apply as individuals who have sensed a call to mission, nearly all supported by their churches. A minority are directed to us by mission agencies. Over half engage in full-time Christian service outside the UK after they have completed their studies, about a quarter do so in the UK and the other quarter serve God in secular employment, mostly within the UK. Many are involved in development work, many in evangelism and church planting, and many in teaching and pastoral care within churches.

Staff:

Redcliffe is staffed academically 75% by full-time, salaried tutors, 15% by part-time, paid lecturers and 10% by volunteers. Most are selected through a formal interview process with a few seconded by a mission agency. Academic qualifications, mission experience and teaching and pastoral skills are all important in the selection of staff since they contribute to the holistic nature of the course. Nearly all of our academic staff have been involved long-term in mission in countries other than their own. While their main ministries have been in teaching and training, they have also engaged in evangelism, church-planting and pastoral care. All are British in origin except two, one full- and one part-time, who come from Asia. The administrative and support staff (about 50% of the whole staff team) are made up of full- and part-time workers, all of whom are committed Christians and a number of whom have had significant cross-cultural experience. The entire staff team consists of around 25 people.

History and Objectives:

Redcliffe was founded in 1892 and is probably the oldest extant interdenominational college in the United Kingdom. It was initially conceived as a women's missionary training college since there were very few openings for women in Bible colleges at that time. In 1984 male students were also admitted. Although changing location several times and upgrading its training to master's level, the aim of the College has remained consistent: to train an international body of students in Christian ministry with a special emphasis on cross-cultural mission.

The present three dimensional focus of the College in terms of "Knowing, Being and Doing" was formulated in the late 1980s, and the current five-term structure with one of these serving as a placement term ("Doing") was inaugurated in 1991, as was a completely revamped curriculum ("Knowing"). A Personal Development Tutor was appointed in the following year to develop the "Being" dimension.

The College relocated from London in 1995 because student growth required larger premises. Its present Gloucester site is well situated in a multi-cultural city which affords numerous ministry opportunities for students.

In the 1990's the College embarked on a process of acquiring validation for its various programs through the local University of Gloucestershire. The Diploma was validated in 1997 and the Honour's Degree in the following year. The Certificate in Applied Theology in Cross-Cultural Contexts followed in 2000. In 2003 the Master's degree in Global Issues in Contemporary Mission was accepted by the University and, in addition, an alternative mode of delivery of this degree involving summer schools and internet discussion groups was validated in 2005.

The current objectives fall into three inter-related areas: course development, partnerships and a building programs.

As far as course development is concerned, the College is developing an Asian studies program to prepare people to work in Asia and among the global Asian diaspora. This will include new courses at both undergraduate and master's levels. We are also implementing a European Mission track in recognition of the increasing importance of this continent as a mission field. One medium-term goal is the introduction of a Ph.D. or Doctor of Missiology degree.

On the partnership front, we aim to work ever more closely with mission agencies, NGOs and mission training institutes in the majority world. The recent appointment of a Director of Partnership Development is a crucial foundation for meeting this goal.

The building program consists of a five-year goal to erect a new library with additional teaching areas, to enhance student accommodation and related facilities.

Connecting these three areas is a coordinated Marketing & Communications program. The overall objective, of course, is continually to improve the College's ability to train the whole person to take the whole Gospel of Jesus Christ to the whole world.

The biggest challenges concern student recruitment and financial resources. Although current recruitment is at record levels, long-term demand for full-time residential mission training is uncertain in a context in which short-term mission is prevalent. In the absence of financial reserves, uncertainties about student recruitment make it difficult for the College to develop its program as it would ideally like to do.

Another challenge relates to the potential threat to Christian organizations from legislation relating to employment, charitable status and freedom of expression. An increasing number of our international students are also finding it difficult to gain visas to enter the UK.

Part 2: Non-formal and Community-Based Learning

How does this training program use non-formal practice and experiential learning to develop skills, and/or how does it intentionally use community to generate growth in character?

We use the image of a three-legged stool to explain our approach to training: knowing, being and doing are the three legs that support what Redcliffe seeks to do in training students. If we neglect any of them, the training will fail in significant ways. Contrary to the experience of some institutions, we have found that validation by a university has helped, rather than hindered, us to achieve this.

Knowing

The majority of our students come with a profession and several years of work experience in a particular area. Most also come with formal qualifications at graduate or postgraduate level and an increasing number arrive with significant cross-cultural mission experience. They want to improve their knowledge of the Bible and link this with spiritual growth, seeing more knowledge as automatically resulting in a more vibrant spiritual life. As you will see below, we feel that much of this development is actually done in other areas of learning. However, we believe that it is important to develop students who have a good knowledge of both Word and world, the message of good news and the context in which the message is to be communicated. So we provide overviews of Old and New Testaments, in-depth studies of various biblical books and contextual readings of various biblical passages as well as courses in globalization and mission, group Bible-study leadership and cross-cultural communication. These subjects are taught using a combination of formal lecturing, seminars, group discussion and presentations and team teaching as appropriate to the subject matter and level of the group. The main aim is to produce informed and thinking students. To help them continue to equip themselves after they have left, the college has developed a missiological e-zine, *Encounters* (www.redcliffe.org/encounters) to provide ongoing "thought food."

Being

With work-overload and workaholic tendencies being major issues for global mission (Hay, R., *Worth Keeping: Global Perspectives on Best Practice in Missionary Retention*, Pasadena: William Carey Library, 2007), it is vital to help students understand who they are, how they behave, where they draw their self-worth and identity from and how they can best resource their own growth and spiritual life. To these ends, all students have to do a Personal Development module that involves meeting with a pastoral tutor each term and with the Personal Development tutor twice a year to agree on personal development goals and to monitor their progress in achieving them. These are non-academic goals, such as developing a more meaningful prayer life, learning how to be more hospitable, increasing fitness and overcoming an addiction or dependency. The student must demonstrate growth and progress in these areas in order to pass this module and the pass is required by the validating university for a student to gain their desired qualification.

As a tool to help students become self-aware, a prerequisite to becoming culturally aware, we offer the Myers Briggs Type Indicator. Students can undertake the assessment and be counseled one-to-one on their results. We refer to the results of these assessments in other parts of the training including the Personal Development and Developing Spirituality modules.

Community living plays a significant role in the training of Redcliffe students. Most live on campus and study, eat, sleep, work and worship in close proximity. This might be quite straightforward in a monocultural setting but with 25 nationalities in a student body of 90 it throws up many challenges that confront students with some of the harsh realities of living and working cross-culturally. All students share in the practical work of the college through the Teamworks program. Teams of six to ten students are responsible for cleaning or maintaining a part of the college and most work together to do this. We add to the value of this with a Teamwork module where all new students learn about cross-cultural teamworking, both being in and leading such teams. We are currently working towards gaining university validation of a Teamworks Programme, in which a mark will be given to a team for how well they achieve their task(s) as well as for a reflective journal on the joys and challenges of working in a team.

In this whole area of "being" we are seeking to create "stressful situations with a safety net." Students will face these realities on the mission field and so part of their development is to learn to deal with them now when a mistake is not fatal and they have support structures around them.

Beyond the formal support structures, the accessibility of tutors is a much valued part of community life. Small tutor groups and sharing from the life of the tutor, reinforced by an open-door policy, use of first names for all staff, and staff and students eating and taking coffee together, means that mentoring relationships can develop that last long after the student leaves college and enters ministry.

Worship is an important part of community life, and regular formal gatherings are supplemented with informal, often spontaneous, student worship-times. In the regular gatherings students often lead and so the community is exposed to a whole cross-section of cultural and denominational styles of worship. These help students value diversity, cope with difference and often provoke lively discussions.

Doing

Redcliffe prepares people for mission, that is, not just to think about mission but also to do it. We want students to become reflective practitioners. So alongside knowing and being, all students get involved in doing. They do a weekly ministry placement for at least two hours. Gloucester is a culturally diverse city and so there are many opportunities such as for prison ministry, schools and youth work, pastoral placements and City Mission work. For six weeks each year the majority do a block placement, gaining experience, often overseas, in hands-on ministry.

For both types of placement, students write a report reflecting on how they handled the experiences they encountered and what they learnt from them. This report, along with a report on their performance by their supervisor, provides the basis for an assessment of their learning from their placements, which is validated and forms an integral part of their overall course. Their report includes sociological and theological analysis of the ministry they were involved in and its context, offering opportunities for applying the knowledge they have gained at college and personal reflection that reveals their personal growth in being.

So each of the three areas of knowing, being and doing are substantial in their coverage, rigorous in their assessment and vital to students' overall training.

Part 3: Program Improvements and Development

How has this training program progressively improved learning activities addressing the development of essential ministry and/or cross-cultural skills, or the formation of attitudes leading to character growth?

As an ongoing validation requirement, the University requires a self-evaluative annual report which stimulates constant reflection on the effectiveness of the training program and consequently the regular improvement of various elements.

This report draws on the proceedings of the Course Committee which meets three times a year and is attended by student representatives who provide student evaluations of all modules.

One of the major tasks in the early years of validation, stimulated by the external examiner's criticisms, was the sharpening of the placement work, particularly in terms of what was expected in students' reflective reports. At first many of them were criticized by the examiner as "pious postcards from abroad" without critical or reflective rigor. Helpfully, tutors were encouraged to challenge students to figure out "what's going on when what's going on is going on!" In other words, to look below the surface both subjectively ("Why am I feeling what I'm feeling?") and objectively ("Why is this ministry functioning as it does?"). Students are now taught methods of reflective practice and sociological analysis to enable them to maximize their placement learning.

However, quality control of this vital element of the College program remains a real problem. Tutors carefully evaluate the written and oral placement reports of students, but obtaining conscientious field supervisors who guarantee excellent ministry experiences remains an ongoing challenge.

Another challenge is setting the parameters of what is an acceptable mission placement. Would a student request to join an intercessory world prayer group be acceptable, for example, or the request to shadow a mission marketing officer? Behind this dilemma is the larger conceptual discussion of what exactly constitutes mission and indeed, what does the notion exclude?

Although many of the taught modules are practically orientated from Cross-Cultural Living to Public Speaking Skills, and the list is growing with recent additions such as Business as Mission and Children's Ministry, students have requested other elements of "how to" training so that extra-curricular workshops are now offered from car maintenance to simple Do It Yourself (DIY) skills.

Turning to the personal development area, again it must be emphasized that much in the regular teaching curriculum encourages students to reflect upon their own spiritual lives and attitudes and there is actually a module entitled Developing Spirituality. In terms of assessment, the College has very few exams, and exercises such as personal journaling facilitate self-awareness, and assessments requiring group presentations enable students to reflect on issues raised by working in cross-cultural teams.

Recent developments have been noted in Part 2 above regarding the Teamworks program.

In many ways, then, Redcliffe has been seeking to use non-formal, experiential and practical learning, not least via the intentional use of "community", alongside rigorous academic practices and standards, to facilitate and ensure students' development of needed skills and growth in character as well as increasing their biblical, theological and missiological understanding. Ongoing monitoring by our external examiners and university validators has indicated that Redcliffe is succeeding while always looking for ways in which to improve.

«13»

Program: ESEPA Seminary and the Cross-Cultural Ministries Center

Country: Costa Rica

Sponsor: Academic institution

Contributor: Paul Mauger

Part 1: Demographics

Name	ESEPA: Seminary and the Cross-Cultural Ministries Center
Address	Seminario ESEPA Apdo 161-1350 San Sebastian San Jose, Costa Rica
Contact information	Phone: +506-227-1958, 226-3684 Fax: +506 227-8974 Email address: registro@esepa.org Web site: www.esepa.org
Other contact	Gary S. Shogren, Rector Email: rector@esepa.org
Language of instruction	Spanish
Affiliations and sponsors	Interdenominational, started by Association of Costa Rican Bible Churches Latin America Mission, Miami, FL, USA Overseas Council International, Indianapolis, IN, USA
Length of program	Diplomado (Bachelor's level certificate)—2 years. Bachillerato (full Bachelor's program)—4 years. Certificado (Diploma for those without secondary education)—16 months in modules. Two year Master's programs are also available in Bible and Theology. Other arrangements can be made according to specific needs. Programs are available for other Christian leaders.
Number of students	ESEPA has approximately 25 students expressly preparing for cross-cultural ministries; 225 in the wider program.

Students:

The student body consists of two basic groups. The first group, about 80% of the students, is comprised of Evangelicals from Costa Rican churches. The second group, the remaining 20%, is made up of Evangelicals from other countries, mainly from Latin America, and a few from Europe and North America.

The entry requirements are both general and specific to the program. General requirements are: the student must be an evangelical Christian, be active in ministry with a calling to continue, have a good pastoral recommendation, and have a satisfactory personal testimony. The specific requirements depend on the program of study. The three programs and their requirements are:

- Diploma level: certificate of completion of primary school.

- Bachelor's level: certificate of completion of secondary education (high school).

- Master's level: diploma and transcripts from bachelor's program.

The kinds of ministries they are involved in or plan to enter include: missions, pastoral, teaching, leadership in the church, and para-church ministries. Our graduates and former students of Cross-Cultural Ministry are serving in east and south Asia, west and central Africa, the Middle East, Europe and indigenous groups of Latin America. Those of other majors are mostly in Latin America.

Staff:

Our staff consists of a mix of Latin Americans from several countries, North Americans, and Europeans. Some are salaried, some are volunteers, and others raise their own support as foreign missionaries. There is generally a good spirit of cooperation among the staff, and this multi-cultural style is accepted as a permanent characteristic of the school.

Teaching staff must be evangelical Christians with calling, gifting, background and commitment to serve full-time. We look for ministry and cross-cultural experience as well as capacity for producing high quality training. The more specialized the subject matter or skill to be taught, the more specific the experience we look for. While it is difficult to generalize the cross-cultural experiences of our staff as a whole, most of our current staff have many years of experience with two, three or more cultures in the Americas, some in Europe and a few have Asian and African experience.

History and Objectives:

While ESEPA has been training Christian leaders in Costa Rica since 1983, it was after 13 years of rich ministry experience when various members of the ESEPA faculty sensed a "second calling" of God to contribute more proactively to the movement of Christian cross-cultural workers going out from Latin America to serve around the world. Cross-Cultural Ministries, ESEPA's youngest but fastest growing major, provides for the formal training needs of the students, while the Cross-Cultural Ministries Center offers a relational and informal complement to the formal program.

ESEPA's training program is unique in that it offers a combination of character formation, practical ministry skills and experience, and high quality training for the whole person. Perhaps the other aspect that makes it useful is our emphasis on realism and missions ministry, rather than mere Missiology.

The objectives of ESEPA are:

- To strive to help our students have a full picture of the remaining steps to reach their cross-cultural ministry field.

- To provide formal training as well as informal components of mentoring and the Cross-Cultural Ministry Center program, described below.

- To continually improve and broaden the program. Via cooperative efforts, we seek out partners who complement our program so that missions candidates have access to all they need.

- To explore options for experiences in significant Hindu, Muslim and other non-Latin American populations in our region. Our desire is to offer a term-abroad program in which students live, serve and study in a very different cultural context.

- To consider a possible multi-language program in the future in order to give candidates the basics in English and/or other major languages they are likely to need early on in their field service. A beginning level of a language such as French, Arabic, or Mandarin could give the confidence and survival boost needed to get through the initial months that are so critical to long-term adaptation.

- To research the best means to put more, perhaps all, of our programs online for the sake of the many workers who feel that they went out without enough training and now have a hard time getting it.

Looking ahead, we face three areas of challenge. These challenges are:

- To assist missions candidates as they face the financial struggle common for Latin American missionaries to endure. We have a burden to see how Latin American missionaries can enjoy better financial and moral support. Churches have a history of weak commitments that are easily broken. We want to facilitate better church-missionary links and foment self-financing options, such as using business to provide both financial stability and ministry context.

- To provide internet delivery of educational programs. The financial and logistical obstacles to getting online are substantial.

- To continually improve the formation program rather than allow it to stagnate.

Part 2: Non-formal and Community-Based Learning

How does this training program use non-formal practice and experiential learning to develop skills, and/or how does it intentionally use community to generate growth in character?

Experiential learning with ESEPA

Since its founding in 1983 to form pastors and Christian leaders as the "School of Pastoral Studies," ESEPA has been oriented toward practical ministry experience. ESEPA has always emphasized getting the Bible into Christian leaders' hearts. We have discarded the myth that the classroom is a head-experience only.

Live it. We seek to help students become better cross-cultural workers, from the inside out. Obtaining knowledge is fine, but we'd rather help Christian leaders give God the space He desires in their lives, that they may be fit channels to bless others. This does happen in the classroom. The secret? Modeling, hard work and prayer.

The toolbox. Our task is to equip leaders to influence others for God's Kingdom. Students learn to preach the Scriptures and make them relevant for listeners in their context. They practice evangelizing by sharing the Gospel with people outside class. They learn the meaning of the Trinity, and appreciate that it matters personally that God exists as an eternal, loving community of three. They find that counseling is not impersonal problem solving, but listening compassionately to real human beings, helping them understand their reality and receive guidance from the living God. Students must dialog about relevant topics with people outside the seminary, thus finding real-world value in what they learn, while personalizing both their faith and how they do ministry. Students can start here and now to relate cross-culturally, to be better equipped for the field. They must interact with people of other cultures by worshipping in churches whose language is neither Spanish nor English, conversing with African and Asian store managers, and seeking out foreigners "on the street."

We expose them to the realities of cross-cultural living and ministry by inviting field missionaries on leave to come and share their best and worst experiences. Students must interview experienced field missionaries about cross-cultural dynamics, ministry ideals and realities of clashing with other values. In-class activities are surprisingly useful for experiential learning. Objectively designed interactive role-plays place students in the position of the other culture. Staged multicultural group activities help students build cultural empathy skills while developing teamwork abilities. Some courses include freestyle projects where students can design any kind of presentation, with professor approval, to demonstrate real-world application of cross-cultural ministry principles and skills.

Almost all our students must participate in organizing a missions mobilization conference in a local church. All students have to engage in ministry or community service, cross-culturally where pertinent and feasible. Students do short-term missions in and outside Costa Rica, to indigenous peoples, Spanish speakers, and others. We promote external opportunities along with ESEPA's own, to give students diverse options.

Flexibility. In the Cross-Cultural Ministry curriculum we included certain flexible courses, constantly molding them according to need. Currently we have a course in basic health care, and plan to launch another in micro-business and development in missions. While we expect bi-vocational ministry students to get their professional training elsewhere, these courses broaden ministry options and link the two vocations.

Jungle foray. We have a long-standing working agreement with a ministry partner that provides outstanding cross-cultural training. In this proven experiential jungle-training program of three courses, students take few belongings, live with indigenous families, practice learning language, and wrestle with an animist worldview. If it were practical to offer more regularly, we would make it a required course.

Relational Ministry at ESEPA

At ESEPA we believe strongly that the best ministry is done through relationships, and we promote this principle by modeling it.

Mentoring. Our ideal for the Missions training program is that each Cross-Cultural Ministry student have mentor(s) for accountability and guidance through the entire preparation process from calling to the field. Candidates should have a personal missions training plan to keep them on track, with realistic expectations about the time and expense necessary to get to the field well-trained.

Both the student division and classes encourage all students to look for mentors and take advantage of those they already have. A few courses actually require students to try out mentoring, and we practice this relational ministry on a regular basis within and outside ESEPA. Our leadership emphasis focuses on relational ministry, accountability, gifting, and character issues. The main message: If you want to influence people for God, be worth following.

Modeling relational ministry outside ESEPA. I am happy to be part of a seminary that knows it needs the wider church. In this spirit, we cooperate with others in missions training. One highlight is partnering with FEDEMEC, the main national sending body for Costa Rica, in holding their Candidate School for those near departure for service. This is both training and critical preventative member care. We also offer a joint training program with FEDEMEC, participate in events of various organizations as well as the Costa Rican Missions Fellowship, whose members are ministries doing missions from Costa Rica.

Relationships should shape buildings, not vice-versa. When people come to our Cross-Cultural Ministry Department office, they repeatedly tell us they feel at home, relaxed; they would like to stay. God in His grace gave us the vision to have a space where people would come in and talk freely – relationally – about God's work in their lives, and about Missions. This became our Cross-Cultural Ministries Center. We keep the coffee maker by the entrance. To the left we have our desks and basic tools required by an academic department. At right, however, is a comfortable living-room setting, framed by a huge world map, books, and other missions resources. All around are posters and photos of real people doing ministry worldwide.

Relationships in class. Finally, we return to the classroom, insisting it is a tool for relational learning. We use small-group activities, conversation and interactive projects in and outside the classroom to encourage students to remember that it's all about people.

Finally, what makes formal training a relational desert? Task-oriented professors. We desire to be warm, compassionate servants who transmit the desire to be more like Jesus.

Part 3: Program Improvements and Development

How has this training program progressively improved learning activities addressing the development of essential ministry and/or cross-cultural skills, or the formation of attitudes leading to character growth?

Training based on needs in our context. ESEPA's Cross-Cultural Ministry training has always addressed current needs of field workers. ESEPA was founded in 1983 to provide training for the leaders of Costa Rican churches, an acute felt need in that period. As ESEPA began to develop a missions program, God blessed us with an astounding mix of experienced missionaries, pastors, and other leaders, from both inside and outside ESEPA, who worked together to develop our curriculum. Naturally, these founders drew on existing training elsewhere, but they avoided the temptation to merely imitate. They adapted training to the unique needs of Costa Rican workers bound for, or on the field. ESEPA emerged from this process with a masterfully complete curriculum. While most elements lasted on paper, some were not so realistic to offer. Not only ESEPA developed its early missions training in this talented group, but also other ministries. Care was taken to avoid duplication and squandering limited resources. ESEPA was willing to release certain courses or emphases when others took them on. I am convinced that this open-handed approach is one of the reasons for ESEPA's own healthy program today.

Second calling. In the 1990's, ESEPA transitioned from training missionaries who happened to be around, to a much more intentional approach. Several of us actually felt a "second calling" to offer help to the missions movement. This led to several concrete changes. First, we injected more missions into every major for all students, to encourage more churches to send and support missionaries. Second, we actively sought out missionary candidates. Third, we updated the seminary purpose statement specifically to include ministry formation of cross-cultural missionaries.

Released to pursue missions training more purposefully, in 1998 the newly formed Missions Department pursued identifying the current needs of field workers. We interviewed workers personally, both on the field and while back on leave. We began with the open question, "What would the ideal, complete missions training program look like?" The answers determined our own new direction, and later became the main source for an ideal training plan laid out by the Costa Rican Missions Fellowship. One incongruity we found in this context was that, while candidates can design a great training plan, they sense such urgency to reach the field that we feel the need to persuade them to stay long enough to finish preparing. We decided to offer a "Missions Certificate," a relatively complete package with Bible, Missions, Theology; General and Cross-Cultural Ministry; Leadership and the practical aspects mentioned in Part 2, all integrated into this two-year program. For those desiring more, we continued developing a four-year bachelor's program, officially launched in 2003. While we prefer to see missionaries with the full program, we feel the certificate was a healthy concession we made to our local reality.

Please help our churches! The interviewed field workers affirmed that our emphasis on involving the local church in missions was essential. From this came the effort to require all students to deeper understanding of missions, doing missions from the local church, and organizing missions conferences in local churches.

We need to talk. Meanwhile, the "second calling" led us on a parallel path to develop a "missions center," now called the Cross-Cultural Ministries Center. We saw a need for personalized guidance in the preparation process in students and candidates, and so we believe God gave us the vision to have a relational and informal complement to the structured classes.

In the Center we invite students and candidates to talk about anything related to missions and character formation. What does a calling look like? What peoples are still unreached? How do I deny my cultural values and adopt those of another culture? These informal moments spent as friends are invaluable for aiding the formation of healthy Christian character. The professors also benefit from it. As we filled out the Bachelor's in Cross-Cultural Ministry, we added components such as folk religion, understanding church and society, empathy for the other culture, multiplying churches that probably will not be like our own. We combined our leadership emphasis with cross-cultural ministry in a Cross-Cultural Leadership course – how to prepare oneself to be a good leader "not in my own eyes but in theirs."

From the inside out. As we receive feedback from field workers and take in findings from studies such as ReMap I and II, we are ever more convinced that character formation is the core of good preparation for Cross-Cultural Ministry. Not only have we strengthened the emphasis in our own program, but also joined in preventative member care with FEDEMEC (see part 2) by developing the Candidate School for those nearing departure. Candidate School currently consists of a retreat of several days, with monthly follow-up meetings. We try to deal with key heart issues that can make or break the missionary on the field, and again try to impress on them the importance of having accountability and mentors for life.

Specific needs. Our drive to offer what students need led to a working agreement with the Iberoamerican Institute for Cross-Cultural Studies in Spain, for preparation in Islamic studies. This exciting option is available now but we hope it will grow significantly. Most recently we faced the challenge of making our dynamic Cross-Cultural Ministry program fit into the overall process of accreditation with the Costa Rican government, to meet the needs of our students for degrees that can help with jobs and further studies. To allow ourselves room to continue to adapt to today's needs, we designed certain courses with flexible descriptions that enable us to offer material targeted toward the needs of those currently being trained, such as the previously mentioned course in health care. The one thing we feel certain about is that tomorrow's Cross-Cultural Ministry training will not look exactly like today's. The basics will change little, but we hope always to vary the program to suit the needs of each generation of workers who prepare to go out. May God give us grace to do so.

Evaluation Tools

«1»

Missionary Training Assessment (MTA) Tool for Training Programs

Organization: The Next Step;[1] USA
Contributor: Jim Roché

In response to the book, *Too Valuable to Lose* (William Taylor, ed., William Carcy Library, 1997), the late Woody Phillips, while general director of United World Mission, initiated discussions about the feasibility of mission agencies, churches, and formal and non-formal educational institutions partnering with each other to provide training for missionary candidates—particularly for the benefit of smaller agencies unable to provide their own in-house training. An initial response of almost 50 persons attended an exploratory meeting in September 1997. They concluded that communicating among partners about the availability of courses or training modules, organizing local gatherings across the country, and sponsoring a larger annual national conference would be an effective strategy.

What we discovered, however, was that the organizers in those cities soon tired of promoting their meetings, which were additional to their own heavy workloads, and local meetings discouraged participation in national gatherings. We found that opening up training modules to other agencies was too difficult to communicate and schedule conveniently for others to attend. We also discovered that there was little enthusiasm for many agencies to expose their self-recognized weaknesses in training to participants from other organizations. Some found much of their training needs were too unique to their own agency culture or fields. So, rather than scheduling

---

1   The Next Step is a partnership among organizations and individuals that has developed into a professional organization of missionary trainers in North America intent upon improving the quality and extent of missionary training for cross-cultural workers.

training opportunities from "provider" to "recipient" agencies, we recognized the greater need in North America was to improve the entire discipline of missionary training through critical evaluation of both effective and ineffective programs. To create improvement required a renewed spirit of transparency among colleagues as to what was and what was not working. We believed in the need and potential of The Next Step, but we clearly needed a new strategy to encourage improvement, as the partnership itself was growing weaker and incapable of influencing the way missionary training was understood and conducted.

In January 2003, The Next Step sponsored the National Missionary Training Forum, a three-day conference with pre-conference seminars. Over 120 missionary trainers attended. Relationships were easily initiated within this larger group and trust emerged due to providing ample time for networking. The large participation in that and the next annual conference provided The Next Step with the financial capability to underwrite a task force to address improvements in missionary training. We invited 14 highly qualified and experienced missionary trainers and educators, representing each of the constituent organizational associations within The Next Step, to meet together for several days in 2004.

We asked the task force to produce a tool to evaluate educational practices without the judgmentalism associated with academic accreditation criterion. However, the tool had to forthrightly state criteria capable of distinguishing that which was excellent from that which was poor. The assessment tool had to be capable of informing trainers of the priorities requiring attention in their educational practices. We wanted the criterion to be free of bias toward the size or nature of the organization (whether school, church, or agency). We wanted the tool to serve as a guide to our Next Step conference planners when considering topics for our annual conferences. We wanted the tool to identify excellent programs, or strong components of programs, so those program developers could competently serve as peer consultants to other organizations requesting help. We wanted the tool to be free of complexity so it could be easily self-administered. Those were many large and complex demands. Under the guidance of task force leader Dr. Steve Hoke, we believe we may very well have succeeded!

At the January 2005 National Missionary Training Forum annual conference, we introduced the concept of "best practices"—an evaluative and improvement process familiar to businesses and non-profit organizations. The task force recognized the value of this approach to their project as it is non-judgmental, focused on the positive, and capable of being employed by any type or size of organization. The task force identified seven criteria (with accompanying statements of areas contributing to that standard) deemed critical to the educational processes of missionary training. Several drafts were distributed in an effort to achieve clarity of thought and intent.

One concept in the criteria—employing adult learning theory and methods—proved to be particularly unclear among members. To address that need, The Next Step contracted Dr. Jane Vella (http://www.globalearning.com), a highly regarded educator and prolific author in the field of adult learning, to introduce her training to the membership at the January 2006 National Missionary Training Forum conference. This was a clear example of how the tool, now introduced as the Missionary Training Assessment (MTA) could be used to guide our conference programming to raise our training standards.

The MTA was distributed among the partnership at the January conference and posted to our website (http://www.thenextstep.org) for downloading. We specifically identified and recruited volunteer training directors within our partnership who would rigorously self-evaluate their training programs and would allow external evaluators to also evaluate them this year.

Additionally, the task force developed an Action Planning Guide to follow the assessment process. The assessment asks for responses to each of the criteria and accompanying contributory statements as either a firm "YES!" indicating they have truly met the criteria, a qualified "Yes" in which the criteria was met but improvements could be made; "Needs Work" to acknowledge identifiable weaknesses, and "Help!" The Action Planning Guide uses those responses with the following guides to take the next step toward improvement:

What "YES!" successes do we want to celebrate?

- What are the key contributors to this strength?
- What does our pattern of "YES!" statements tell us or what can we learn from this?

What qualified "Yes" or new successes can we both celebrate and build on?

- What does our pattern of "Yes" statements tell us? What can we learn from this?
- What do we need to keep improving in this area?
- What are the key contributors to this strength?
- Delegate or find "champions" to research, plan and implement corrective action.

What are the "Needs Work" areas of our training?

- What does our pattern of "Needs Work" statements tell us?
- What do we need to do to improve in each area?
- Rank the priority in which we should attack these issues.
- Find "champions" to research, plan and implement corrective action.

In what areas do we desperately need "Help!"?

- What does our pattern of "Help!" statements tell us? What can we learn from this?
- What root problems can we identify through a SWOT (Strengths, Weaknesses, Opportunities and Threats) Analysis?
- What do we need to do to improve in each area?
- Rank order the priority in which we should attack these issues.
- Find "champions" to research, plan and implement corrective action.

This project remains "in progress" as we anticipate continuing improvements through this year. The Next Step is committed to the value of collegial partnership; sharing both what has worked and what has failed is critical to improvement. Expanding our emerging Next Step partnership in North America to networking internationally may be a jump in our vision, but does not change our values, and is absolutely essential to our commitment to global evangelism. We sincerely invite additional thoughts and suggestions for improvements by this worldwide partnership through submitting ideas at out website, www.thenextstep.org.

Missionary Training Assessment[2]
An Instrument for Evaluating and Improving Training Programs

Explanation of the MTA: The MTA is a self-assessment tool that employs seven (I-VII) standards of excellence of missionary training. Under each standard, critical areas are identified that contribute to that standard—e.g., "We regularly (annually, bi-annually, etc.) identify learners' needs."

Response Categories: You may indicate the degree to which each statement describes your training by checking (☑) one of five response categories:

- YES!: This strong positive response indicates the standard is clearly in place and operating effectively.
- Yes: This positive response indicates the standard is recognized and progress is being made.
- Needs Work: This response indicates the standard is not yet fully recognized or assistance is needed in knowing how to move forward.
- HELP!: This strong negative response indicates the standard does not exist or is not recognized and significant help is needed to know how to improve.
- N/A: The "Not Applicable" response should be used only when your organizational structure does not accommodate the critical area stated.

Organization:_____ Name: _____

Name of Program:_____ Date:_____

We are a: ___ congregation ___ mission agency ___ school ___ nonformal training organization

	YES!	Yes	Needs Work	Help!	N/A
I. NEEDS IDENTIFICATION **An excellent program of missionary training identifies the learning and performance needs of the learners, the organization, and other stakeholders.**					
A. We regularly (annually, biannually, etc.) identify learners' needs.	❑	❑	❑	❑	❑
B. We regularly identify training needs within the organization.	❑	❑	❑	❑	❑
C. Our training program is sensitive and responsive to the needs of our stakeholders.	❑	❑	❑	❑	❑
D. Our training program adapts to learners' needs (including spiritual, emotional, physical, and financial) and ministry skills.	❑	❑	❑	❑	❑

---

2   The MTA is the product of a task force of missionary trainers commissioned by the Next Step. This tool is offered as a document "in process" intended for further refinement and adaptation. Suggestions may be made to our website (www.thenextstep.org), which also offers the latest version of the MTA for free download.

	YES!	Yes	Needs Work	Help!	N/A

II. ALIGNMENT

An excellent program of missionary training is aligned with the mission, values, and vision of the parent organization.

	YES!	Yes	Needs Work	Help!	N/A
A. Our organization has clearly stated mission, values, and vision.	☐	☐	☐	☐	☐
B. We align our training program with organizational mission, values, and vision.	☐	☐	☐	☐	☐
C. We keep our training programs aligned with changes in organizational goals and objectives.	☐	☐	☐	☐	☐
D. Our training leadership has direct access to executive leadership.	☐	☐	☐	☐	☐

III. CORE VALUES

An excellent program of missionary training intentionally promotes spiritual formation, dependence on God, and Christian community.

	YES!	Yes	Needs Work	Help!	N/A
A. We model earnest prayer and obedience to God in all phases of training.	☐	☐	☐	☐	☐
B. Our trainers are characterized by humility, depending on God for effectiveness and training results.	☐	☐	☐	☐	☐
C. We ensure that learning happens in a safe, "grace-filled" environment.	☐	☐	☐	☐	☐
D. We build community identity and commitment.	☐	☐	☐	☐	☐
E. We provide varied opportunities for growth in personal and corporate spiritual life.	☐	☐	☐	☐	☐

	YES!	Yes	Needs Work	Help!	N/A

IV. TRAINING DESIGN

An excellent program of missionary training employs adult learning theory and methods.

		YES!	Yes	Needs Work	Help!	N/A
A.	We respect our learners by utilizing their abilities and background.	❏	❏	❏	❏	❏
B.	Our training is based on an analysis of the knowledge, skills and character of effective missionaries.	❏	❏	❏	❏	❏
C.	Our learning activities help learners develop capacity for life-long growth in knowledge, skills, and character for ministry.	❏	❏	❏	❏	❏
D.	The scope of our program assures training for all levels and roles in our organization.	❏	❏	❏	❏	❏
E.	Our staff models cross-cultural sensitivity in training methods and manners.	❏	❏	❏	❏	❏
F.	We expect trainers to actively engage in ministry beyond the training program.	❏	❏	❏	❏	❏
G.	Our trainers stay current by intentionally increasing their knowledge and skills.	❏	❏	❏	❏	❏
H.	Our training values are made clear in what and how we teach.	❏	❏	❏	❏	❏

V. RESOURCE STEWARDSHIP

An excellent program of missionary training makes careful use of spiritual, human, and financial resources.

		YES!	Yes	Needs Work	Help!	N/A
A.	Our staff's spiritual gifts and experiences are fully utilized.	❏	❏	❏	❏	❏
B.	Our program efficiently uses available financial resources (whether large or small).	❏	❏	❏	❏	❏
C.	Our program measures the cost effectiveness of training against improved ministry performance.	❏	❏	❏	❏	❏
D.	Our leaders encourage shared learning within the organization.	❏	❏	❏	❏	❏
E.	We share training techniques and resources reciprocally with other trainers and organizations.	❏	❏	❏	❏	❏
F.	We partner with receiving churches, receiving teams, sending churches, agencies, and schools.	❏	❏	❏	❏	❏

	YES!	Yes	Needs Work	Help!	N/A

VI. EVALUATION STRATEGY

An excellent program of missionary training will have a clear, measurable, and feasible evaluation plan.

	YES!	Yes	Needs Work	Help!	N/A
A. We have a plan for regular (e.g., annual, biannual) evaluation of our training program.	❏	❏	❏	❏	❏
B. Our evaluation of learners goes beyond knowledge alone to measure skills and character.	❏	❏	❏	❏	❏
C. Our evaluation addresses four levels: reaction, learning, behavior, and organizational results, not degree of satisfaction only.	❏	❏	❏	❏	❏
D. Our evaluation assesses the extent to which training contributes to personal and organizational effectiveness.	❏	❏	❏	❏	❏
E. Our evaluation looks at various program elements including time, delivery system, accessibility, user friendliness, and stewardship of organizational resources.	❏	❏	❏	❏	❏
F. We use evaluation to make program improvements.	❏	❏	❏	❏	❏

VII. ACCOUNTABILITY

An excellent program of missionary training is accountable to stakeholders and peers.

	YES!	Yes	Needs Work	Help!	N/A
A. We have procedures in place for reporting to stakeholders on the efficiency of our training programs.	❏	❏	❏	❏	❏
B. We have procedures in place for reporting to stakeholders on the effectiveness of our training programs.	❏	❏	❏	❏	❏
C. We periodically invite review of our training program by a panel of our peers.	❏	❏	❏	❏	❏

«2»

Assessing Missionary Training in a National Context

Organization: Global Connections and Redcliffe College
Contributor: Simon Steer

Following its conference in May 2004, Global Connections (the United Kingdom's evangelical missions network) ran a series of discussions to explore issues raised at the conference. In particular, a forum was held in October 2004 focusing on missionary training. One of the issues raised at this forum was the lack of awareness, even amongst training institutes, of the current situation in terms of the supply and demand of mission training. One of the key recommendations from this forum was to undertake research to explore a range of issues being faced by training providers and users alike.

Also in 2004, Redcliffe College began a strategy development project. As part of this work, the College wanted to understand its own provision of mission training within the wider UK and even global context. Redcliffe commissioned a piece of research to examine these issues. Redcliffe discussed this project with Global Connections and it was agreed that the research should be conducted under the banner of Global Connections to widen its scope and provide impartiality. Esther Vaughan of Vaughan Consulting conducted the research and this Executive Summary report was published electronically and made available at www.globalconnections.co.uk. The full report can be ordered from the Global Connections online store by following the links on that site.

Mission Training Review: Piecing Together the Puzzle
Executive Summary Report Produced on Behalf of Global Connections
February 2006

The Pieces of the Puzzle

Finding the Pieces

Background
- Initiated by Redcliffe College as part of their strategy review and Global Connections following their 2004 conference, this review started from a position of trying to understand what we do and do not know about mission training in the UK today.

- The primary concern of this review is to provide enough information to inform the rambling discussions on mission training and put together a framework for a new Global Connections Training Forum who will take these discussions forward.

- As the scope of the project is wide, the depth of the findings is understandably shallow. However, important insights have been highlighted and a more robust framework for the current comments provided.

Methodology
- The survey responses were collected using an online facility which in itself provides great opportunities (in increased response and reduced costs) albeit with some limitations (accessibility for overseas workers).

- The groups included in the surveys were: UK training institutions, UK mission organizations, college students, mission workers, college bursars and church leaders. Whilst the review also sought information from Europe via EEMA leaders, no information was forthcoming.

Understanding the findings

- For ease of understanding, the findings of this review have been split into four sections:

  1. Current demand for mission training.

  2. Current supply of mission training.

  3. Perceptions of trends and developments within mission training.

  4. Views on quality of mission training.

- The key findings for each of these have been provided below. It is important to note that this data consists of the views and perceptions of the different groups surveyed. No attempt has been made to validate any of the assumptions or figures provided by respondents.

- It is also important to read the data carefully—some of the sections have very small bases of respondents and so the findings may be skewed by a few of these respondents. The bases have been noted for each section to help with understanding the scope of the findings in the full report.

Executive Summary Key Findings

Demand for Mission Training

Decreased demand:

- The emphasis on the need for training from mission agencies has decreased alongside a decrease in the number of candidates interested in long-term mission service.

Value of mission focused colleges:

- The importance of mission focused colleges and courses has been highlighted by students and mission workers who value training provision where there is an explicit focus on cross cultural mission, an international community and lecturers with mission experience.

Mission training in ministerial colleges:

- Demand for cross-cultural mission training is coming from ministerial college respondents who would like to see this integrated with their current training.

Importance of flexibility:

- The need for flexibility in all areas of training (length, subject areas, method etc) has been raised by mission organizations.

Supply of Mission Training

Financial sustainability:

- Mission colleges are finding financial concerns an increasing burden, which may lead to a consolidation of colleges offering mission training.

A change of approach:

- The value of the current approach of pre-field/ongoing training has been questioned by mission organizational personnel.

Foreseen Trends, Developments and Threats

Collaboration:

- The need for more collaboration has been highlighted (especially among mission training colleges; between mission colleges and ministerial colleges and between mission colleges and mission organizations).

Greater input from overseas:

- This has been highlighted in terms of non-western teaching staff, students from overseas and potentially moving mission training to the Global South.

Political and social threats:

- Increasing censorship and the rise of political correctness is seen as a potential threat to mission training in the UK. This has been highlighted alongside comments about the declining UK Church.

Financial threats:

- The financial issues faced by students and colleges is likely to prompt a more radical alignment of UK mission training.

Perceived Quality

Positive feedback:

- The findings were generally positive, particularly from mission workers and current mission students, who have found their training to be helpful (some have even commented 'essential').

The whole package:

- The perceived quality of mission training is often wider than the content of the lectures. An international student body and lecturers with mission experience were highlighted as key, whereas mission workers generally discouraged attending colleges that do not specifically focus on mission training.

Balance of mission and theology:

- Getting the balance right between theology and mission elements is important. There are differences of opinion amongst mission organizations as to which of these elements training institutions are doing well.

Questions Raised:

For colleges with mission courses:

- Is it time to re-think the current training structure?
- Is there enough room for all the colleges – is consolidation needed?
- As Christian colleges, what is your kingdom responsibility in terms of duplicating courses?
- Is the role of the UK Christian college as a mission training provider declining?
- Are training institutions meeting the demands of modern day candidates and mission organizations—should they?
- Why are mission organizations choosing to provide the training themselves?

For ministerial and other theological colleges:

- How can cross-cultural mission be incorporated as an integral part of courses?

For churches

- Are churches doing enough to promote and support mission training?

- How can church leaders be encouraged in the value of mission training?

- Do churches have a financial responsibility to those they encourage to train?

For mission organizations:

- What are mission organizations' responsibilities in encouraging mission training?

- How can mission personnel be used to develop the courses provided by training institutions?

- Is there a need to re-think current recommendations for mission training particularly in the light of advice given by mission workers and current students?

- If the receivers of training rate the cross-cultural experience of college so highly, why are mission organizations encouraging short courses and distance learning?

- Are mission personnel up-to-date with current mission training programs?

- How is the quality of internal programs assessed?

For the Global Connections network:

- Who should be working together? / How can this be achieved?

- How can the profile of mission training be raised within the different network groups?

- As a network, what is our responsibility to retain credible, affordable mission training in the UK?

Recommended Next Steps

1. **Mission Training Day Conference**
   - It is recommended that Global Connections hold a day conference to discuss the findings of this survey, along with other relevant information, and seek to address the questions raised.

2. **Mission Training Forum**
   - As a result of the day conference it is suggested that a Mission Training Forum should be created to provide a framework for continued discussion in these areas and development of new initiatives and collaborations.

   - This needs to include representatives from mission and ministerial training institutions, church leaders and mission organizations.

   - The questions thrown up by this review should be discussed by this forum and further research work undertaken in specific areas to gain a better understanding of the current and future potential for training.

Conclusion

A follow-up day conference was held in May 2006 at which 60 people from a variety of training programmes and mission agencies discussed the findings of the research and suggested ways in which to take it forward. It was also recognized that there is a need to develop more effective collaboration on training amongst the organizations within the Global Connections network. One possibility is the creation of a Mission Training Forum to provide a context for continuing discussion about the issues raised and to identify further research that might be required. The research has already proved its value to a number of the participating training providers and, more broadly, has helped to place mission training much higher up the agenda of the Christian community in the UK.

An intriguing question remains: would similar research be beneficial if conducted by other national movements, or at an international or global, level? There is no doubt that this is something the International Missionary Training Network will want to encourage amongst our constituencies.

«3»

Module Evaluation by Participants

Organization: Gateway Missionary Training Centre
Contributor: Rob Brynjolfson

Evaluating learning experiences is one of the important steps in the ongoing evaluation of a training program but designing an evaluation form is not as easy as it may look. A training program needs objective feedback from participants if it is to make improvements that are based on more than intuition. So, how can a training center retrieve useful and effective information from the students that serves to evaluate and improve the training program? Here are some suggestions including a sample evaluation form.

Take the time. Trainees will better understand the value of their input if a school schedules adequate time for trainees to respond. Sometimes the forms are handed out and students are asked to fill them in at their leisure and return them later to the office, indirectly communicating to the student that the evaluation is not valued. Best results are achieved when instructors finish their last class early enough to allow students ample time to complete the forms.

Keep the outcomes in mind. An outcomes-based training program should be committed to measuring the achievement of the desired end results. Designing evaluations around outcomes for specific modules or learning experiences assumes that those teaching understand the specific outcomes they want to achieve. This is an important way to keep congruency between outcomes and trainers. When outcomes are addressed specifically and intentionally, they can be evaluated. If the outcomes were not achieved, the training should be modified.

Make it useful. Complicated forms only serve to complicate matters. Long forms will usually be set aside or at best completed hurriedly. If you don't know how the information can be used to improve the program, don't waste the participant's time asking for it. Determine what you actually need to know, and how you can best retrieve the information you actually need. Evaluations can be useful for (a) needs assessment, (b) determining training objectives, (c) shaping content, (d) improving delivery, and (c) assessing potential application.

Keep it simple. The simplest and quickest evaluations use numeric scales. Scales can include almost any range of numbers, but even-numbered scales are best to keep students from landing on the middle "neutral" number, and forcing either a positive or negative response. Numeric scales are simple to use, but may create ambiguity if the numbers don't mean the same thing to participants. Some people think that 7 out of 10 is disgraceful and others see a 5 as quite satisfactory. Greater accuracy may be achieved by using word descriptions rather than numeric values. If a numeric scale is used, identifying each numeric value with a word statement may help to gather more accurate information.

Try to reduce the personality factor. It is very difficult to take "personality" out of the equation. Some people are more easily satisfied than others. Some people are "critical thinkers" and others are not. Persons will be in different moods as they give their responses. Some cultural groups find it very difficult to be critical of "teachers" in any way. Since evaluations are usually anonymous, it is difficult to know how to measure the importance of any individual rating. When using a numeric scale, averaging all the responses is useful in removing some of this personality variable. Another practice is to remove the "outliers"—those responses that are so extreme that they may skew the overall results.

Allow for written responses. The most useful information usually comes from written responses. Since the information is to be used to improve the program, it is most useful to ask for practical suggestions rather than simply eliciting students' feelings, or what they liked or did not like. More useful questions to ask may be: "What would have been more helpful...?" or "How would you improve...?"

Keep it anonymous. The best evaluations are based on forthright response. Students are less likely to be candid, however, if they believe their evaluations may impact their grade or the opinion of a teacher. So keeping results anonymous will generally provide more accurate data. The downside of this approach is that occasionally, some issue is raised that could be pursued further for clarification or to garner greater insight. Giving students the option of signing their evaluation if they want to, may be a way of allowing participants to work at their own comfort level in this respect. Some programs are so small that maintaining anonymity is also a challenge. In these cases, the responses can be collated and summarized by one person who assures confidentiality is maintained.

Use the information. People will not take the time to fill out a form if they think no one intends to use the information. Programs and schools need to demonstrate to trainees how improvements have been made because of previous evaluations received. During the module introduction, instructors should be encouraged to describe how the content and delivery of the module evolved into its present state by including useful evaluations from previous students.

The editors of this manual debated whether or not to include an actual sample evaluation form. We are convinced that every program needs to design its own evaluation instruments. On the other hand, an example may help illustrate some of the above guidelines. Furthermore, the following form can become a starting point for adapting it to a particular context. The fact that the specific outcomes and learning objectives are reviewed is important. This evaluation form could be strengthened (though made significantly longer) by making it module specific and including specific outcomes and learning objectives. The following form is designed to be more "generic" and can be used with the syllabus for the module in hand.

Sample Form

Module Evaluation

Module: *(Title)*　　　　　　**Facilitator:** *(Name)*

Please give careful consideration to the following items. Your honest answers and insights are needed to help us improve this course and program of training. If you want to remain anonymous, you do not need to write your name on this page.

Section 1: Syllabus Review, Content and Delivery

Please review the syllabus provided with this evaluation and give your response to the following questions, indicating the degree of agreement or disagreement according to the following scale: **1 = strongly disagree, 2 = disagree, 3 = agree, 4 = strongly agree**	1, 2, 3, 4
1. I feel I was able to learn what I really needed to learn regarding the subject matter.	
2. The readings and other assignments for this module were appropriate for this subject.	
3. The readings and other assignments for this module were not too long.	
4. The instructor was well prepared.	
5. The content of this module was challenging and thought provoking.	
6. The instructor was interesting and made use of a variety of teaching methods.	
7. I believe the general outcomes specified on the syllabus for this module were achieved.	
If you disagree, please indicate which outcomes were not achieved to your satisfaction and why. (If you need more space, please continue writing on the back of this sheet.) _____ _____ _____	

8. I believe the specific learning objectives designated on the syllabus were achieved.

If you disagree, please indicate which objectives were not achieved to your satisfaction and why.

(If you need more space, please continue writing on the back of this sheet.)

_____

_____

_____

9. Which of the following teaching methods were most useful to you and why? Lecture, class discussion, work in groups, question and answers, case studies, role play, simulations, drama, multimedia or other (please specify).

_____

_____

_____

_____

_____

Section 2: Sample Narrative Questions

Your thoughtful response to the following questions will help the school and instructor to make improvements for future classes.

Needs assessment:

    A. Describe your expectations for this module as you prepared to take it. Were they met?

    B. If not, what improvements to this module could have ensured that your expectations were met?

Training objectives:

    A. To what degree do you feel the module accomplished its stated outcomes and objectives?

    B. How would you improve this module to ensure that the training outcomes and objectives could be met?

Content:

    A. How would you describe the content of the module in terms of organization, thoughtfulness, and degree of usefulness?

    B. What suggestions would you make to improve the content of this module?

Delivery:

    A. List the teaching methods employed during the delivery of this module. Which were most useful and why?

    B. What suggestions would you make to improve the way this module was taught?

Application:

    A. Related to your ministry aspirations, what did you learn that was new?

    B. In what way has this module impacted your life and ministry plans?

«4»

Student Assessment in an Outcomes-Based Program

Organization: Gateway Missionary Training Centre
Contributor: Rob Brynjolfson

The best evaluation of a training program is the assessment of its students. When assessment results are compiled and tracked over time for all the outcomes, specific program strengths and weaknesses can be identified. But how can this be done effectively with integral training programs? One of the hallmarks of formal education is that knowledge acquisition can be measured quite easily. Likewise, non-formal skill outcomes can be assessed on the basis of recognized performance. But how do we measure outcomes that relate to character and spiritual formation? The difficulty of assessing spiritual and character growth is one of the factors that causes educators to undervalue its importance in training curriculum.

Outcomes-based training programs must assess development and progress in all of the outcomes, not just those that are easily tested. If a program description claims to produce growth in character, spiritual formation and attitudes, an attempt must be made to determine whether or not this growth occurs. By failing to assess all of the outcomes, a training program places itself in peril. The first danger is that of building on unproven assumptions. If the growth is not measured, how can one be certain that the training goals are achieved? And how can a program be improved if there is no indication of needed change? The second danger is one common to all integral training programs. Over time the tendency is to become imbalanced with a growing dependency on academic and classroom-related learning activities because these are familiar and more easily measured.

The assessment form included below attempts to evaluate student growth based on all of the stated outcomes of the training program at the Gateway Missionary Training Centre in Canada (see Program Description 9, p. 171). This form does not take the place of specific assignments, tests, competence assessments or other methods of evaluating student performance. It is typically used as a self-assessment tool or by mentors, peers, and training staff in determining field readiness. Assessment forms like this sample require conscious effort to minimize subjectivity. Some steps can be taken to add elements of objectivity such as performing the assessment periodically and comparing the results with previous assessments. Having two or three assessors evaluate the trainee independently and then comparing those results is very helpful in overcoming judgment errors and bias. Significant discrepancies can be discussed between assessors and a consensus position reached before evaluation results are shared with the trainee and/or others concerned.

Self-assessment: One of the goals of affective learning is to produce self-awareness. Training programs will be surprised at the level of self-awareness that can be achieved by asking trainees to complete a self-assessment at the beginning and at the completion of the training. Gateway requires a self-assessment upon entry into the program. When trainees have been asked to repeat the self-assessment at the end of the training, in almost every case trainees assessed themselves less positively in a number of areas after receiving the training. This surprise might lead some to think the training failed, but on the contrary, it demonstrated that the trainees arrived at a more realistic concept of their own abilities and preparedness for overseas service. The training had dispelled their naiveté.

Peer assessment: Peer evaluation is one of the most common informal means of assessing behavior. When done formally, it is often received with trepidation. Peers operate in a give-and-take environment. Hunches and suspicions of what others think about us may be confirmed through a more formal process. A director of a mission agency stated that acceptance into the mission ought to include the assessments of fellow candidates because they are the ones who will have to work together on the field. One training school in Africa requires written peer assessments from every student for every student and staff member. Hard as it is to receive criticism, assessment, together with the gracious working of the Holy Spirit, can produce self-awareness, humility, and repentance, which are pre-conditions to real change and growth.

Assessment by trainers: As with the comments regarding peer assessment above, an outcomes assessment form like the one below serves the staff of a training program to systematically monitor and evaluate growth. This can be done by mentors or coaches, but should be reviewed by a group or committee to minimize errors in judgment that could be made if only one person was performing the assessment. At Gateway, the individual's mentor evaluates the person and reviews this with other staff members, looking for agreement and consensus. These evaluations may be shared with the trainee's sponsoring church or mission agency.

Using the Gateway Assessment

The purpose of training is to produce growth. Growth is not static. So the most useful application of this sort of assessment is to use it periodically with some indication of what kind of progress has been made. Some outcomes indicate a level of proficiency that cannot possibly be achieved in the limited duration of many training programs. At Gateway, the form intends to assess field entry readiness.

The segment of the assessment form provided below shows that the trainee demonstrated an evident lack of the fruit of the Spirit at the beginning of the program, but showed a marked improvement at the end of the program. This is indicated by an arrow. The trainee also seemed responsive to God's guidance on entering the program, but later demonstrated insecurity, and a lack of perseverance.

Sample assessment of one outcome area:

Outcome Area: Spiritual Maturity	Growth				Final
	0	1	2	3	Assmnt
Knows & loves God & exhibits fruit of Spirit		└→			2
Spontaneously worships God; growing in personal & corporate worship			└→		3
Responsible to God's guidance; exhibits endurance, etc.		←┤			1

GATEWAY

Training for Cross-Cultural Service

21233 32nd Ave., Langley BC V2Z 2E7

Student Assessment

Trainee:		Date:	
Mentor:		Term:	

Gateway Outcomes	Field Readiness Rating	
The following is a list of Gateway program outcomes.	0	Needs much work
Our program is designed to produce growth towards field readiness in each of these areas of knowledge, character and skill development.	1	Needs some work
	2	FIELD READY
Indicate where you believe your mentoree currently stands in each of the following areas:	3	Exceptional
	NA	Not Applicable
	U	Unknown

SPIRITUALITY: Demonstrates growth in relationship with God	Rating
• Maintains a regular quiet time	
• Demonstrates an active prayer life	
• Shows evidence of spiritual discernment	
• Knows how to study and apply Scripture well	
• Identifies and deals with issues that affect a growing relationship with God	
• Rises to challenges in faith	
• Nurtures a vital relationship with God in order to thrive in ministry throughout life	
• Discerns and obeys the will of God	
• Values the counsel and direction of others in the body of Christ	
• Knows and uses Spiritual gifting wisely	
• Understands and is abler to apply principles of spiritual warfare	

CHARACTER: Reflects Christ-likeness in attitude and action	Rating
• Demonstrates growth in the fruit of the Spirit	
• Is a person of integrity (moral, reputable, dependable, responsible, accountable, disciplined)	
• Has a learning attitude	
• Willingly responds to encouragement and correction	

	Rating
• Shows forbearance toward cultural, theological or church differences	
• Shows flexibility & adaptability to new or changing circumstances	
• Shows servant attitude	

INTER-PERSONAL SKILLS: Demonstrates ability in relating to others	Rating
• Is aware of his/her own personality strengths and weaknesses	
• Exercises conflict management skills	
• Works at maintaining good relationships – understands and relates well	
• Is a team player	
• Functions effectively in a multi-cultural team	
• Is skilled at building bridges and forming friendships	
• Is sensitive to the feelings of others	
• Is aware of how he/she affects others and makes appropriate adjustments	
• Listens attentively (attempts to understand people he/she relates to)	

PHYSICAL AND EMOTIONAL HEALTH: Evidences a balanced holistic approach to life	Rating
• Demonstrates emotional stability	
• Is open to advice and counsel in these areas	
• Is willing to adjust to different diets	
• Is able to identify and deal with stress	
• Is aware of health issues overseas	
• Participates in some form of regular exercise	
• Is emotionally resilient, able to live positively in difficult circumstances	
• Is secure, having a healthy self-image	

CHURCH: Demonstrates commitment to the universal body of Christ locally and globally	Rating
• Is committed to, and participates in, a local church	
• Works at his/her relationship with the home church	
• Embraces the biblical concept of the universal church	
• Recognizes critical issues relating to church planting	
• Is able to develop a basic church planting strategy	
• Is aware of the role and extent of the missionary involvement in the growth of the church	
• Maintains good relationships with the national church (i.e. avoids paternalism, dependency, etc.)	

BIBLE & THEOLOGY of MISSIONS: Has a firm grasp of the Bible and mission theology	Rating
• Demonstrates commitment to the authority of the Bible	
• Demonstrates a keen interest and thirst for the Word of God	
• Is able to think biblically, applying Scripture in life and practice	
• Understands and can describe the biblical basis of missions	
• Is able to understand and defend the theological foundations of missions	
• Demonstrates a passion for missions	

TEAM WORK: Able to function effectively on a team	Rating
• Is aware of roles, spiritual gifting and personality types as they relate to ministry on a team	
• Exhibits servant leadership with co-workers and nationals	
• Practices mutual submission (Eph. 5:21) with co-workers and nationals	
• Demonstrates leadership potential as: (indicate which) visionary leader, team builder, manager/administrator	

CROSS-CULTURAL ADAPTATION: Understands and values cultural differences and demonstrates adaptability	Rating
• Understands the missionary adaptation process and its importance	
• Is sensitive to other cultural norms and makes appropriate adjustments to dress and behavior	
• Adapts to different surroundings, people and cultures	
• Identifies symptoms of culture shock and can apply coping strategies	
• Shows respect and appreciation for cultural differences	
• Adopts values and standards consistent with a missionary calling	
• Embraces and values cultural differences without a tendency to prejudge	
• Is inquisitive and interested in understanding and enjoying cultural differences	
• Is perceptive and observant of cultural clues both verbal and nonverbal	

CONTEXTUALIZATION: Understands the culture and adapts the Gospel message to communicate it effectively	Rating
• Is aware of significant differences in worldview and how this affects the transmission of the gospel	
• Understands the challenges of communicating cross-culturally	
• Is able to adjust method or form in order to improve communication	
• Understands contextualization and its role in cross-cultural ministry and is able to express his/her personal convictions	

LANGUAGE LEARNING: Demonstrates competence in acquiring another language	Rating
• Is committed to learning another language	
• Develops a personal language learning strategy	
• Demonstrates progress in learning another language, communicating with local language and thought patterns	

COMMUNICATION: Communicates effectively in a variety of settings	Rating
• Communicates clearly with organized thoughts	
• Is creative in seeking to maintain the interest of the audience	
• Communicates his/her vision with enthusiasm	
• Prepares well for different settings	
• Uses e-mail to communicate effectively	
• Writes interesting prayer letters	

EVANGELISM: Intentionally seeking opportunities to introduce people to Jesus Christ	Rating
• Understands the crucial elements of the gospel and can present them effectively	
• He/she shares his/her testimony clearly	
• Is eager to see people won to Christ	
• Is able to witness clearly but with tact and sensitivity	
• Is able to lead someone to Christ	

DISCIPLESHIP: Is a disciple and makes disciples of Jesus	Rating
• Committed to the task of making disciples	
• Knows what is involved in being and making a disciple	
• Is able to disciple individuals or small groups using Bible study methods	

PRACTICAL SKILLS: Willing to learn and to perform activities related to daily living	Rating
• Demonstrates adequate life skills to maintain a healthy life overseas	
• Shows a servant's attitude when fulfilling service obligations	
• Meets mission job description or "tentmaking" requirements	

FAMILY & SINGLE LIFE: Understands and demonstrates what family and or single life involves here and on the mission field	Rating
• Maintains a balance between personal life and ministry	
• Is sensitive to the needs of single or married co-workers	
Family Life:	
• Is sensitive to the needs of spouse and children	
• Understands implications of raising a family overseas	
• Prepares family for life overseas	
Single Life:	
• Able to deal effectively with singleness	

PRE-FIELD MINISTRY: Knows the steps and practices skills/activities that are essential to getting to the field	Rating
• Is effective in raising ministry partners	
• Develops and initiates a plan to get to the field	

Comments:

Suggestions:

Index